THE USBORNE INTERNET-LINKED
BOOK OF
KNOWLEDGE

Edited by Emma Helbrough

With thanks to Sarah Cronin

CONSULTANTS:

Astronomy and space: Stuart Atkinson and Cheryl Power
Planet Earth: Dr. Roger Trend and Dr. William Chambers
Plants and animals: Dr. Margaret Rostron and Dr. John Rostron
The human body: Dr. Laura Prtak
Science and technology: Dr. Tom Petersen
Maps: Craig Asquith
World history dates: Dr. Anne Millard, Gary Mills
and Dr. David Norman
Americanization: Carrie Seay

SCHOLASTIC INC.

New York Toronto London Auckland Sydney
Mexico City New Delhi Hong Kong Buenos Aires

CONTENTS

4 Internet links

ASTRONOMY AND SPACE

8 The Universe
10 Our Solar System
12 The Sun
14 The Earth
16 The Moon
18 Eclipses
20 Star groups
22 Star patterns
24 The night sky in spring
26 The night sky in summer
28 The night sky in fall
30 The night sky in winter
32 Famous constellations
33 Map of the Moon

PLANET EARTH

36 Inside the Earth
38 The Earth's crust
40 Rocks, minerals and fossils
42 Rivers
44 Seas and oceans
46 The Earth's atmosphere
48 What is weather?
50 Water and clouds
52 Climate

PLANTS AND ANIMALS

56 Plants
58 Flowering plants
60 Animals
62 Ecosystems

64 Life cycles
66 Natural cycles
68 Evolution
70 Classification

THE HUMAN BODY

76 The skeleton
78 The circulatory system
80 Digestion
82 Food and diet
84 The respiratory system
86 The nervous system
88 The brain
90 Skin, nails and hair
92 Eyes
94 Ears
96 The nose and tongue
98 Genes and DNA
100 Gene science

This is a bottlenose dolphin. Its smooth, streamlined shape helps it to glide through the water quickly.

SCIENCE AND TECHNOLOGY

104 Solids, liquids and gases
106 The elements
108 Energy
110 Sound
112 Light
114 Color
116 Electricity
118 Magnetism
120 Flight
122 TV and radio
124 Telephones
126 Computers
128 The Internet

MAPS

132 World political
134 World physical
136 North America

138 South America
140 Australasia and Oceania
142 Asia
144 Europe
146 Africa

COUNTRIES AND FLAGS

150 Gazetteer of states

WORLD HISTORY DATES

166 Prehistoric world
168 Ancient world
170 Medieval world
172 The last 500 years

FACTS AND LISTS

178 Time zones
179 Measurements
180 Measuring nature
182 Scientific laws
183 Geometrical shapes
184 World records
186 Scientists and
    inventors
190 Key dates in science
192 Glossary
198 Index
204 Acknowledgements

INTERNET LINKS

This book contains descriptions of many recommended websites where you can find out more about the subjects covered in the book. For links to these sites, go to the Usborne Quicklinks Website at **www.usborne-quicklinks.com** and enter the keyword "knowledge."

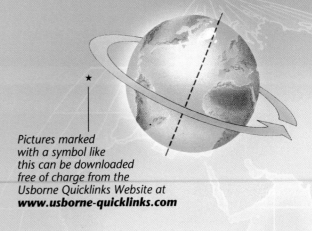

Pictures marked with a symbol like this can be downloaded free of charge from the Usborne Quicklinks Website at **www.usborne-quicklinks.com**

SITE AVAILABILITY

The links on the Usborne Quicklinks Website will be reviewed and updated regularly. If any of the sites become unavailable, we will, if possible, replace them with suitable alternatives.

Occasionally, though, you may get a message saying that a website is unavailable. This may be temporary, so try again a few hours later, or even the next day.

Internet links

You'll find descriptions of recommended websites in boxes like this one throughout the book. For links to all the websites, and for free downloadable pictures, go to **www.usborne-quicklinks.com** and enter the keyword "knowledge."

HELP

For general help and advice on using the Internet, go to Usborne Quicklinks and click on "Net Help."

To find out more about using your web browser, click on your browser's Help menu and choose "Contents and Index." You'll find a searchable dictionary containing tips on how to find your way around the Internet easily.

For more up-to-the-minute technical support for your browser, click on "Help" and then "Online Support." This will take you to the browser manufacturer's website.

DOWNLOADABLE PICTURES

Some of the pictures from this book can be downloaded from the Usborne Quicklinks Website and printed out for your own personal use. For example, you could use them to illustrate homework or a project. They must not be copied or distributed for any commercial purpose. Downloadable pictures have a ★ symbol beside them. To print out these pictures, follow the instructions on the Usborne Quicklinks Website at **www.usborne-quicklinks.com**

WHAT YOU NEED

The websites described in this book can be accessed using a standard home computer and a web browser (the software that enables you to display information from the Internet). Here's a list of basic requirements:

- A PC with Microsoft® Windows® 98 or later version, or a Macintosh computer with System 9 or later

- 64Mb RAM

- A web browser, such as Microsoft® Internet Explorer 5, Netscape® 6 or later versions

- Connection to the Internet via a modem (preferably 56Kbps) or a faster digital or cable line

- An account with an Internet Service Provider (ISP)

- A sound card to play sound files

INTERNET SAFETY

When using the Internet, please make sure you follow these simple guidelines:

• Ask your parent's or guardian's permission before you connect to the Internet.

• If you write a message in a website guest book or on a message board, do not include your email address, real name, address or telephone number.

• If a website asks you to log in or register by typing your name or email address, ask the permission of an adult first.

• If you do receive email from someone you don't know, tell an adult and do not reply to the email.

• Never arrange to meet anyone you have talked to on the Internet.

EXTRAS

Some websites need additional programs, called plug-ins, to play sounds, or to show videos, animations or 3-D images. If you go to a site and you do not have the necessary plug-in, a message should come up on the screen.

There is usually a button on the site that you can click on to download the plug-in. Alternatively, go to Usborne Quicklinks and click on "Net Help." There you can find links to download plug-ins. Here is a list of plug-ins that you might need:

• QuickTime – lets you play video clips.

• RealOne™ Player – lets you play video clips and sound files.

• Flash™ – lets you play animations.

• Shockwave® – lets you play animations and enjoy interactive sites.

NOTES FOR PARENTS

The websites described in this book are regularly checked and reviewed by Usborne editors and the links in Usborne Quicklinks are updated. However, the content of a website may change at any time and Usborne Publishing is not responsible for the content of any website other than its own.

We recommend that children are supervised while on the Internet, that they do not use Internet chat rooms, and that you use Internet filtering software to block unsuitable material.

Please ensure that your children read and follow the safety guidelines on the left. For more information, go to the Net Help area on the Usborne Quicklinks Website at **www.usborne-quicklinks.com**

COMPUTER VIRUSES

A computer virus is a program that can damage your computer. A virus can get into your computer when you download programs from the Internet, or in an attachment (an extra file) that arrives with an email.

We strongly recommend that you buy anti-virus software to protect your computer and that you update the software regularly, as new viruses are being invented all the time.

You can buy anti-virus software at computer stores or download it from the Internet. To find out more about viruses, go to Usborne Quicklinks and click on "Net Help."

See for yourself

In some sections of this book, you'll find experiments and activities in boxes like this one. Always read through the experiment before you begin and if it involves anything that you would normally do under supervision, then ask an adult to help you.

The dark shape below is a nebula, a cloud of dust and gas in space. This one is called the horsehead nebula because it is shaped like the head of a horse.

ASTRONOMY AND SPACE

THE UNIVERSE

The Universe is the name that we use to describe the collection of all the things that exist in space. It is so huge that its size is hard to imagine. It is made of many billions of stars and planets, and enormous clouds of gas, separated by gigantic empty spaces.

LIGHT YEARS

Distances in space are huge. They are usually measured in light years. One light year is the distance that light travels in a year, which is approximately 5.88 trillion miles. Light travels at a speed of 186,000 miles per second.

Internet links

For a link to a website where you can go on a virtual journey around the Solar System, go to
www.usborne-quicklinks.com

GALAXIES

A galaxy is an enormous group of stars. Galaxies are so big that it can take a ray of light thousands of years to travel across one. Earth is in the Milky Way galaxy. This galaxy is about 100,000 light years across. Distances between galaxies are much greater.

On a clear night, you can see a broad, dense band of stars stretching across the sky. This is the Milky Way. In ancient times, people thought the band looked like a trail of spilt milk, which is how our galaxy got its name.

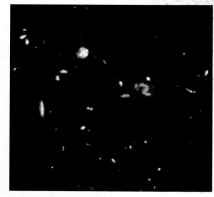

The smudgy little shapes in this photograph are some of the most distant galaxies ever seen.

HOW BIG?

Nobody knows how big the Universe is. It contains millions and millions of galaxies. As astronomers develop new, more powerful telescopes, they discover even more galaxies. So far, astronomers have spotted galaxies that are up to 15,000 million light years away.

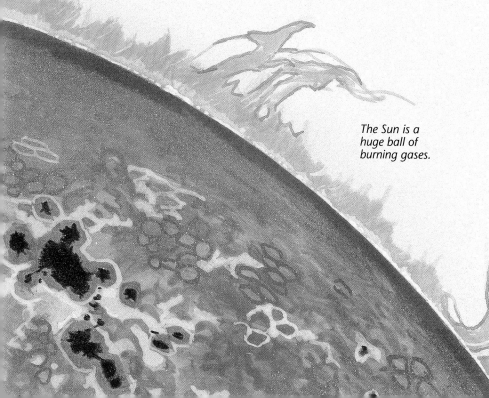

The Sun is a huge ball of burning gases.

PLANET EARTH

The Earth is one of nine planets that travel around, or orbit, the Sun. Together, the Sun and everything that is in orbit around it are called the Solar System. The closest natural object to the Earth is the Moon, which orbits the Earth. It takes a ray of light 1 1/2 seconds to travel from the Moon to the Earth.

On a clear, dark night, you can see several thousand stars in the sky.

This diagram shows the Moon in orbit around the Earth.

The Moon

The path of the Moon's orbit

STARS IN SPACE

There are billions of stars in every galaxy. A star is a ball of gas that produces heat and light. Some stars are much brighter than others. They vary in color too.

The color of a star depends on how hot its surface is. Stars can be red (these are the coolest), orange, yellow, white or blue. Blue ones are the hottest of all.

The closest star to Earth is the Sun. It is about 93 million miles away. A ray of light takes eight minutes to travel from the Sun to Earth. The second-closest star to Earth is Proxima Centauri. It is about 4 1/4 light years away – that is, 25 trillion miles.

Earth

OUR SOLAR SYSTEM

The word solar means "of the Sun." Our Solar System lies about 28,000 light years away from the middle of the Milky Way. As well as the Sun and the nine planets that orbit it, it is made up of moons, chunks of rock and huge amounts of dust, metal and icy debris.

THE SUN

The Sun is bigger than everything else in the Solar System put together. It is a yellow star, which means it is fairly cool compared with many other stars in our galaxy. The Sun applies a pulling force, called gravity, to everything within a range of around 3,730 million miles, locking them into orbit around it.

This picture shows the planets in orbit around the Sun. They are not drawn to scale.

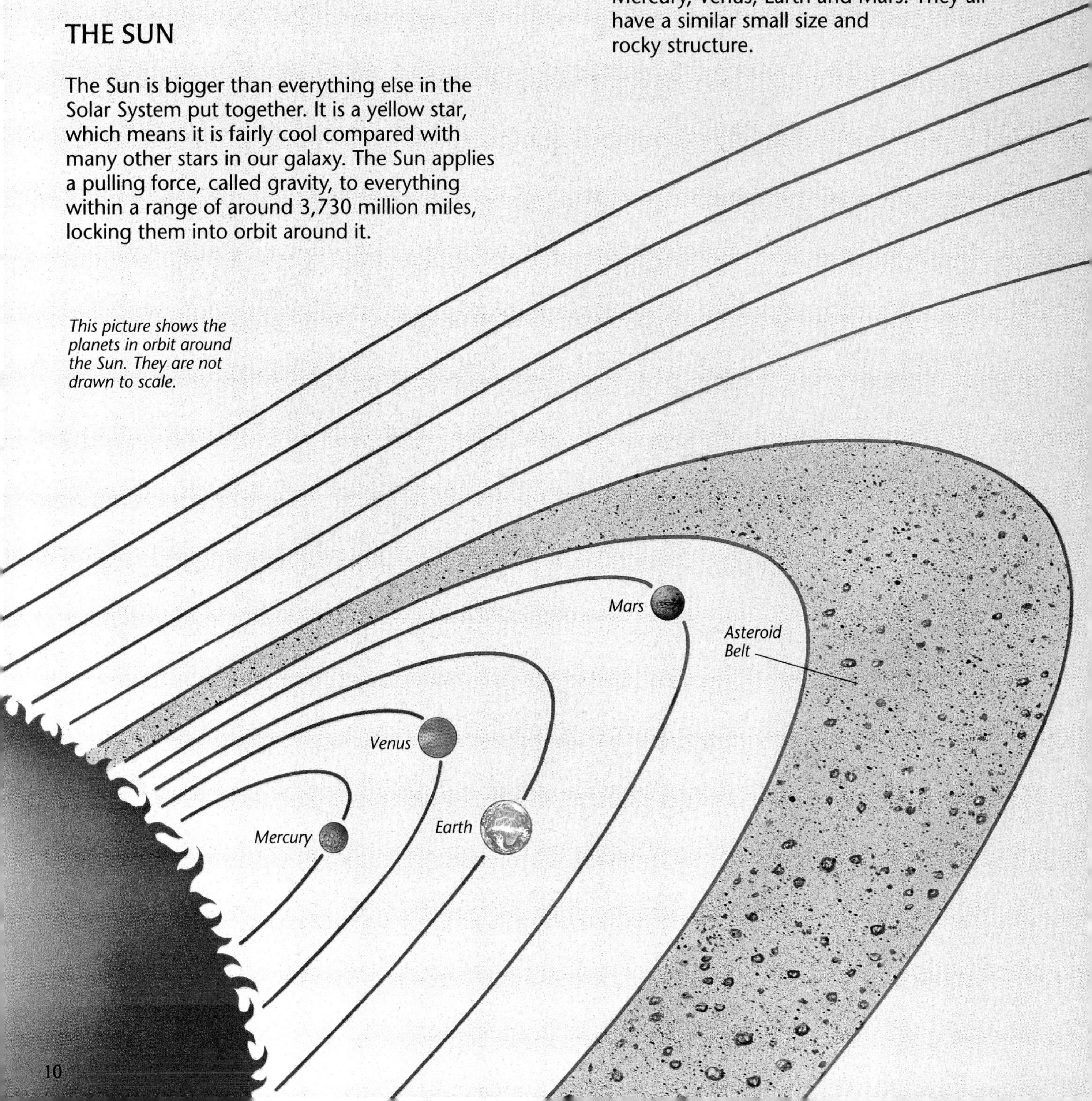

THE INNER PLANETS

The largest objects that orbit the Sun are the planets. At the moment, scientists only know of nine of them, but there may be more that haven't been discovered yet. You can see five of the planets in the night sky; they look like bright stars. The four planets closest to the Sun are known as the inner planets. These are Mercury, Venus, Earth and Mars. They all have a similar small size and rocky structure.

Mars

Asteroid Belt

Venus

Mercury

Earth

THE OUTER PLANETS

The planets farther away from the Sun are called the outer planets. These are Jupiter, Saturn, Uranus, Neptune and Pluto. They are made of ice, gas and liquids, and all except Pluto are larger than the inner planets.

Pluto

Neptune

Uranus

Jupiter

Saturn

Internet links

For a link to a website where you can read a guide to the objects in our Solar System, go to **www.usborne-quicklinks.com**

ASTEROIDS

Asteroids are large chunks of rock, or rock and metal. They were formed along with the rest of the Solar System around 5,000 million years ago. They orbit the Sun like the planets. Some asteroids have a long, oval-shaped orbit which takes them far away from the Sun. Others travel ahead of or behind the planets. But most lie between Mars and Jupiter in a band called the Asteroid Belt.

COMETS

Comets are huge lumps of dirty ice, mixed with dust and grit. Most of them only come near the Sun for short periods of time. When a comet is near the Sun, the Sun's rays heat it up and it starts to melt. As it melts, it releases gases and dust trapped in its ice. They stream out behind the comet, creating a long tail.

MOONS

Many planets have moons that orbit them in the same way that our Moon orbits the Earth. Some planets have many moons; for example, Jupiter has at least 50.

There are different types of moons. Some are rocky; others contain ice and liquid as well as rock. Most moons have craters, mountains and valleys, just like our Moon. Some we know little about, because they have not been photographed in much detail.

METEOROIDS

Small pieces of debris floating around in the Solar System are called meteoroids. When they fall to Earth, they burn up and make a bright streak across the sky. Falling meteoroids are called meteors. Some meteors actually hit the Earth's surface. These are called meteorites.

THE SUN

The Sun gives the planets their heat and light, so the farther a planet is away from the Sun, the colder the planet is. The Sun has been burning for over 4,000 million years and will probably continue to burn for around another 5,000 million years. The temperature in its core is incredibly hot, reaching more than 59 million °F.

HOW BIG?

The Sun measures about 870,000 miles across. Inside, it could hold more than a million planets the size of the Earth. But compared with some of the other stars in the Universe, the Sun is not all that big. This picture shows the size of the Sun compared with one of the biggest stars – Betelgeuse (also known as Alpha Orionis). Stars that are smaller than our Sun are called dwarf stars, while stars larger than our Sun are known as giant stars. The biggest of all are called supergiant stars. Betelgeuse is a supergiant star.

Sun ·

Betelgeuse

THE STRUCTURE OF THE SUN

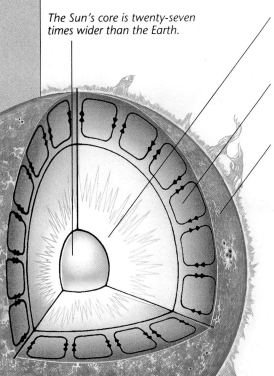

The Sun's core is twenty-seven times wider than the Earth.

The radiative zone surrounds the core. Heat produced in the core spreads through this part.

The convective zone carries the Sun's energy up to the surface. The arrows show its churning motion.

The photosphere is the Sun's surface. It is made of churning gases.

Internet links

For a link to a website where you can see amazing movie clips of solar flares and find out more about the Sun, go to **www.usborne-quicklinks.com**

★

SUNSPOTS

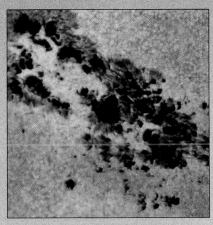

This sunspot was photographed from Earth using special equipment.

The Sun's surface is sometimes marked with small, dark patches, called sunspots. They are areas of the Sun's surface that are slightly cooler than their surroundings. Sometimes, lots of sunspots join together to cover an enormous area. The largest area yet seen covered in sunspots was over 7,000 million square miles.

FIERY FLARES

Sometimes, when energy builds up in an area on the outer layer of the Sun, it flares up, heating gases to millions of degrees and blasting jets of burning gas into space. These violent explosions look like flames and are known as solar flares and prominences. Prominences can shoot out as far as 31,000 miles from the surface of the Sun.

This photograph shows the Sun's endlessly churning surface.

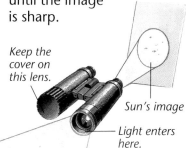
STRANGE LIGHTS

This is an aurora, a display of moving light caused by solar wind. Auroras can be seen from areas in the far north and the far south of the Earth.

The Sun blows a constant stream of invisible particles into space, in all directions. This is known as solar wind. Some of the particles blow against the Earth, but you don't feel them, because the Earth has a magnetic shield around it, known as the magnetosphere. This deflects and soaks up most of the energy from the solar wind. When particles become trapped near the Earth's north and south poles, they create a beautiful light display, called an aurora. In the north, this is called the aurora borealis, or the northern lights. In the south, it is called the aurora australis, or the southern lights.

THE EARTH

The Earth's distance from the Sun makes it just the right temperature for water to exist as a liquid. Earth is also surrounded by a breathable layer of gases. All these things create the right conditions for life to exist on Earth.

LIFE ON EARTH

Earth is the only planet in the Solar System that is known to support life. Animals and plants need water in order to live, but it has yet to be found on the surface of any other planet. If scientists could find evidence of water or ice on their surfaces, it could show that they are or were once home to primitive life.

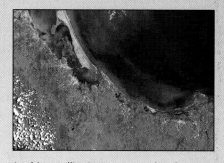

In this satellite image, water has been shaded in blue. Without water, forests (shown here in red and green) and other plant and animal life could not exist on Earth.

In this satellite image of the Earth, you can see central and western Europe through the clouds.

THE ATMOSPHERE

The blanket of gases surrounding Earth is called the atmosphere. It works like a shield, filtering out harmful rays from the Sun. Nitrogen makes up 78% of the atmosphere, and oxygen, which living things use to breathe, makes up 21%. The remaining 1% is made up of small amounts of several other gases.

From space, Earth's atmosphere looks like a very thin blue layer around the planet. It appears blue because of the way sunlight is filtered through atmospheric gases.

SPINNING EARTH

The Earth turns as it orbits the Sun, spinning at 1,000mph. It takes 24 hours, or one Earth day, for it to complete a full spin.

As the Earth spins, the part that is facing the Sun is constantly changing. In the part that is turned toward the Sun it is daytime and in the part that faces away it is nighttime.

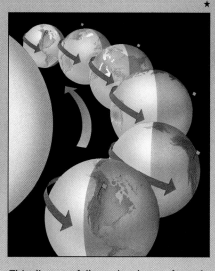

This diagram follows the change from day to night in one place (marked by the green flag) as the Earth spins. The blue arrow indicates the path of the Earth's orbit around the Sun, and the pink arrows show which way the Earth is spinning.

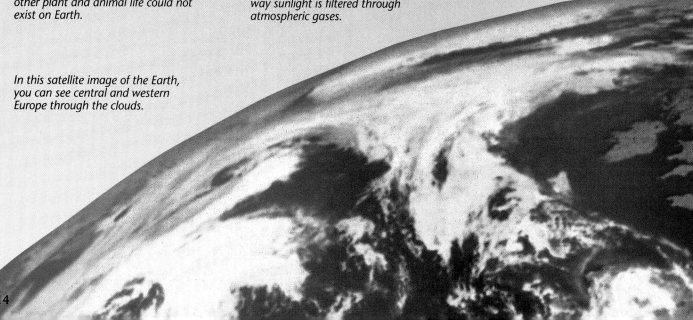

SEASONS

The Earth takes exactly 365.256 days (one Earth year) to complete an orbit. As it makes its journey, different parts of the Earth receive different amounts of heat and light. The Earth is tilted at an angle too, so one half of it is usually closer to the Sun than the other. In this half, it is summer, while in the other it is winter. As the Earth moves around the Sun, the part that is closest changes and the seasons change.

This diagram shows how the seasons change as the Earth orbits the Sun.

March: Neither hemisphere is tilted toward the Sun.

Spring

Autumn — Sun's rays

Summer

Winter

Winter

Summer

Autumn

Spring

June: When the northern hemisphere is tilted toward the Sun, it is summer there. In the southern hemisphere, it is winter.

September: As in March, neither hemisphere is tilted toward the Sun.

December: When the northern hemisphere is tilted away from the Sun, it is winter there. In the southern hemisphere, it is summer.

EARTH FROM SPACE

Today, we are learning more and more about our planet from information sent back by satellites and space stations. For example, weather forecasters use information collected by satellites to predict weather patterns and to warn people of severe weather anywhere in the world.

Satellite pictures can also help scientists observe the effects people have on the environment, for example, the destruction of the rainforests in South America.

This satellite picture shows hurricane clouds approaching the east coast of the U.S.A.

Internet links

For a link to a site where you can see satellite views of Earth, go to **www.usborne-quicklinks.com**

15

THE MOON

The Moon is about 239,000 miles away from Earth. Most moons are very small compared with the planets that they orbit, but our Moon is large compared with Earth – about a quarter of its size. The Moon has no atmosphere and its surface is rocky, dusty and gray all over.

This is what the Earth looks like when seen from the Moon.

HIDDEN VIEWS

The Moon spins around as it orbits the Earth. It takes the same time for the Moon to spin once as it does for it to orbit Earth. This means that the same side of the Moon is always facing us.

It takes just over 27 days for the Moon to complete an orbit of the Earth.

In 1969, the U.S. Apollo 11 space mission landed people on the Moon for the first time in history.

An Apollo astronaut exploring the Moon

MASSIVE CRATERS

This is Copernicus, one of the Moon's biggest craters.

The Moon's surface has many craters, which were made by comets, asteroids and meteoroids hitting it. Some of them are so large that an entire city could fit inside them, though there are lots of tiny craters too.

On a clear night, when there is a full Moon, you can see the biggest craters with the naked eye, though binoculars will give a much better view.

Many of the Moon's craters are surrounded by pale-looking lines, called rays. The rays were made by dust that was thrown out when objects such as meteoroids landed.

SEAS ON THE MOON?

There are lots of dark patches on the Moon's surface. From the Earth, these flat areas look like seas. Early astronomers thought they actually were seas, so they called them *mares* (pronounced *mar-ays*), which means "seas" in Latin. In fact, these "seas" are areas of lava which poured out of volcanoes and then cooled to become solid rock.

Most of the Moon's "seas" are on the side that always faces Earth.

MOUNTAINS

The Moon's surface is very mountainous. Its mountain ranges are named after ranges on Earth. The highest range of mountains is called the Apennines. One of its peaks is nearly as high as Mount Everest, the highest mountain on Earth.

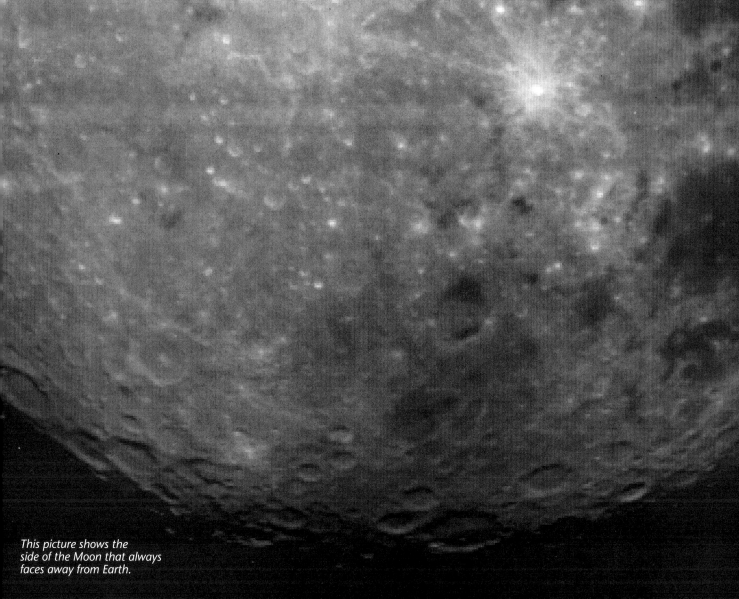

This picture shows the side of the Moon that always faces away from Earth.

TEMPERATURES

On Earth, the atmosphere works like a roof. It stops the Sun from making things too hot during the day, and at night, it prevents heat from escaping.

As the Moon has no atmosphere to protect it, the Sun's rays can make the temperature rise to 253°F, which is hotter than boiling water. When the Sun is not shining on the Moon, the temperature can fall to -189°F.

Internet links

For a link to a website where you can see the Moon's current phase, go to
www.usborne-quicklinks.com

PHASES OF THE MOON

The Moon does not make its own light, but it reflects the Sun's rays. It can look very bright in the night sky.

The shape of the Moon seems to change from night to night. This is because, as the Moon orbits the Earth, different amounts of its sunlit side are visible to us. Sometimes, you can't see its sunlit side at all. The different shapes are known as the phases of the Moon.

The diagram on the right shows the different phases of the Moon. Look at the moon tonight and see if you can tell

Direction of sunlight *Moon* *Earth*

The pictures below show what the Moon looks like from Earth when it is in each of the numbered positions shown in the diagram above.

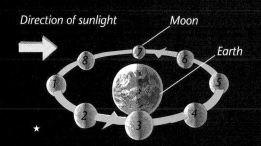

1. New moon
2. Crescent
3. Half moon
4. Waxing

5. Full moon
6. Waning
7. Half moon
8. Crescent

ECLIPSES

As the Earth and Moon move in space, they sometimes block each other from the Sun's light. This is known as an eclipse. Every now and then you can see an eclipse. It is an exciting event and often makes the news. There are two types – a lunar eclipse and a solar eclipse.

LUNAR ECLIPSES

When the Earth passes between the Sun and the Moon, and the Moon moves into Earth's shadow, a lunar eclipse occurs. The Moon looks dim in the sky. There is usually one lunar eclipse a year. You can see a lunar eclipse from the side of the Earth that is in darkness.

The Moon often turns a reddish shade during a lunar eclipse.

TOTAL LUNAR ECLIPSE

Like any shadow, the Earth's shadow is lighter at the edges and darker in the middle. If the Moon passes into the darker part, called the umbra, a total eclipse takes place. When this happens, the Moon looks very dark.

Sun   Earth   Moon

During a total lunar eclipse, the Moon is completely in the Earth's shadow.

A PARTIAL LUNAR ECLIPSE

This diagram shows what happens during a partial lunar eclipse.

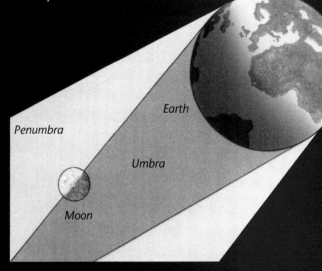

Earth

Penumbra

Umbra

Moon

★

A partial lunar eclipse happens when part of the Moon stays in the lighter part of the shadow, the penumbra. The Moon doesn't look as dark during a partial eclipse as it does during a total eclipse.

A partial eclipse also occurs if the Moon misses the umbra completely and only goes through the penumbra, but it is much less noticeable.

The big photograph on this page shows a total eclipse of the Sun, or solar eclipse (see opposite). The Sun is blocked out completely by the Moon's shadow.

Internet links

For a link to a website where you can see photographs of eclipses, go to **www.usborne-quicklinks.com**

SOLAR ECLIPSES

A solar eclipse happens when the Moon passes between the Sun and the Earth, blotting out sunlight to part of our planet. Solar eclipses only happen about once every three to four years and usually only last for two to three minutes. During a total solar eclipse, you can see a bright glow of light around the Moon. This is the corona, the outer part of the Sun's atmosphere.

An annular eclipse occurs when the Moon passes directly in front of the Sun but has a ring of sunlight visible around it. Some eclipses can look either total or annular depending on where they are seen from. These are called hybrid eclipses.

SEEING THE ECLIPSE

A total solar eclipse can only be seen from the places on Earth that are covered by the Moon's umbra. This area is called the zone of totality. The zone of totality is only up to about 250 miles in diameter. This means that relatively few people have ever seen a total eclipse.

This series of pictures shows what happens during a solar eclipse. The red arrows show the direction of the Moon.

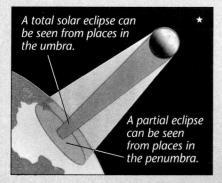

A total solar eclipse can be seen from places in the umbra.

A partial eclipse can be seen from places in the penumbra.

1. The Moon approaches the Sun.

2. The Moon starts to slide over the face of the Sun.

3. The Sun's light is partly blocked out. This is a partial eclipse.

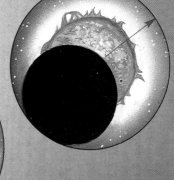

4. In a total eclipse, the Sun is blocked out. Only the corona can be seen.

LOOKING SAFELY

The best way to see a solar eclipse is to project an image of it (see page 13). DO NOT look straight at the eclipse, or view it through tinted glass, binoculars or a telescope. The rays from the Sun are so powerful that they may blind you.

A DAZZLING EFFECT

Immediately before the Sun disappears from view behind the Moon during a solar eclipse, a final flash of light shines out. This is known as the diamond ring effect because it looks like a sparkling diamond. This occurs again when the Sun reappears on the other side of the Moon.

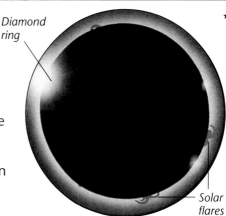

Diamond ring

Solar flares

STAR GROUPS

Galaxies are groups of billions of stars that can form in different shapes. Within a galaxy, stars often group together in clusters, and galaxies are themselves generally grouped together too.

Internet links

For a link to a website where you can go on a virtual tour of galaxies and learn about some unusual ones, go to **www.usborne-quicklinks.com**

GALAXIES

On the right, you can see four of the most common galaxy shapes: spiral, barred spiral, elliptical and irregular. A third of all known galaxies are spiral shaped. Most astronomers think that the Milky Way is a barred spiral galaxy.

The force of gravity keeps all the stars in a galaxy together. In the same way that the planets are locked in orbit around the Sun, the Sun is locked in orbit around the middle of the Milky Way.

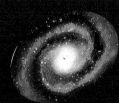

A spiral galaxy has a bright middle and two or more curved arms of stars.

A barred spiral galaxy has a central bar with an arm at each end.

An elliptical galaxy varies in shape from circular to oval.

An irregular galaxy doesn't really have any fixed shape. It just looks like a cloud of stars.

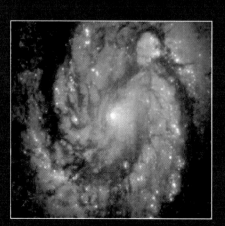

This is the spiral galaxy M100. It is 30 million light years away from Earth.

NEAREST GALAXIES

The galaxies closest to the Milky Way are the Large and Small Magellanic Clouds (LMC and SMC). These are small, irregular galaxies.

The nearest large galaxy is the Andromeda Galaxy. This spiral galaxy is the most distant object visible to the naked eye. It is 2.9 million light years away.

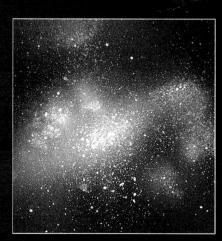

This is the Large Magellanic Cloud.

SEEING GALAXIES

When you look at a galaxy, you see the combined light of its billions of stars. Through small telescopes, most galaxies appear as smudges of light. They can be seen much more clearly through very powerful telescopes, although these can be very expensive.

GALACTIC GROUPS

The group of galaxies that contains our galaxy is called the Local Group. It is relatively small and only contains about thirty galaxies, stretching across five million light years. Some groups, such as the Virgo cluster, which is 60 million light years away, contain up to 2,500 galaxies.

STAR CLUSTERS

Stars within a cluster move at the same speed and in the same direction. There are two types of star clusters. Open clusters are found in areas of space that are rich in gas and dust. They can contain up to a thousand bright young stars, which are scattered loosely in the cluster.

This is the Pleiades group of stars, in the constellation Taurus. It is an open cluster.

Globular clusters are much larger than open clusters and tend to be found above and below the central bulge of a galaxy. They contain up to a million stars, densely packed together in sphere-shaped clumps. There are about 150 known globular clusters in our galaxy.

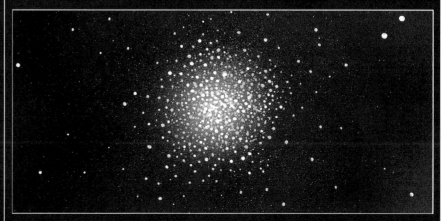

This is a globular cluster. Globular clusters look like very faint stars to the naked eye.

This is a Hubble Space Telescope image of the Cartwheel Galaxy. It is 500 million light years away.

SPACE COLLISION

The Cartwheel Galaxy (shown above) is an enormous galaxy, 150,000 light years across. Its rare shape was formed when a smaller galaxy smashed into it. The outer ring is an immense circle of billions of new stars. These formed from the gas and dust that expanded from the core after the collision. Its original spiral shape is now starting to reform.

STAR PATTERNS

Since the earliest civilizations, people have noticed patterns of bright stars in the sky. These patterns are called constellations. At first glance, you may only see what looks like a jumble of twinkling stars. But with practice you can pick out the shapes of constellations.

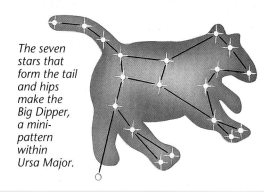

The seven stars that form the tail and hips make the Big Dipper, a mini-pattern within Ursa Major.

This is Ursa Major, or the Great Bear. Here, the imaginary shape of a bear has been drawn around the constellation.

USING STAR MAPS

You can use star maps, like those on pages 24–31, to help you identify constellations. In this book, there are different maps for each season, because as the Earth orbits the Sun, the part of the sky we can see changes. There are also different maps for the northern and southern hemispheres, as many of the stars you can see from each of these are different.

To use the star maps, choose the right hemisphere and season and look in the direction indicated on the map. On each pair of maps, the dates and times when the star maps will match up exactly with the night sky are noted. The star maps don't show the planets or the Moon because their positions change from month to month. If you see something that looks like a star, but isn't shown on the maps, it's probably a planet.

HUGE DISTANCES

Constellations are made up of the most prominent stars in the sky. From Earth, the stars in each constellation look fairly close to one another. In reality, they are extremely far apart.

The stars in the constellation Orion, for example, vary between less than 500 and over 2,000 light years away from Earth. They only look as if they are near to each other because they all lie in the same direction.

SMALLER PATTERNS

Within constellations, there are smaller patterns, called asterisms. The Big Dipper, or Plough, is a famous asterism. It is part of the constellation Ursa Major (see top picture).

POINTERS

Stars in certain constellations form pointers that will help you to find other constellations in the sky.

For instance, if you imagine a line running through the two end stars of the Big Dipper in Ursa Major, the line points to Polaris, the North Star. These two useful stars are known as the Pointers.

This diagram shows the constellation Orion as it looks in the sky (left), where the stars seem close together, and how the stars are really positioned in space (right).

The Pointers in the Big Dipper line up with Polaris in the constellation Ursa Minor.

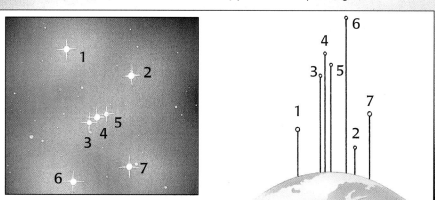

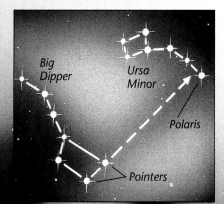

STARS ON THE MOVE

Stars move through space at extremely high speeds, but they are so far away that any motion is impossible to detect, except with very powerful equipment. This is why constellations seem to be fixed in the sky.

100,000 years ago, the stars of the Big Dipper were shaped like this.

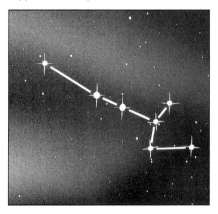

This is how the Big Dipper looks today.

In another 100,000 years, the shape will have altered greatly.

NAMING THE STARS

Many of the brightest stars have both a Greek or Latin name and an English name. The brightest star of all is called Sirius, a name of Greek origin, which means "scorching." Its English name is the Dog Star.

ALL IN ORDER

Stars are also known by the name of their constellation, plus a Greek letter. Usually, the brightest star in a constellation is given the first letter of the Greek alphabet, alpha (α). The next brightest is given the second letter, beta (β), and so on.

There are only 24 letters in the Greek alphabet, so if a constellation has more than 24 stars, the rest are numbered.

GREEK SYMBOLS AND THEIR NAMES

α	alpha	ν	nu
β	beta	ξ	xi
γ	gamma	o	omicron
δ	delta	π	pi
ε	epsilon	ρ	rho
ζ	zeta	σ	sigma
η	eta	τ	tau
θ	theta	υ	upsilon
ι	iota	φ	phi
κ	kappa	χ	chi
λ	lambda	ψ	psi
μ	mu	ω	omega

This is an illustration of the five main stars of the constellation Cassiopeia. These stars make up its W-shape, which is easy to recognize. Each star is labeled with a letter from the Greek alphabet, which indicates how bright it is compared with the others.

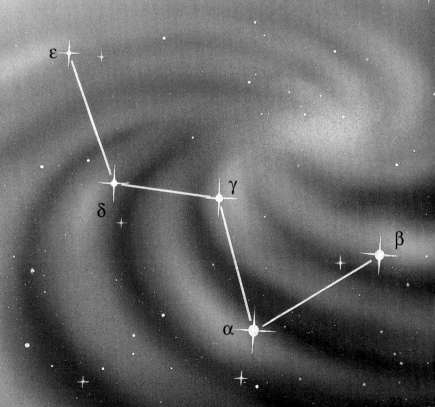

THE NIGHT SKY IN SPRING

STAR MAPS FOR THE NORTHERN HEMISPHERE

The only star in the sky that doesn't seem to change its position is Polaris, in the middle of the top map. Polaris is flanked by Capella and Aldebaran on its left, and Deneb and Vega on its right.

Look for Ursa Major (the Great Bear) overhead and Taurus (the Bull) in the west. The bright streak in the sky is the starry trail of the Milky Way.

March 15th 11:00pm
April 15th 10:00pm
May 15th 9:00pm

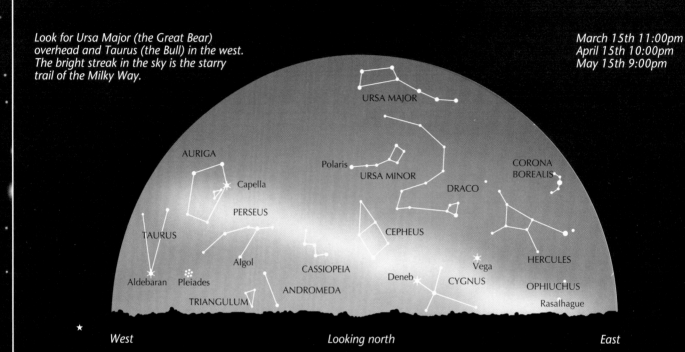

West   Looking north   East

Regulus is the bright star in the middle of the sky. It is part of the constellation of Leo (the Lion).

East   Looking south   West

STAR MAPS FOR THE SOUTHERN HEMISPHERE

The most famous constellation is Crux, or the Southern Cross. It can never be seen from the northern hemisphere. Facing north, the constellations of Pegasus and Andromeda dominate the sky.

Internet links

Website 1 Find tips on how to observe the night sky.

Website 2 View amazing interactive star maps.

For links to these websites, go to
www.usborne-quicklinks.com

M31, just above the horizon, is a spiral-shaped galaxy.

September 15th 11:00pm
October 15th 10:00pm
November 15th 9:00pm

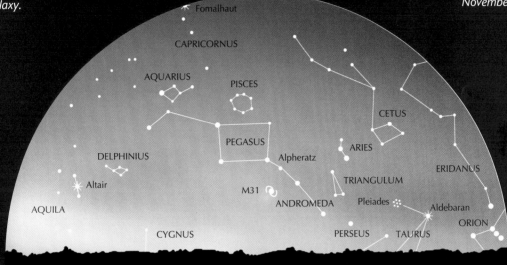

West — Looking north — East

Sirius is the brightest star in the sky. Canopus is the second brightest.

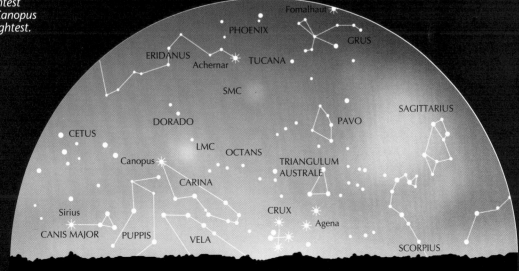

East — Looking south — West

25

THE NIGHT SKY IN SUMMER

MAPS FOR THE NORTHERN HEMISPHERE

The sky never really gets dark in summer, so only the brightest stars show up clearly. If the sky is clear on August 12th, stay up to watch shooting stars coming from the constellation of Perseus.

Capella, Regulus and Deneb are the brightest stars in the northern sky at this time of year.

June 15th 11:00pm
July 15th 10:00pm
August 15th 9:00pm

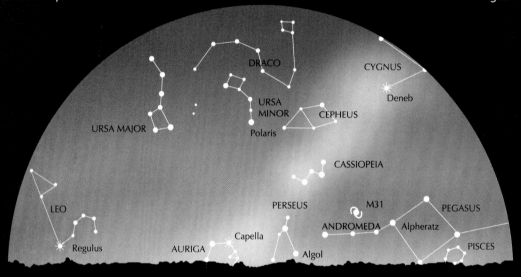

West   Looking north   East

Look for Antares shining brightly above the southern horizon.

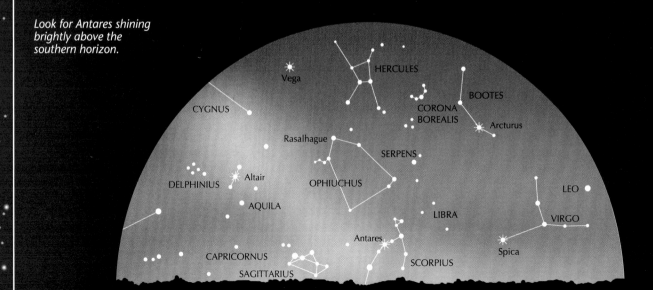

East   Looking south   West

MAPS FOR THE SOUTHERN HEMISPHERE

Facing north, the easiest constellations to spot are Orion and Canis Major (the Great Dog) and over to the east you can see Leo (the Lion). Sirius (the Dog Star), one of the stars in Canis Major, is the brightest star in the sky.

Internet links

Website 1 See a different NASA picture of the Universe each day.

Website 2 Find constellation charts and star maps for each month.

For links to these websites, go to
www.usborne-quicklinks.com

Look for the cluster of stars known as Pleiades, or Seven Sisters, in the constellation of Taurus.

December 15th 11:00pm
January 15th 10:00pm
February 15th 9:00pm

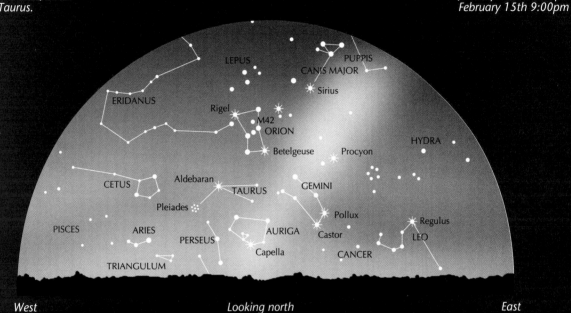

West   Looking north   East

LMC and SMC stand for Large and Small Magellanic Cloud. These are small galaxies.

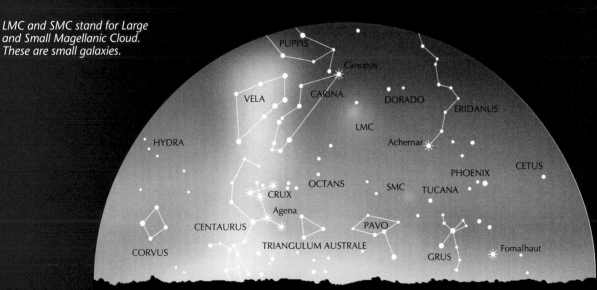

East   Looking south   West

27

THE NIGHT SKY IN FALL

MAPS FOR THE NORTHERN HEMISPHERE

Facing north, look for Ursa Major, which is below Polaris and parallel with the horizon. Looking south, you should be able to see Pegasus (the Winged Horse), which has a square of stars in the middle.

In the east, the winter stars are beginning to rise, including the red star Aldebaran.

September 15th 11:00pm
October 15th 10:00pm
November 15th 9:00pm

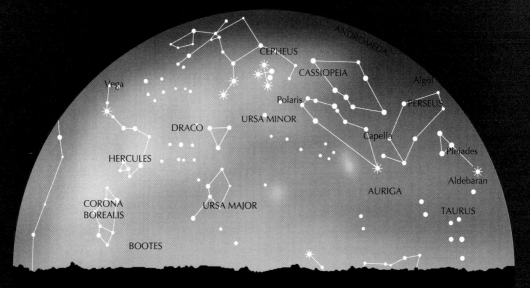

West Looking north East

This is the best time to see M31, a huge distant galaxy. It is just visible with the naked eye, but binoculars will show it as a misty oval.

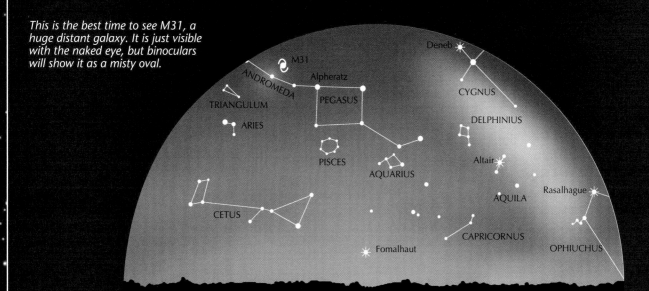

East Looking south West

MAPS FOR THE SOUTHERN HEMISPHERE

Facing north, a triangle of three bright stars dominates the sky: Regulus, which is blue, yellow Arcturus and blue-white Spica. Facing south, the Milky Way crosses the sky in a wide band.

Internet links

Website 1 Find out more about stars and see amazing pictures of them.

Website 2 Find out what's inside a star and why stars twinkle.

For links to these websites, go to
www.usborne-quicklinks.com

Look for the constellations of Virgo (the Virgin) and Leo (the Lion).

March 15th 11:00pm
April 15th 10:00pm
May 15th 9:00pm

West — Looking north — East

Above Crux (the Southern Cross) is Centaurus (the Centaur). A centaur was a mythical creature that was half man and half horse.

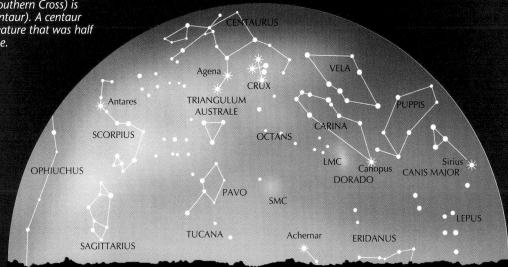

East — Looking south — West

THE NIGHT SKY IN WINTER

MAPS FOR THE NORTHERN HEMISPHERE

Winter is a good time to look for shooting stars. Set your alarm for just before dawn on December 14th to see shooting stars coming from Gemini. Looking south, you can see Orion, one of the brightest constellations.

Facing north, look for Ursa Major balancing on its tail, and Cygnus (the Swan).

December 15th 11:00pm
January 15th 10:00pm
February 15th 9:00pm

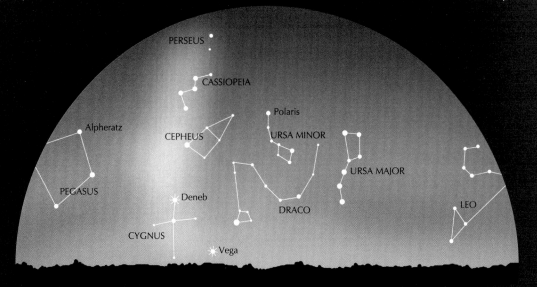

West   Looking north   East

If you find the bright constellation of Orion, it will help you locate the other constellations.

East   Looking south   West

MAPS FOR THE SOUTHERN HEMISPHERE

There are plenty of bright stars to look for at this time of the year. Try to spot Deneb, Spica, Altair, Vega and Fomalhaut. The Milky Way is seen at its best, cutting the sky in half.

Internet links

Website 1 Find out about different kinds of equipment you can use for stargazing.

Website 2 Go on an amazing virtual journey through the stars.

For links to these websites, go to **www.usborne-quicklinks.com**

Look for Ophiuchus (the Serpent Bearer), a very large group of stars, and Hercules, named after a Greek hero.

June 15th 11:00pm
July 15th 10:00pm
August 15th 9:00pm

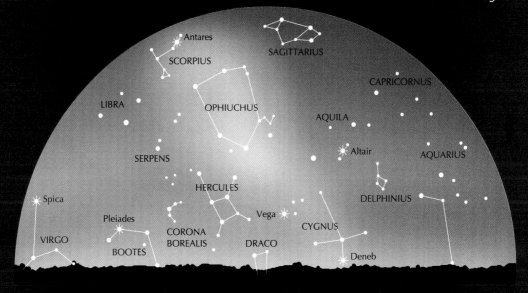

West   Looking north   East

The Milky Way runs through Crux (the Southern Cross) and Centaurus (the Centaur).

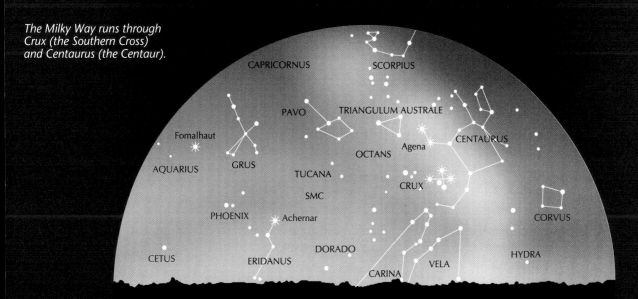

East   Looking south   West

FAMOUS CONSTELLATIONS

H ere are some famous constellations with
drawings of the things that they are
supposed to represent. Compare the shape of
the constellation to the drawing. You'll see that
often the star pattern does not look much like
the shape it represents.

Internet links

For a link to a website where you can
play a constellation game, go to
www.usborne-quicklinks.com

ORION THE HUNTER

The star scene shown on the right is dominated by
Orion, a great hunter in Greek mythology. Armed
with a club and a shield of lion skin, he faces a
charging bull, Taurus. The easiest part of Orion to
spot is the line of three stars that forms his belt.
Below it lie two stars, which represent his sword.
Orion's two faithful hunting dogs, Canis Major and
Canis Minor, stand behind him. At his feet is Lepus
the hare, the animal he most enjoys hunting.

Aldebaran

TAURUS

Procyon

Betelgeuse

ORION

CANIS MINOR

Rigel

Sirius

LEPUS

CANIS MAJOR

*The shape of Canis Major, the
large dog, is fairly easy to make
out. However, you need more
imagination to see the shape of
the little dog, Canis Minor.*

PEGASUS

Enif

ANDROMEDA

Algol

THE STORY OF PERSEUS

To ancient Greek astronomers, the stars on the
left represented the myth of Perseus. He killed
Medusa, a creature so ugly that anyone who
looked at her turned to stone. On his way home
he found Andromeda, daughter
of Cassiopeia and Cepheus.
She was chained to the
rocks, waiting to be
devoured by the dreaded
sea monster Cetus. Perseus
showed Medusa's head to
Cetus, who immediately
turned to stone, and so
Andromeda was saved.

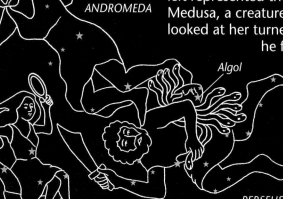

*Perseus cleverly used a
mirrored shield to help him
kill Medusa without looking
straight at her. As Perseus
cut off Medusa's head, the
white-winged horse, Pegasus*

PERSEUS

MAP OF THE MOON

The map below shows the side of the Moon that always faces the Earth. Look at the Moon on a clear night and see how many of these features you can see.

Internet links

Website 1 Explore interactive maps of the moon.

For links to these websites, go to
www.usborne-quicklinks.com

Most astronomical telescopes make things look upside down. If you are using a telescope, turn this picture upside down to make it look like what you see.

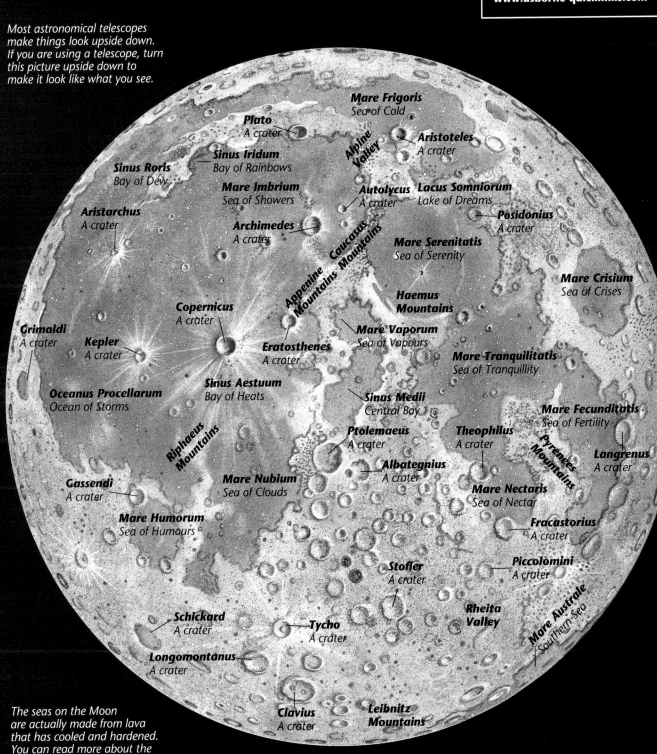

Mare Frigoris
Sea of Cold

Plato
A crater

Aristoteles
A crater

Alpine Valley

Sinus Iridum
Bay of Rainbows

Sinus Roris
Bay of Dew

Mare Imbrium
Sea of Showers

Autolycus
A crater

Lacus Somniorum
Lake of Dreams

Posidonius
A crater

Aristarchus
A crater

Archimedes
A crater

Caucasus Mountains

Mare Serenitatis
Sea of Serenity

Mare Crisium
Sea of Crises

Copernicus
A crater

Appenine Mountains

Haemus Mountains

Eratosthenes
A crater

Mare Vaporum
Sea of Vapours

Grimaldi
A crater

Kepler
A crater

Mare Tranquilitatis
Sea of Tranquillity

Oceanus Procellarum
Ocean of Storms

Sinus Aestuum
Bay of Heats

Sinus Medii
Central Bay

Mare Fecunditatis
Sea of Fertility

Riphaeus Mountains

Ptolemaeus
A crater

Theophilus
A crater

Pyrenees Mountains

Langrenus
A crater

Gassendi
A crater

Mare Nubium
Sea of Clouds

Albategnius
A crater

Mare Nectaris
Sea of Nectar

Mare Humorum
Sea of Humours

Fracastorius
A crater

Stofler
A crater

Piccolomini
A crater

Schickard
A crater

Tycho
A crater

Rheita Valley

Mare Australe
Southern Sea

Longomontanus
A crater

Clavius
A crater

Leibnitz Mountains

The seas on the Moon are actually made from lava that has cooled and hardened. You can read more about the Moon's seas on page 16.

This is Wonder Lake in Denali National Park, Alaska. The mountain behind it is Mount McKinley, the highest mountain in North America.

PLANET EARTH

INSIDE THE EARTH

T he Earth has a solid surface, but is not solid all the way through. Inside, it is made up of layers, some of which are partly molten (melted). If you sliced through the Earth, you would see four main layers: the crust, the mantle, the outer core and the inner core.

Internet links

For a link to a website where you can find out how compasses work using the Earth's magnetism, and learn how to make your own compass, go to **www.usborne-quicklinks.com**

CRUST AND MANTLE

The thin layer of solid rock that covers the Earth is called the crust. This is the thinnest of the Earth's layers, at between 3 miles and 43 miles thick.

Beneath the crust is the mantle, which is made of silicon and magnesium. Within the mantle, there is a thin layer called the asthenosphere. This is mostly solid rock, but a small amount is molten rock, or magma. The crust and the upper part of the mantle, together known as the lithosphere, move around on this layer.

INTO THE CORE

The Earth's core is an incredibly hot ball of iron and nickel, with a temperature of around 9,000°F. It has two parts. The outer core, which is about 1,400 miles thick, is molten. The inner core is solid. It is about 800 miles thick.

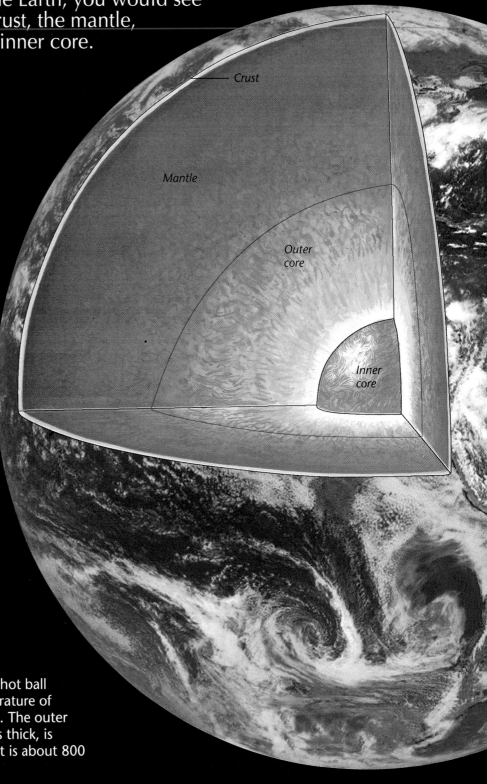

Crust

Mantle

Outer core

Inner core

THE EARTH'S CRUST

There are two different types of crust. Thick continental crust forms land and much thinner oceanic crust makes up the ocean floors. Continental crust is made of light rock such as granite, sandstone and limestone. Oceanic crust is made of heavier rock such as basalt and dolerite.

The Earth's crust is made up of oceanic and continental crust.

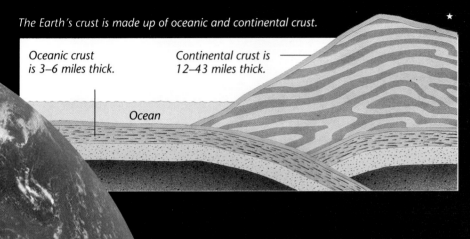

Oceanic crust is 3–6 miles thick.

Continental crust is 12–43 miles thick.

Ocean

INVESTIGATING THE EARTH

It's difficult to find out about the inside of the Earth. Geologists, who study rocks, find out about areas near the surface by drilling holes into the crust and collecting rock samples. But, they can still only drill a short distance below the surface.

DEEPER DOWN

Volcanic eruptions provide some information about material deep inside the Earth. But the main way that geologists find out about the Earth's structure is by studying earthquakes.

During an earthquake, vibrations called seismic waves travel through the Earth. As they pass through different materials, they change speed and direction. By studying records of earthquakes, called seismograms, geologists try to determine what rocks are found at different depths.

Earthquake

Paths of waves

This diagram shows how seismic waves change direction as they pass through the Earth.

MAGNETIC EARTH

The Earth is magnetic. This is thought to be caused by molten iron circulating in its core. Imagine that there is a huge bar magnet running through the Earth. The ends of this "magnet" are called the magnetic poles. They are not in exactly the same place as the geographic North and South Poles.

This diagram shows the Earth's magnetic field, the area affected by its magnetism. The lines show the direction of the magnetic field.

Magnetic North Pole

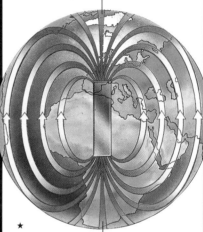

Magnetic South Pole

You can see the Earth's magnetism at work when you use a compass. The compass needle, which is magnetic, always points north. This is because it is pulled, or attracted, by the magnetic North Pole.

Compass needles point to the Earth's magnetic North Pole.

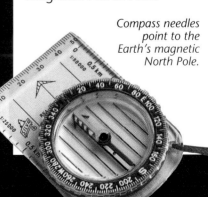

37

THE EARTH'S CRUST

The lithosphere is broken up into large pieces called plates, which are constantly moving. Many of the Earth's most spectacular features have been formed by the gradual movement of these plates.

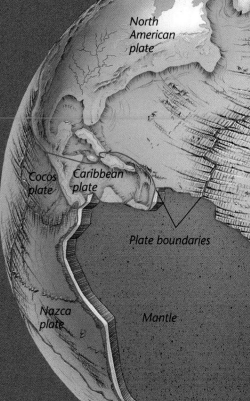

North American plate

Cocos plate

Caribbean plate

Plate boundaries

Nazca plate

Mantle

A MOVING SURFACE

There are seven large plates and many smaller plates. Each one is made up of either continental or oceanic crust, or both. The areas where the plates meet are called plate boundaries. The plates move very slowly on the asthenosphere, at a rate of about 2in a year. As they all fit together, the movement of one plate affects the others. The study of these plates and the way they move around is called plate tectonics.

Internet links

Website 1 See an animated picture showing how the Earth's plates have moved.

Website 2 Read about the causes and effects of earthquakes and volcanoes, and watch some video clips.

For links to these websites, go to **www.usborne-quicklinks.com**

OCEAN RIDGES

As plates below the ocean move apart, magma from the mantle rises and fills the gap. It cools and hardens to form a mountain range, or ridge, of new crust. As the movement continues and more magma wells up, the ridge spreads out sideways, becoming a spreading ridge. Boundaries where new crust is formed are called constructive boundaries.

This diagram shows how ridges and trenches form.

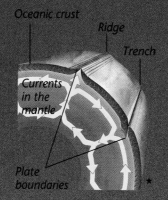

Oceanic crust

Ridge

Trench

Currents in the mantle

Plate boundaries

TRENCHES

When an oceanic and continental plate move together, the heavier oceanic plate is forced beneath the lighter continental plate, and a trench forms where they meet. As the plate sinks, some of it melts and becomes magma. These boundaries are called destructive boundaries. The deepest trench, the Mariana Trench in the Pacific Ocean, is deeper than Mount Everest is tall.

SHIFTING CONTINENTS

As plates shift, the position of the oceans and continents on the Earth's surface changes. The maps on the right show how geologists think the continents may have shifted.

Geologists think that there was once a single supercontinent, which we call "Pangaea."

As new rock formed at plate boundaries, the floor of the Atlantic Ocean probably widened.

Today, South America and Africa are drifting apart at a rate of 1.5in each year.

Atlantic Ocean

Africa

South America

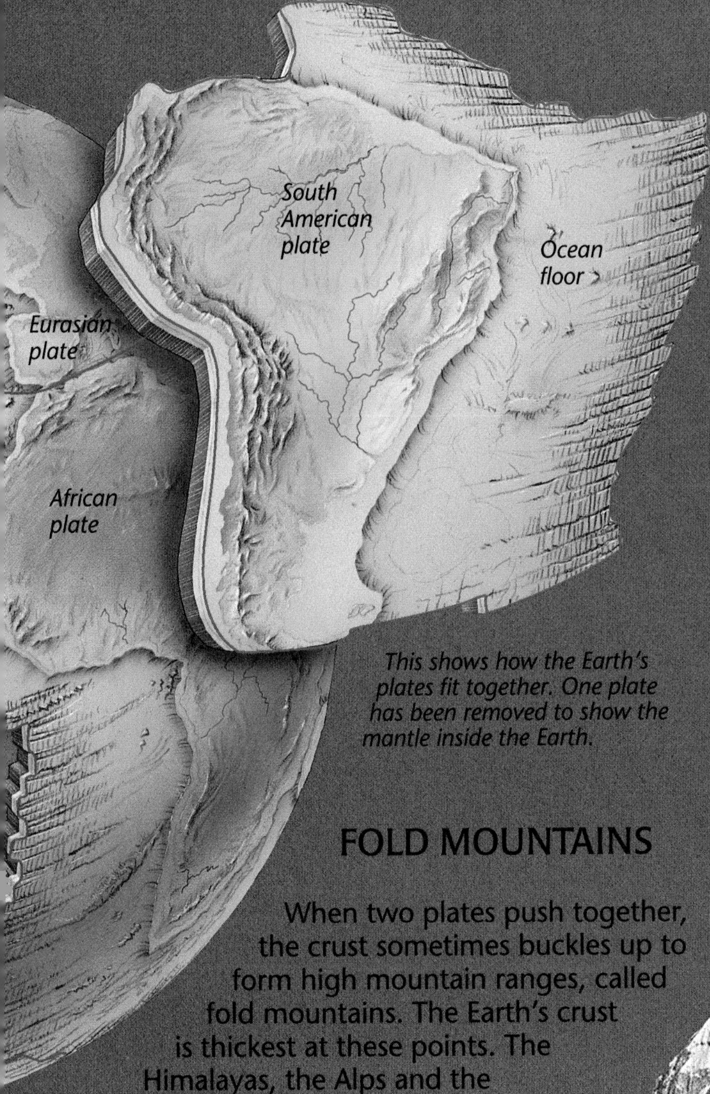
South American plate
Ocean floor
Eurasian plate
African plate

This shows how the Earth's plates fit together. One plate has been removed to show the mantle inside the Earth.

FAULTS

As plates move, the strain of the movement sometimes causes brittle rock to crack. These cracks are called faults. When two faults are close together, the chunk of crust between them can sometimes collapse, to form rift valleys. The raised parts on either side form mountains called block mountains.

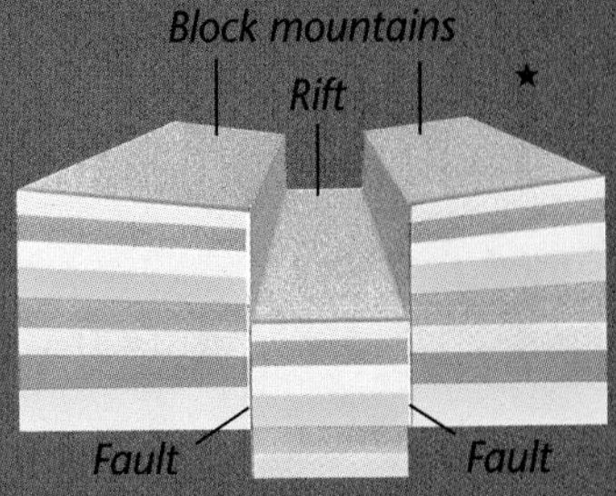
Block mountains
Rift
Fault
Fault

This picture shows a fault in the Great Rift Valley in Africa.

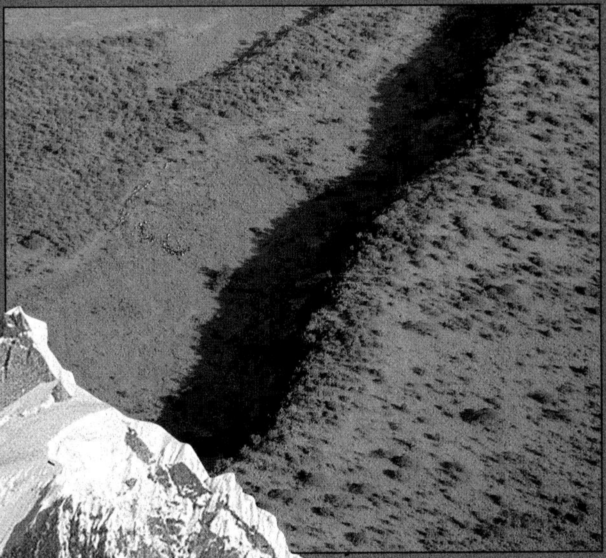

FOLD MOUNTAINS

When two plates push together, the crust sometimes buckles up to form high mountain ranges, called fold mountains. The Earth's crust is thickest at these points. The Himalayas, the Alps and the Andes are all fold mountains

This is part of the Himalayas mountain range in Asia, which is the highest in the world.

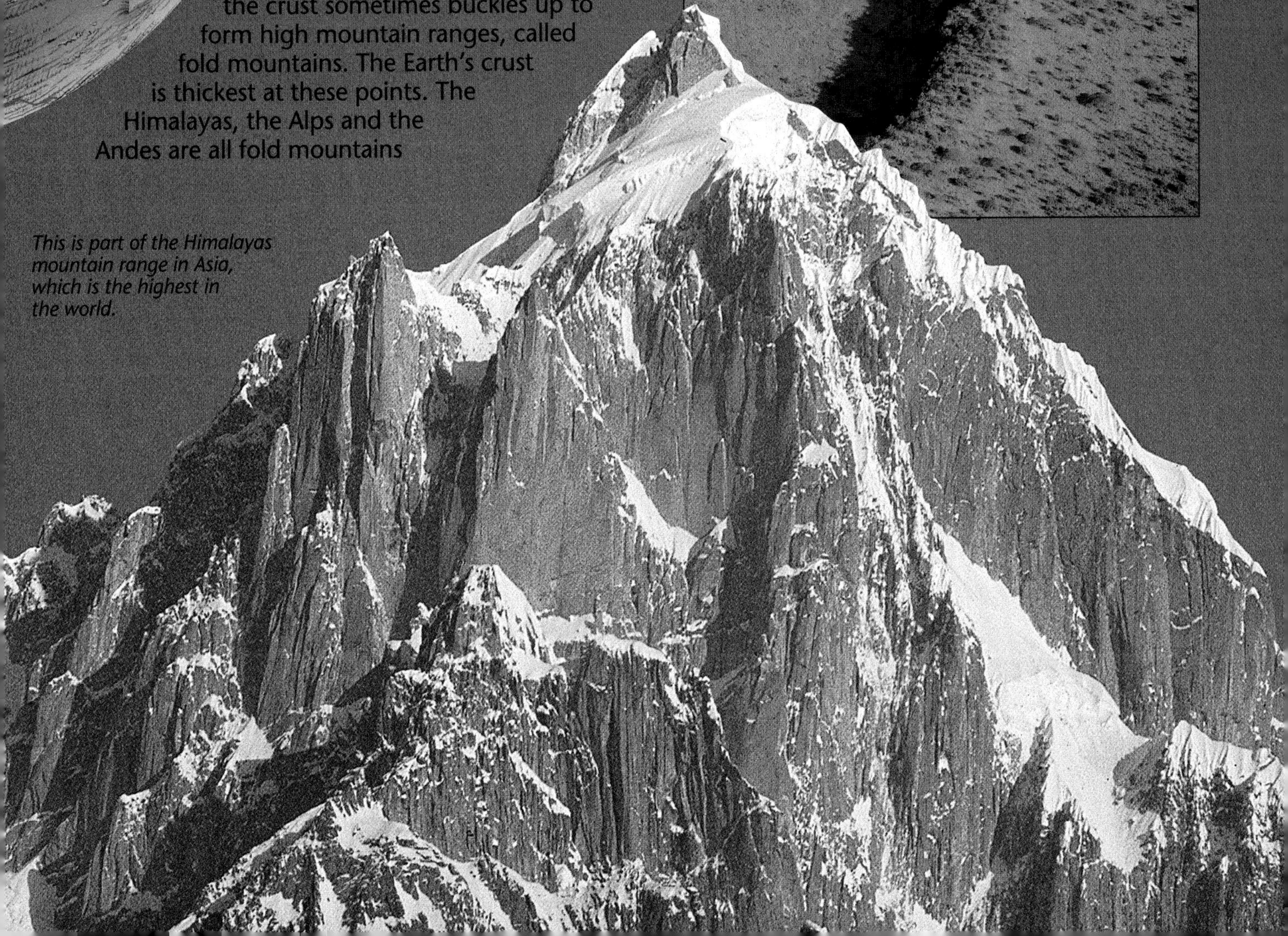

ROCKS, MINERALS AND FOSSILS

The Earth's crust is made of rock, which is made of chemical substances called minerals. There are three kinds of rocks: igneous, sedimentary and metamorphic. Over many years, rocks are sometimes transformed from one kind to another.

IGNEOUS ROCK

Igneous rock is formed from magma. There are two different kinds of igneous rock: intrusive and extrusive. Intrusive igneous rock is formed when magma cools inside the Earth. It may appear on the Earth's surface if the overlying rocks are worn away. Extrusive igneous rock forms from magma that has cooled on the Earth's surface, for example after it has been thrown out during a volcanic eruption.

Tuff is an igneous rock made from pieces of volcanic rock and crystals compressed together.

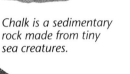
Obsidian is a shiny igneous rock formed when magma cools very quickly.

SEDIMENTARY ROCK

Sedimentary rock is made from pieces of older rock and the partly decayed remains of plants and animals. Rain, wind and ice wear away these fragments, which are called sediment, from exposed areas of rock. They are then blown by the wind, or carried by rivers, glaciers or landslides, to the sea, where they sink. There they build up in layers called strata. The water and upper layers of sediment press down on the lower layers until, eventually, they become solid rock.

Chalk is a sedimentary rock made from tiny sea creatures.

Sandstone is a sedimentary rock made up of sand grains.

The Grand Canyon, in the U.S.A., is a gorge formed by the Colorado River. You can clearly see the different layers of rock.

METAMORPHIC ROCK

Metamorphic rock is rock that has been changed – for example, by heat from magma, pressure caused by plate movement, or both heat and pressure from very deep burial. It can be formed from igneous, sedimentary or other metamorphic rocks.

Marble is a metamorphic rock formed from limestone.

Mica schist is a metamorphic rock that tends to split into layers.

MINERALS

Minerals are made of elements, which are simple substances that can't be broken down into any other substance. Some minerals, such as gold, are made of only one element, but most are made of two or more. Certain minerals are cut and polished to be used as gemstones.

These pictures show minerals in rocks and as gemstones.

Opal can be milky white, green, red, blue, black or brown.

Turquoise runs through rock in the form of veins.

Carnelian is a dark red stone.

Internet links

For a link to a website where you can see different kinds of rocks and find out how they formed, and try some fun quizzes, go to **www.usborne-quicklinks.com**

FOSSILS

The shapes or remains of plants and animals that died long ago are sometimes preserved in rocks. They are called fossils. When plants and animals die, they often decay or are eaten. Fossils form when they are buried by sediment, which then turns to sedimentary rock.

Sometimes, actual parts of the plant or animal are preserved, for example hard parts such as teeth, shells and bones. But most parts usually rot away, leaving a space. This then fills up with minerals, which preserve the shape.

This is the fossil of an ammonite (an extinct sea creature).

RIVERS

The water in rivers comes from rainfall, from snow and ice melting, and from water inside the Earth, called groundwater. Rivers carry this water downhill, along with vast amounts of rock, sand, soil and mud, to lakes and oceans. Rivers can carve through solid rock, eroding deep gorges and huge waterfalls.

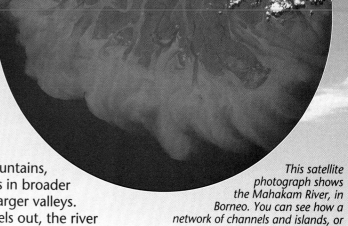

A RIVER'S COURSE

A river changes as it flows downhill along its path, or course. The beginning of a river is called its source. Many rivers begin in mountain areas, where rain and melting ice run into steep, clear streams. These streams cut narrow, deep valleys and join together as they flow downhill. Smaller streams and rivers that flow into a bigger river are called tributaries.

Away from mountains, the water flows in broader channels and larger valleys. As the land levels out, the river starts to form large bends, or meanders. Finally, the river widens out into a broad estuary, or splits to form a network of channels called a delta, before flowing into the sea or a lake. The part of a river where it meets the sea is called the river mouth.

This satellite photograph shows the Mahakam River, in Borneo. You can see how a network of channels and islands, or a delta, is formed where the river runs into the sea.

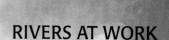

RIVERS AT WORK

As a river flows, the water sweeps along any rocks in its way. The rocks slide and bounce along, chipping away at the riverbed and making it deeper and wider. They also grind against each other, which wears them down and breaks them into smaller pieces.

As a river flows downstream, the riverbed becomes smoother, so the water flows slightly faster. It starts to drop, or deposit, sand, silt and then mud. This is why the lower sections of a river have muddy riverbeds. Near the sea, the sediment may build up to form whole islands. This is when the river splits up to forms a delta.

These rocks have been smoothed and rounded by the action of the water in the river.

CHANGING COURSE

Rivers flow faster around the outside of a meander than on the inside. The outside edge is gradually eroded, while the river deposits sediment on the inside edge. This means that the meander grows longer and narrower over time.

Eventually, the two sides of the meander meet each other, and the river cuts through to form a new, straighter course. The entrance to the meander gradually fills up with sediment, and the loop is cut off, leaving a lake called an oxbow lake, or billabong.

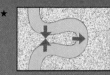

A river erodes the outside of a bend and deposits sediment on the inside, making a loop.

The loop grows longer and narrower until the river finally breaks through.

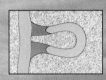

The river flows past the ends of the loop and they slowly become silted up.

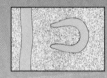

Eventually, the loop gets cut off completely and forms an oxbow lake.

This is the Horseshoe Falls, part of Niagara Falls, which is a huge waterfall on the border between Canada and the U.S.A. The waterfall moves upstream by around 11ft per year.

Internet links

For a link to a website where you can learn more about rivers and find out which are the longest in the world, go to **www.usborne-quicklinks.com**

WATERFALLS

Waterfalls begin when a river flows from an area of hard rock onto soft rock. The river wears away the soft rock more quickly and creates a ledge. Water falling over the ledge erodes a hollow at the bottom called a plunge pool. The bigger the ledge, the greater the force of the water crashing down.

The action of the water and pebbles churning in the plunge pool can undercut the hard rock, creating an overhanging ledge. Chunks of the overhanging rock break off and very gradually, over hundreds of years, the waterfall moves backward, cutting a deep valley called a gorge.

This diagram shows how a waterfall is formed.

Waterfall cutting back

Falling water cuts away at the soft rock below.

Hard rock

Plunge pool

Softer rock

Spray undercuts here.

SEAS AND OCEANS

More than two-thirds of the Earth's surface is covered with salt water. The Earth's five oceans and its seas are all connected, so sea water flows freely between them. Oceans are very important to life on Earth, and are home to huge numbers of living things. For thousands of years, they have provided people with food, and passengers and goods are often carried by sea.

The ballan wrasse fish is found mainly near rocky shores in Europe.

EXPLORING THE SEA

Scientists visit the seabed in mini-submarines called submersibles, or explore it from the surface using robots called remote operated vehicles (ROVs). They also map the seabed using sonar. This sends out sounds, which are bounced back as echoes, showing how deep the seabed is.

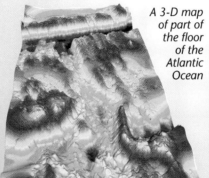

A 3-D map of part of the floor of the Atlantic Ocean

UNDER THE SEA

Near land, the seabed slopes gradually downhill, forming a wide shelf called the continental shelf. It then drops away to the deeper part of the ocean floor, the abyssal plain, which has valleys, hills, mountains and even volcanoes, just like the land.

CHANGING COASTS

The coast is constantly being broken down and built up by the action of waves. Over many years, this action changes the shape of countries' coastlines.

When waves crash against cliffs, any debris they are carrying is flung against the rock, wearing it down, or eroding it, into bays. These are called destructive waves. But when waves break onto flat beaches, they slow down and drop debris, which then builds up gradually to form beaches. These are called constructive waves.

Sea level can also change, which affects coastlines. At the moment it is rising by about 0.04in each year. (You can find out more on page 53.)

This diver is retrieving a rock from a remote operated vehicle (ROV). The ROV has returned to shallow waters after collecting rock samples from the seabed.

LIFE IN THE OCEANS

Seas and oceans contain a huge variety of plant and animal life, from the surface all the way down to the deepest trenches.

The loggerhead turtle lives in warm, shallow seas and comes ashore to lay its eggs.

The main food source in the sea is phytoplankton, which is microscopic plant life. Billions of phytoplankton drift near the surface of the sea, and make their food from sunlight, water, gases and minerals.

This is part of a coral reef in the Red Sea, which lies between Egypt and Saudi Arabia.

CORAL REEFS

Coral reefs are amazing undersea structures that form in warm, shallow seas. They look like plants, but they are actually made of the skeletons of tiny animals called coral polyps. When old polyps die, new ones grow on top of the skeletons, and over many years a huge reef builds up.

Internet links

For a link to a website where you can discover more about the diverse life in the world's oceans, go to **www.usborne-quicklinks.com**

OCEAN ZONES

The deeper down you go in the ocean, the darker and colder it is, and the fewer plants and animals there are. Different plants and animals live at each level.

Sunlit zone
Sea plants and many animals live here.

Down to 650ft

Twilight zone
Many different kinds of fish live here.

Down to 3,300ft

Sunless zone
Animals feed on dead food that falls from above.

Down to 13,100ft

Abyssal zone
The water is cold and dark. Few creatures live here.

Down to 16,400ft

THE EARTH'S ATMOSPHERE

Earth's atmosphere is about 500 miles thick and has an enormous effect on our weather and climate. When energy from the Sun reaches the atmosphere, most filters through, but some is reflected back into space. Our atmosphere is made up of five layers: the troposphere, stratosphere, mesosphere, thermosphere and finally the exosphere, which extends out into space.

THE TROPOSPHERE

The troposphere is the layer of the atmosphere nearest to the Earth's surface and is where the weather is produced. It gets its name from the Greek word *tropos,* which means "a turn." This is because the air there is constantly circulating.

The troposphere contains 80% of all gases in the atmosphere, as well as clouds, dust and pollution. From the Earth's surface, it extends to around 6 miles above the poles and 12 miles above the Equator. Temperatures are high near the Earth because the air is heated from below by the Earth's surface, which is warmed by the Sun. Higher up, the air is thinner and can't hold as much heat, so temperatures decrease.

Internet links

For a link to a website where you can find out why we need the ozone layer and how we can stop damaging it, go to **www.usborne-quicklinks.com**

THE ATMOSPHERE'S STRUCTURE

The gases that surround the Earth are held by its gravity. The atmosphere's layers are divided up according to the temperature of these gases. These extend out from Earth and fade into space.

This diagram shows some of the layers in the Earth's atmosphere. The outermost layer, the exosphere, is not marked; it is around 310 miles from Earth.

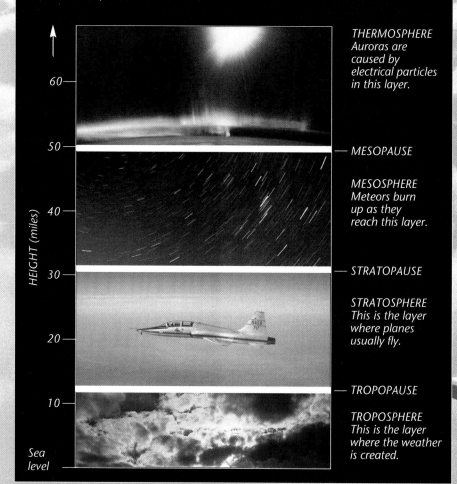

HEIGHT (miles)

60 —
50 —
40 —
30 —
20 —
10 —
Sea level

THERMOSPHERE
Auroras are caused by electrical particles in this layer.

— MESOPAUSE

MESOSPHERE
Meteors burn up as they reach this layer.

— STRATOPAUSE

STRATOSPHERE
This is the layer where planes usually fly.

— TROPOPAUSE

TROPOSPHERE
This is the layer where the weather is created.

THE STRATOSPHERE

The upper limit of the stratosphere is around 30 miles from the Earth's surface. Planes usually fly in this layer because the air is very still.

The stratosphere contains about 19% of all the atmosphere's gases. The temperature there is high because it contains the ozone layer. Ozone gas is very important, as it absorbs the harmful ultraviolet rays from the Sun, preventing them from reaching the Earth. These rays can cause skin cancer and damage to the eyes.

THE MESOSPHERE

The mesosphere reaches to a height of around 50 miles. Temperatures there are the coolest in the atmosphere because there is very little ozone, dust or clouds to absorb energy from the Sun. It is warmer at the bottom, as there is more ozone there.

When you fly in a plane in the stratosphere, you can often see the clouds in the troposphere below.

THE THERMOSPHERE

The Space Shuttle orbits in the thermosphere. The temperature in this layer can be extremely high, reaching up to 2,732°F. This is because it contains a high proportion of a gas called atomic oxygen, which heats up as it absorbs energy from the Sun.

THE OZONE LAYER

The layer of ozone gas in the stratosphere is being damaged by chemicals called chlorofluorocarbons (CFCs), which are used in some spray cans and refrigerators. At certain times of year, a hole in the ozone layer appears over Antarctica, and in other areas the ozone layer becomes very thin. This damage means that more of the Sun's harmful ultraviolet rays reach the Earth's surface.

The bright pink areas in this picture show a hole in the layer of ozone gas over Antarctica.

WHAT IS WEATHER?

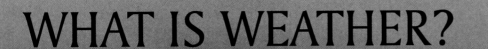

Weather is the way the Earth's atmosphere behaves, whether it is hot or cold, windy or still, raining, snowing or hailing. It affects people's everyday lives in all kinds of ways.

WEATHER EFFECTS

Anything from crops to summer vacations can be ruined if the weather behaves unexpectedly. Weather is also a factor in many of the world's worst disasters, such as floods, landslides, droughts and famines. For thousands of years, people have worshiped weather gods and used rituals to try to affect the weather. But even with modern technology, it is almost impossible to control.

PREDICTING WEATHER

Although we can't control the weather, weather scientists (meteorologists) can try to predict how it will behave. They measure temperature, atmospheric pressure and the amount of rainfall at weather stations around the world, and satellites in space help them to track the movements of clouds.

But they can only predict weather a few days in advance, and weather can change so quickly that the forecasts are sometimes wrong.

This Japanese dancer wears a special costume to perform a traditional dance which is meant to make the rain fall.

Internet links

For a link to a website where you can find out what causes wild weather such as hurricanes, blizzards and thunderstorms, go to **www.usborne-quicklinks.com**

WEATHER SYSTEMS

Weather is made up of three main ingredients: temperature, the movement of the air and the amount of water in the air (see pages 50–51). These factors are always changing and affecting each other. They combine to make complicated patterns, known as weather systems.

THE SUN'S ROLE

The Sun plays the most important part in causing the weather. It heats up the land, which in turn heats up the atmosphere. If the Sun is hidden by clouds, or if a cold wind is blowing, the temperature is cooler.

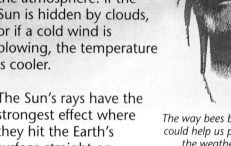

The way bees behave could help us predict the weather.

The Sun's rays have the strongest effect where they hit the Earth's surface straight on, around the Equator. Farther away from the Equator, the rays spread out over a larger area, so their effect is weaker.

AIR AND WIND

Wind is caused by the Sun too. As air gets hotter, it expands, gets less dense, and rises. A mass of colder, heavier air rushes in to replace it, making wind. Huge windstorms called hurricanes sometimes form over the sea near the Equator where the air is warm and damp.

Paper umbrellas, called parasols, have been used for hundreds of years to protect people from the Sun.

TRADITIONAL SIGNS

Clouds like these usually appear when the weather is warm and sunny.

Before satellites and computers were invented, people predicted the weather by observing natural signs, such as the way clouds look and the way animals behave. For example, white, fluffy clouds called cumulus clouds usually mean sunny weather, and bees usually go home to their hives before a storm.

WEATHER FACTS

• The heaviest hailstones, weighing up to 2lb 2oz, fell in Gopalganj, Bangladesh, in 1986.

• The wettest place in the world is Mawssynrma, India. It gets nearly 40ft of rain a year.

• The biggest recorded snowflakes were 15in across and fell on Montana, U.S.A., in 1887.

• The driest place is the Atacama Desert, Chile. In some spots, there has been no rain for 500 years.

• The hottest place is the El Azizia desert, in Libya. In 1922, the temperature reached 136°F.

WATER AND CLOUDS

The amount of water on Earth doesn't change, but water changes its state in a process known as the water cycle. It exists as a liquid (water) in seas, rivers and clouds; it freezes into a solid (ice) as snow and hail; and it also exists as an invisible gas in the air.

Snowflakes form when water droplets freeze into ice crystals. These snowflakes have been tinted so you can see their six-sided shapes more clearly.

This diagram explains how water is recycled between the Earth and air.

THE WATER CYCLE

When the Sun heats up water in rivers, lakes and seas, it changes from a liquid into a gas called water vapor. This process is known as evaporation. As the water vapor rises, it cools. This makes it condense (or turn into liquid again) to form tiny droplets, which can be seen as clouds. As the cloud droplets move around, they collide with each other and grow bigger. When they are heavy enough, they fall as rain, and the water flows back into rivers, lakes and seas.

Plants suck up water from the ground and this then escapes from their leaves as water vapor. People and animals breathe out water vapor too. You can see this when you breathe heavily on a mirror. The water vapor cools when it hits the mirror and turns back into tiny droplets of water.

When cloud droplets become heavy, they fall as rain, snow or hail.

Water flows down to the sea in streams and rivers.

As water vapor rises, it cools and forms clouds.

Plants and animals take in water that has fallen as rain.

Water evaporates from rivers and seas in the heat of the Sun.

CLOUDS

The way clouds look depends on how much water is in them and how much the air is moving up and down.

When clouds form in calm air, they spread out across the sky in sheets. On hot days, they puff up into heaps, following the rising air. Clouds full of big droplets look darker.

Cumulus clouds form puffy heaps high in the sky in warm, sunny weather.

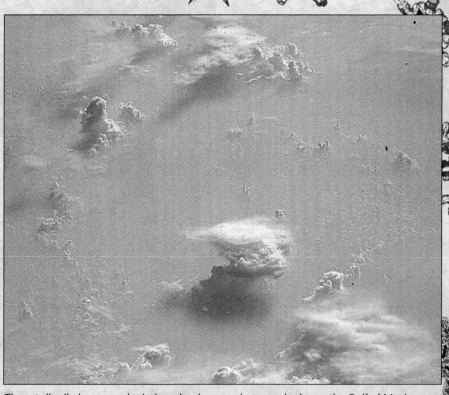

These tall, piled-up cumulonimbus clouds were photographed over the Gulf of Mexico. A cumulonimbus cloud is freezing at the top, but warmer at the bottom.

Stratus clouds form low, flat layers and often block out the sunshine.

Cirrus clouds are high and wispy. (The word cirrus means "like wispy hair" in Latin.)

RAIN, HAIL AND SNOW

Water that falls onto the Earth's surface is called precipitation. Rain is the most common kind. There are many types of rain, from light drizzle to heavy monsoon rains.

In freezing weather, precipitation sometimes takes the form of snow, hail or sleet instead of raindrops. Sleet falls from clouds as snow, but it starts to melt on its way down.

Internet links

For a link to a website where you can find out more about clouds and download pictures for free, go to **www.usborne-quicklinks.com**

Hail begins as ice crystals in giant cumulonimbus clouds. This diagram shows how it forms.

Air currents push the crystals up and around inside the cloud.

As they move, the crystals bump into water droplets, which freeze around them in layers, like the layers of an onion.

The layers of ice build up until they form heavy hailstones, which fall to Earth.

CLIMATE

An area's climate is its typical pattern of weather conditions and temperature over a long period of time. One type of climate may affect a large region, or a small, local area, where it is called a microclimate. Climates depend on latitude, distance from the sea and height above sea level.

Banana trees grow in equatorial areas.

CLIMATIC REGIONS

A climatic region is a large area on the Earth within which the climate is generally the same. The world's major climatic regions are described on this page.

Polar climates are harsh and change little throughout the year. The temperature is very low and there is little rain or snowfall. Hardly any plant life can grow in these conditions.

Polar bears have thick fur to keep them warm.

Tundra regions have harsh winds and low winter temperatures, averaging from -22°F to -4°F. Summer temperatures can be fairly warm.

Tough, low-growing land plants such as lichens are examples of tundra vegetation.

In temperate regions, rain falls throughout the year, and the temperature varies with the seasons. Day-to-day weather changes are a feature of temperate regions.

Deciduous trees, which lose their leaves in the fall, are found in temperate areas.

Tropical regions have a warm climate all year round. In many places there are two seasons: dry and wet. Temperatures are around 70°F to 86°F.

Grasslands in tropical regions are mostly made up of scattered trees and tall grasses, which die off in the dry season.

Mediterranean areas are warm and wet in winter but hot and dry in summer. Their climate is heavily affected by currents of air that move between the land and sea.

Citrus fruits grow well in Mediterranean climates. Their thick skins prevent them from drying up during the hot summers.

Continental areas, such as the central parts of Asia and North America, have hot summers and cold winters.

Equatorial regions have a constantly hot and wet climate, which supports rainforests in many areas. The temperature never drops below around 63°F, creating ideal growing conditions for huge numbers of plants.

Desert climates are generally very dry, with less than 10in of rainfall per year. Daytime temperatures in the hottest deserts may be over 100°F, although some become much cooler in winter.

Cacti and many other desert plants store large amounts of water in their thick, fleshy leaves.

MOUNTAIN CLIMATES

In mountain areas, temperatures drop as height above sea level (altitude) increases, producing different climates and vegetation at different altitudes. Trees can't survive on high mountain slopes because there is little soil, and the ground may be frozen and blasted by harsh, icy winds.

The direction which a mountainside faces (called its aspect) also affects its climate. If one side of a mountain receives more sunlight than the other, more vegetation may grow there.

Small, low-growing plants, such as moss and lichens, grow on the high mountainside.

Above a certain level, called the treeline, it is too cold for trees to grow.

Trees

COASTAL CLIMATES

In coastal areas, the land and sea gain and lose heat at different rates during the day and night. The air above them constantly circulates, creating a mild, wet climate. This is known as a coastal or maritime climate.

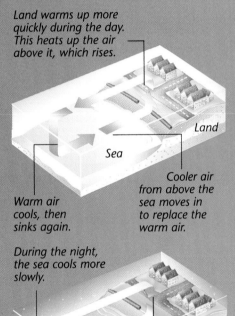

Land warms up more quickly during the day. This heats up the air above it, which rises.

Land

Sea

Cooler air from above the sea moves in to replace the warm air.

Warm air cools, then sinks again.

During the night, the sea cools more slowly.

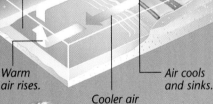

Warm air rises.

Air cools and sinks.

Cooler air moves out.

Internet links

For a link to a website where you can find out more about desert climates, their geography and animal life, go to **www.usborne-quicklinks.com**

CITY CLIMATES

Cities tend to be warmer than the areas surrounding them. This is because concrete absorbs more heat than vegetation. It also holds heat for longer. The ground beneath a city also tends to be drier, as roads and pavements prevent water from draining into the soil beneath.

GLOBAL WARMING

Scientists think the Earth is becoming warmer. This is known as global warming. Industrial processes and other pollution are increasing the amount of gases called greenhouse gases in the atmosphere. These gases trap heat from the Sun, making temperatures rise.

Scientists predict the average temperature will increase by around 3.6°F in the next century. This will affect climates all over the world. Some areas may become warmer and drier, and others wetter. There may also be an increase in extreme weather, such as strong winds and rainstorms.

The temperature rise is also causing ice in the polar regions to melt, which in turn is leading to a rise in sea level. Over time, the shape of coastlines will alter, as more and more land becomes submerged.

PLANTS AND ANIMALS

PLANTS

There are millions of different kinds of living things on Earth. They fall into two main groups: animals and plants. Most plants use sunlight to make their food, while animals feed on plants, or other animals that have eaten plants.

The Earth's land looks green from space because of the billions of plants on its surface.

The Sun provides energy, in the form of light.

PLANT FOOD

The process by which plants make food is called photosynthesis, which means "building with light." For it to happen, plants need water, carbon dioxide and sunlight. The water is absorbed by the roots and it then travels up the stem to the leaves. Tiny holes in the leaves, called stomata, take in carbon dioxide.

Photosynthesis takes place mainly inside a plant's leaves. The leaves contain a green substance called chlorophyll, which absorbs sunlight and converts it into a form of energy. The carbon dioxide and water are combined using this energy, and converted into glucose, a kind of sugar, which plants store as food. Oxygen is also produced.

A plant's flowers contain parts that make seeds. These grow into new plants.

Leaves convert water and carbon dioxide into glucose and oxygen.

This part of the underside of a leaf has been magnified.

The stem carries water from the roots to the leaves and flower.

Tiny holes called stomata let carbon dioxide in, and water and oxygen out.

Internet links

Website 1 Learn about plants by solving mysteries in a game.

Website 2 Discover how plants have adapted to live in harsh places.

For links to these websites, go to
www.usborne-quicklinks.com

WHY WE NEED PLANTS

Plants are essential for life on Earth. Animals cannot make their own food, so they have to eat plants, or other animals that have eaten plants, in order to survive. Plants also give out oxygen, which animals and people need.

Plants are important in many other ways too. We use them to make medicines, fabrics and perfumes, and we get wood from trees. Plants' roots also hold soil together and stop it from being washed away into the sea.

The aloe is one of the thousands of plants we use to make cosmetics and natural medicines.

PLANT EVOLUTION

Plants have been on the Earth for many millions of years. The first plants evolved more than 500 million years ago, which is well before the dinosaurs first appeared.

The first plants only grew in water. Modern algae, which are simple plants without stems, roots and leaves, are related to these early water plants.

Plants began to grow on land around 400 million years ago. The first land plants were spongy mosses. Then came giant tree ferns, which many dinosaurs relied on for food. Flowering plants only started to appear around 135 million years ago.

TYPES OF PLANTS

Different types of living things are called species. There are about a million species of plants, from tiny herbs to enormous trees called giant sequoias, which are the biggest living things on Earth. Different species are suited, or adapted, to living in different parts of the world. In deserts, for example, many plants have very small, needle-like leaves called spines, which lose very little water. This enables these plants to make the most of the scarce water.

Giant sequoia trees are found mainly in California, U.S.A. Some live for over 2,500 years.

FLOWERING PLANTS

Many plants reproduce by growing flowers and making seeds. There are over 250,000 different kinds of flowering plants, including grasses, wild flowers, shrubs and trees.

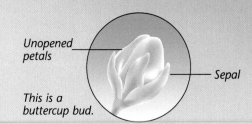

Unopened petals

Sepal

This is a buttercup bud.

BUDS TO FLOWERS

All flowers start as a bud, which grows from the tip of a stalk, called the receptacle. The petals are tightly packed inside the bud, and they are surrounded and protected by special leaves called sepals. When the bud opens into a flower, the sepals either remain as a ring around the petals, or wither and fall off. For example, buttercups keep their sepals, but poppies lose them once the bud has opened.

Flowers are made up of many specialized parts. They have male parts (stamens) and a female part (the pistil). In most flowers, the petals are arranged in a circle, around the male and female parts. Petals are often scented and brightly colored. They have areas of cells called nectaries at their base. These produce a sweet liquid called nectar, which attracts insects and other animals.

Here you can see the different parts of a buttercup flower.

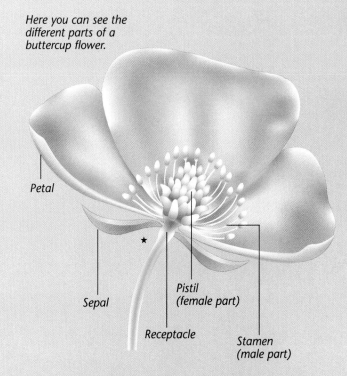

Petal

Sepal

Receptacle

Pistil (female part)

Stamen (male part)

MALE AND FEMALE PARTS

Some species of plants have both their male and female parts in the same flower; others have male parts in one flower and the female part in another. There are also species that grow the female part on one plant and the male parts on another. A stamen is made up of a long tube with a pod at the end, called an anther. Pollen grains, the male reproductive cells, are made inside the anthers. A pistil can be made up of one or more carpels, each of which has a sticky area called the stigma. The stigma traps grains of pollen. It is attached to a tube called the style, which is long in some flowers, but very short in others. The style leads into an ovary, where ovules (eggs) are stored. Seeds are made inside the ovaries.

This picture shows the male parts of a buttercup.

This is a cutaway of an anther.

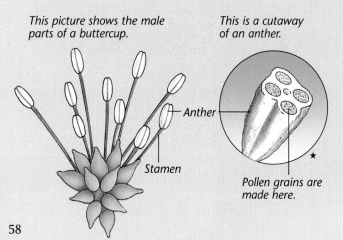

Anther

Stamen

Pollen grains are made here.

This is a diagram of the carpels of a buttercup.

This is a cutaway of a carpel.

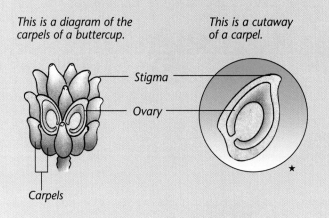

Stigma

Ovary

Carpels

This hummingbird is drinking the nectar inside a flower. As it drinks, pollen sticks to its beak. This will rub off onto the next flower the hummingbird visits.

POLLINATION

Pollen has to be transferred from a stamen to the stigma of a plant of the same kind before a seed can start to form. This is called pollination. The pollen can be carried from flower to flower by wind, water or animals. Once some pollen has landed on a stigma, it travels down the style and into the ovary, where it joins with an ovule and starts to form a seed.

SEEDS AND FRUIT

Seeds have a hard shell with a young plant inside. Most seeds grow inside a fruit, which protects the seeds until they are fully grown. There are two kinds of fruit: succulents and dry fruit.

Succulent fruits have thick, fleshy layers and are often tasty to eat. They include apples, berries and plums. Dry fruits have a tough, dry case. Nuts are a kind of dry fruit. They contain only one seed surrounded by a hard shell. A dry fruit with seeds attached to its inside wall is known as a pod. The fruit of the pea plant are pods. The peas are the seeds.

These are sunflower seeds. Their hard shells are starting to split open, revealing the young plants inside.

SPREADING SEEDS

Seeds need to be scattered far apart, so the new plants won't compete with each other for space, light and water. Some seed pods explode, flinging their seeds far away. Some seeds are carried by water or wind. Others are spread by animals. Sometimes, they stick to an animal's fur, or they may be eaten by an animal and then spread in its droppings.

Coconut seeds grow inside a large waterproof shell. They float in the sea until they are washed up on shore.

ANIMALS

There are millions of species of animals. They include insects, fish, birds, reptiles, amphibians and mammals, which include humans. Unlike plants, most animals are able to move from one place to another to find food.

The bald eagle is a carnivore. It feeds mainly on fish, swooping down and snatching its prey from lakes and rivers.

FINDING FOOD

Different animals eat different kinds of food. Herbivores eat plants and carnivores eat animals. Animals that eat both plants and animals, such as brown bears, are called omnivores. Most humans are omnivores. Some species of animals eat different foods depending on where they live. For example, although brown bears usually eat plants, fruit and meat, if there is a river nearby, they will eat fish too.

Honeyeaters are herbivores. They feed on nectar inside flowers.

PREDATORS

Most animals have to watch out for predators, which are other animals that want to eat them. Their bodies have to be adapted for running fast or hiding. Some animals, such as zebras, are camouflaged, which means they are patterned so that they blend in with their background and are harder for predators to see. But some predators are also camouflaged, so they can creep up on their prey (the animals they eat).

TOOLS FOR EATING

Animals' bodies are adapted to suit the kind of food they eat. Herbivores usually have flat, broad teeth designed for munching plants, while most carnivores have sharp teeth to help them grip their prey and pierce raw flesh. Omnivores usually have a mixture of both kinds.

Cape fur seals are carnivores. In the photograph of a cape fur seal skull below, you can see long, sharp teeth at the front, which the seal would have used for gripping and slicing through fish.

Horses are herbivores. In the photograph of a horse's skull above, you can see flat molar teeth, which the horse would have used for grinding plants.

ANIMAL TALK

Animals communicate with each other in many ways. Most messages are connected with finding mates or giving warnings to other animals.

Sounds are a common way for animals to communicate. Birds sing to attract a mate or to warn other birds to keep away from their territory. Some animals produce sounds using different parts of the body. For example, male crickets rub their wings together to make a shrill chirping noise, which attracts females.

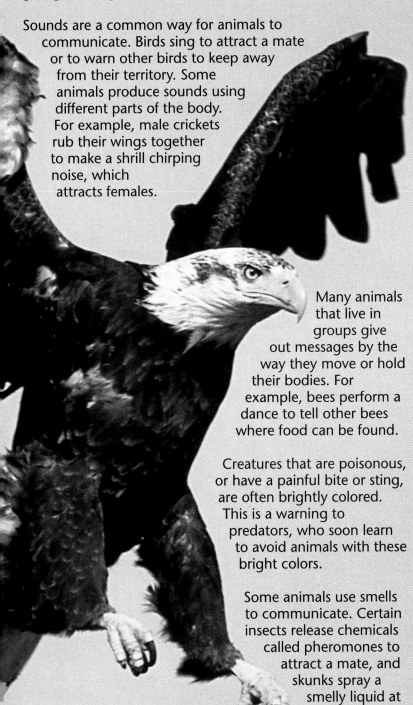

Many animals that live in groups give out messages by the way they move or hold their bodies. For example, bees perform a dance to tell other bees where food can be found.

Creatures that are poisonous, or have a painful bite or sting, are often brightly colored. This is a warning to predators, who soon learn to avoid animals with these bright colors.

Some animals use smells to communicate. Certain insects release chemicals called pheromones to attract a mate, and skunks spray a smelly liquid at enemies to warn them to stay away.

Internet links

For a link to a website where you can play games to find out more about some of the amazing animals around the world, go to **www.usborne-quicklinks.com**

Bald eagles have good eyesight and strong, sharp claws, or talons, which help them to catch their prey.

BREATHING

As well as eating food, animals need to breathe oxygen, a gas which is found in air and water. Animals take oxygen into their bodies, in a variety of different ways.

Fish have gills, which filter oxygen from the water as it flows through them.

Gills

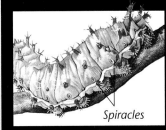

Insects take in oxygen through tiny holes in their bodies, called spiracles.

Spiracles

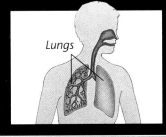

Lungs

Humans and many other animals have lungs, which extract oxygen from the air.

HUMAN THREATS

Animals are very useful to humans, providing meat, milk, eggs, wool, silk, leather and even medicines. Many animals are farmed carefully, but some species are in danger of becoming extinct. This can happen when people kill too many of them or destroy their homes and food supplies, for example by cutting down forests.

Guanacos are hunted for their thick, warm wool.

ECOSYSTEMS

The world can be divided up into areas called biomes, each of which has a distinct climate and a network of plants and animals. These are further divided into many smaller communities of plants and animals called ecosystems. The place where an individual animal or plant lives is called its habitat.

Snowy owls and lemmings are part of the Arctic biome. The Arctic has a cold, icy climate.

Meat-eaters survive by eating other animals found in their habitat. These cheetahs are chasing a Thomson's gazelle.

BIOMES

Some biomes can sustain an enormous variety of plants and animals, while others contain a fairly limited number of species. For example, tropical rainforest biomes have a very warm, wet climate, which many plants an animals thrive on. In contrast, tundra biomes contain a narrow range of plants and animals. This is because few can survive in thei cold, harsh climate.

This diagram shows part of a food web in a mountain forest in a northern country, such as Canada.

FOOD CHAINS

The animals and plants in an ecosystem depend on each other for food. One species eats another, and is in turn eaten by another. This is called a food chain. Plants form the first link in a food chain, because they make their own food. Herbivores then eat the plants and carnivores eat herbivores and other carnivores. A series of interlinked food chains is known as a food web. Many food chains are linked because very few animals feed on just one thing.

Each blue arrow points from a species that is eaten to a species that eats it.

TROPHIC LEVELS

The position of a plant or animal within a food chain is called its trophic level. There are different kinds of plants or animals on each level.

The Sun provides light and energy for plants.

Tertiary consumers
Animals that eat other meat-eating animals

Secondary consumers
Animals that eat plant-eating animals

Primary consumers
Animals that eat plants

Producers
Plants that use the Sun's energy to manufacture food

Decomposers
Organisms that feed on dead plants and animals and break them down in the soil

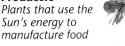

ENERGY

Only a little of the energy an animal gains by eating food is stored; the rest is used up by its body. When an animal is eaten, the consumer only gains the stored energy. Therefore much less energy is available at each trophic level in a food chain, so each level has far fewer consumers than the previous level.

Internet links

Website 1 Read about the major biomes of the world.

Website 2 Find out about endangered animals living in different habitats.

For links to these websites, go to **www.usborne-quicklinks.com**

COMPETITION

Each type of plant or animal has a unique place in its ecosystem, known as a niche. If two different species try to compete for the same food, the stronger or more skilled hunter survives, and the other one either has to change its diet or move away, or it will die out.

Different species in an ecosystem can survive side by side by eating slightly different types of food. For example, in African grasslands, elephants reach up to eat the higher branches of trees and bushes, gerenuks eat leaves lower down and warthogs nibble grasses on the ground.

BALANCE

In an ecosystem, the number of producers and consumers is usually balanced, which means that there is enough food for all. However, the balance is easily upset. If a disease kills all the primary consumers, this affects all the other members of the food chain. For example, plants (producers) might grow better, but secondary consumers might die because there isn't enough food.

An elephant's long trunk allows it to reach to the tops of trees to collect food, while other animals eat the leaves lower down.

LIFE CYCLES

Many changes take place between the beginning and end of an animal's life: it grows, develops and produces young. These patterns of growth and behavior are called a life cycle. Some animal life cycles take years to complete, but some insects complete their life cycle in a few months.

Locust is now fully grown.

Female lays eggs, which hatch into nymphs.

Locust nymph, called a hopper

Hopper sheds its skin several times.

This shows the life cycle of a locust (incomplete metamorphosis).

CHANGING SHAPE

Some animals, such as insects and frogs, change their form in the course of their life cycle. This is called metamorphosis. There are two kinds of metamorphosis: complete and incomplete. In complete metamorphosis, the young form looks very different from the adult form.

Insects such as butterflies, moths and ladybugs undergo complete metamorphosis. Their young, called larvae, feed and grow, then they turn into pupae, which have a hard case. Inside the hard case, they change into adults.

Eggs

Larva, called a caterpillar

Pupa

Adult emerges from pupa.

This shows the life cycle of a butterfly (complete metamorphosis).

Other insects, such as locusts, go through incomplete metamorphosis. This means that the young, called nymphs, look similar to their parents, although some body parts, such as their wings, are not yet formed. A nymph sheds its skin several times as it grows, and its wings and reproductive organs develop. The adult form of an insect that has gone through either complete or incomplete metamorphosis is known as the imago.

Female lays eggs called spawn in water.

Young frog leaves water and grows to full size.

Eggs hatch into tadpoles.

Front legs grow; tail will disappear.

Back legs and lungs develop.

This shows the life cycle of a frog (complete metamorphosis).

Internet links

Website 1 Find out how brown bears prepare for hibernation.

Website 2 See pictures showing the life cycles of different kinds of butterflies.

For links to these websites, go to
www.usborne-quicklinks.com

Like almost all geese, Canada geese migrate to their breeding grounds every year.

MAKING A JOURNEY

At some stage in their life cycles, many animals travel long distances in large groups, usually to breed or find food. This journey is called migration. Many birds migrate twice every year (to their breeding or feeding grounds and back). They use the position of the Sun, stars and features of the land to find their way. Many land animals move with the seasons to find food.

Huge numbers of wildebeest migrate together. They often have to cross rivers and difficult terrain during migration.

MIGRATION IN WATER

Some animals, such as salmon and eels, may only migrate once in their lifetime. The journey they make is long and hard, and few fish survive to breed again.

Salmon travel upstream to breed. They swim from the sea to the rivers where they hatched.

When they arrive, the females lay eggs in the riverbed, in hollows dug out by the males, using their tails.

The young salmon live in the rivers for about three years before swimming to the sea, where they remain until they are ready to breed.

A LONG REST

Many animals that do not migrate survive seasons of cold or drought in a sleep-like state called dormancy. Dormancy during a drought is called aestivation. Dormancy in winter is called hibernation.

Before hibernating, animals collect food. Some eat it all and develop a layer of body fat to keep them alive through the winter. Others store the food and wake occasionally to eat.

Hibernating animals, such as this dormouse, settle down in a safe, well-hidden place.

The animal's breathing and heartbeat slow down, and its body temperature drops. It becomes active again in spring, when food is available.

NATURAL CYCLES

Some substances, such as nitrogen and carbon, are constantly changing form as they move around in huge cycles. This exchange of substances is essential to life on Earth. The air, land, water, plants, animals, and even your own body, all form a part of these cycles. However, natural cycles are easily disturbed, especially by human activities.

This magnified part of a pea plant root contains bacteria which convert nitrogen from the air into a form the plant can use.

KEEPING A BALANCE

Living things take in substances such as oxygen, nitrogen, carbon and water from the world around them through food, soil and air. They use them to live and grow. When a plant or animal dies and decays, its body is broken down and gases are released. The cycle continues, with these substances being used again and again. This process maintains the balance of gases in the air.

This dung beetle is feeding on animal dung. Insects like this help to break down plant and animal matter.

THE NITROGEN CYCLE

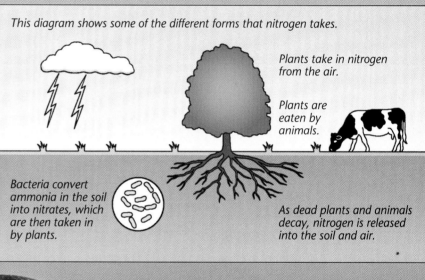

This diagram shows some of the different forms that nitrogen takes.

Plants take in nitrogen from the air.

Plants are eaten by animals.

Bacteria convert ammonia in the soil into nitrates, which are then taken in by plants.

As dead plants and animals decay, nitrogen is released into the soil and air.

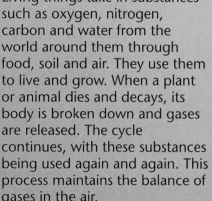

All living things need nitrogen to make essential substances called proteins. Before they can use the nitrogen, it must be combined with oxygen to form nitrates. Certain types of bacteria make nitrates. They mostly live inside the roots of vegetables called legumes, for example peas and beans.

Animals obtain nitrogen by eating plants or animals that have eaten plants. When plants and animals die and decay, fungi and bacteria break down their remains and nitrogen is released back into the soil and air.

One form that carbon can take is charcoal, as shown here. Charcoal can be burned as a fuel. When it is burned, it gives out carbon dioxide.

THE CARBON CYCLE

All living things need carbon to live and grow. Plants obtain it from carbon dioxide in the air. They take in carbon dioxide during the day and use it to help them make food substances called carbohydrates. At night, when food is not being produced, they give out carbon dioxide. Animals obtain carbon by eating plants or animals that have eaten plants. They release carbon in their waste and when they breathe out. Carbon dioxide is also released when plants and animals die and decay. Carbon can be stored in the form of fossilized remains. Eventually, these may form fossil fuels such as coal and oil, which release carbon dioxide when burned.

UPSETTING CYCLES

People can upset the balance of natural cycles in various ways. In some parts of the world, forests are burned down to make way for farms or buildings. Burning releases carbon, which forms carbon dioxide in the air. This then builds up in the atmosphere and traps the Sun's heat, creating what is known as the greenhouse effect. This is believed to cause global warming (see page 53).

Farming also affects the nitrogen cycle. When farmers harvest crops, they remove plants which have taken in nitrates from the soil. Because the plants are not allowed to decay naturally, the nitrogen is not returned to the soil, and the cycle is broken. Farmers often use chemical fertilizers to replace nitrates in soil, but if too much is added, it can seep through the soil into rivers, where it can affect plants and animals.

The algae in this canal are thriving because of excess nitrates running into it from fertilizer used on nearby farmland.

This diagram shows some of the different forms that carbon takes.

Plants take in carbon dioxide from the air to help them make food. At night, they give out carbon dioxide.

When fossil fuels are burned, carbon dioxide is released.

When dead plants and animals decay, carbon dioxide is released into the air.

Animals take in carbon when they eat plants. They breathe out carbon dioxide.

Internet links

For a link to a website where you can find out more about how human activities affect the environment, go to **www.usborne-quicklinks.com**

EVOLUTION

Most scientists believe that life on Earth started with very simple creatures and developed gradually, through a long series of changes. This idea is called the theory of evolution. By studying existing plants and animals alongside prehistoric remains, scientists try to explain how and why living things have changed.

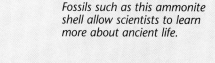

Fossils such as this ammonite shell allow scientists to learn more about ancient life.

EVOLUTION

According to most scientists, the first tiny organisms on Earth were bacteria, which first existed around 3.5 billion years ago. They suggest that, over the course of many millions of years, living things developed to become the first animals, as shown here.

500 million years ago, the first fish evolved, with thick skin and no jaws. About 150 million years later, bony fish evolved.

Sacabambaspis

410 million years ago, the first wingless insects appeared. About 110 million years later, winged insects evolved.

Meganeura

370 million years ago, some water-dwelling creatures began to breathe air, and became the first amphibians.

Ichthyostega

250 million years ago, the first reptiles appeared. Dinosaurs evolved around 200 million years ago, and lived for 135 million years, before they rapidly died out.

Riojasaurus

200 million years ago, the first small mammals appeared. After the dinosaurs died out, larger mammals started to evolve.

Megazostrodon

150 million years ago, the first birds evolved from small species of dinosaurs.

Archaeopteryx

FOSSIL RECORD

Scientists find out about plants and animals that lived millions of years ago by studying fossils. All the fossils found so far are together known as the fossil record. The fossil record shows us how life on Earth has changed over time.

These diagrams show how some fossils form.

When an animal dies, its flesh rots away.

Layers of sand and mud cover the skeleton, and turn into rock. The shape of the skeleton is preserved inside.

★

Internet links

For a link to a website where you can find out more about how dinosaurs evolved and why they became extinct, go to
www.usborne-quicklinks.com

NATURAL SELECTION

In the 1850s, a British scientist named Charles Darwin put forward the theory of natural selection to explain how evolution takes place. He suggested that individual animals and plants have some qualities that help them to survive.

For example in a green forest, a green bug would probably survive longer than a brown bug, because its camouflaged appearance would help it to avoid being seen and eaten by predators.

The individuals that survive longest are likely to have more babies, and will pass on their useful qualities to them. Over a very long period of time, each species will gradually develop all the most useful qualities for surviving in its habitat.

Darwin's theory was rejected by most people when he first made it public, but it has since become widely accepted by scientists.

Large reptiles, such as this Baryonyx, died out, along with many other animals, around 65 million years ago.

Peppered moth (dark variety)

A type of moth called the peppered moth is often used to show how natural selection takes place. During the nineteenth century, many peppered moths rested on trees that had become blackened by soot from factories.

Dark and pale peppered moths resting on a soot-covered tree trunk

Moths with pale wings were seen and eaten by birds, but the rare moths with dark wings survived, bred and increased in numbers. Now, however, there is less pollution from soot and the moths with pale wings are increasing again.

Peppered moth (pale variety)

MASS EXTINCTION

Many scientists suggest that there have been at least five major events in the Earth's history during which huge numbers of living things died at once. These are known as mass extinctions.

These mass extinctions are thought to have happened as a result of sudden, dramatic changes in the Earth's climate. Many organisms could not adapt to these changes, and so they died out. Dinosaurs may have been killed off when a large asteroid hit the Earth, causing major climate changes.

Every mass extinction so far has been followed by a major burst of evolution. For example, the death of the dinosaurs left room for mammals to take over.

CLASSIFICATION

To make living things easier to study, biologists divide them into groups with similar features. This is called classification. For example, an elephant and a mouse are both species that belong to the mammal group, because they have hair and produce milk for their young.

Although an elephant and a mouse look very different from each other, they are both types of mammals.

BIOLOGICAL KEYS

Scientists can identify an organism by looking at its main features and deciding how these are different from those of a similar species. They use a biological key to help them do this. A typical biological key is arranged in branches, as in the example below. At each branch the scientist asks "Does the specimen have...?" and there is a choice between two or more features. Each response leads to another set of options until the organism is identified.

This is a biological key showing how some animals can be grouped according to the features they share.

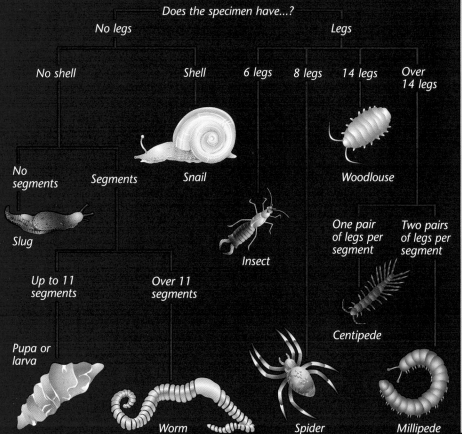

Does the specimen have...?

No legs — No shell — No segments — Slug
No shell — Segments — Up to 11 segments — Pupa or larva
No shell — Segments — Over 11 segments — Worm
Shell — Snail
Legs — 6 legs — Insect
Legs — 8 legs — Spider
Legs — 14 legs — Woodlouse
Legs — Over 14 legs — One pair of legs per segment — Centipede
Legs — Over 14 legs — Two pairs of legs per segment — Millipede

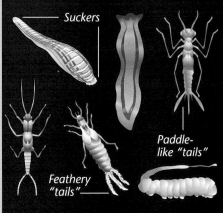

THE FIVE KINGDOMS

The largest groups into which living things can be sorted are called kingdoms. Many scientists currently divide living things into five main kingdoms, though there is some disagreement about this. The five kingdoms are: plants, fungi, animals, protists and monerans. This method of classifying organisms is called classical taxonomy. Viruses are not included in classical taxonomy. Although they can exist independently, they are only able to reproduce within the cells of living things.

PLANTS

Plants are organisms such as trees, grass and flowers, which use sunlight to make their own food.

Rosy periwinkle

FUNGI

Fungi are organisms such as yeast and toadstools, which are plant-like, but can't make their own food. Instead, they mostly feed on dead plants and animals.

Fly agaric

ANIMALS

Animals include fish and birds. They have more than one cell, which are the tiny units that make up all living things. They can usually move around, and eat plants or other animals for food.

Corkwing wrasse

PROTISTS

Protista are single-celled organisms such as euglena, which share features with both plants and animals.

Euglena

MONERANS

Monera are microscopic, single-celled organisms, such as bacteria. They are simpler in structure than protista and they reproduce by splitting in half.

This salmonella bacterium has been magnified thousands of times.

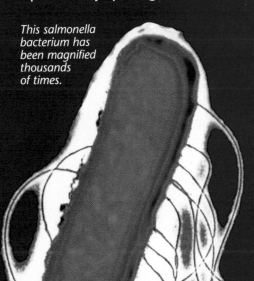

DIVIDING KINGDOMS

Each kingdom can be broken down into levels called taxonomic ranks or taxa. The first rank is called a phylum. Each phylum breaks down into groups called classes. Classes are divided into orders, then families, then genera (singular: genus).

Each genus contains a number of species, which are groups of animals that are similar enough to breed together.

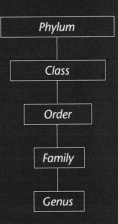

Phylum
Class
Order
Family
Genus

In some cases, there are also midway groups, such as subkingdoms and subphyla.

Some phyla cannot be broken down in this way, because they have too few members. The next group after the phylum may therefore be an order, family, genus or even a species.

Internet links

For a link to a website where you can find out more about the animal kingdom and its subdivisions, go to **www.usborne-quicklinks.com**

71

THE ANIMAL KINGDOM

The animal kingdom contains a number of phyla, the main eight of which are shown below. These can be sorted further into classes, orders, families, genera and species (see previous page). Below, you can see how a single species, such as a timber wolf, can be traced from one of the phyla. Each step down becomes more specific and includes fewer animals than the one before.

PHYLA

Annelids
Worm-like, with round, segmented bodies

Flatworms
Worm-like, with flat, unsegmented bodies

Arthropods
Segmented bodies, jointed legs, hard body covering (exoskeleton)

Nematodes
Worm-like, no segments

Chordates
Body supported by a stiff rod called a notochord

Echinoderms
Spiny skin, sucker feet and a five-rayed body

Mollusks
Soft-bodied creatures, most of which have shells

Cnidarians
Water-dwelling creatures with like bodies and single opening

CLASSES

Fish
Animals that live in water, have scales and fins and breathe with gills

Reptiles
Scaly, cold-blooded animals that lay eggs

Mammals
Warm-blooded animals that suckle their young with milk

Amphibians
Cold-blooded, soft-skinned animals that live on land and in water

Birds
Warm-blooded, egg-laying animals with feathers and wings

(Others)

ORDERS

Primates
Monkeys, apes and similar creatures with hands and feet that grip

Carnivores
Meat-eating animals, such as lions and foxes

Rodents
Mammals with long front teeth for gnawing, such as rats and squirrels

(Others)

FAMILIES

Felines
All types of cats and cat-like mammals

Canines
All types of dogs and dog-like mammals

(Others)

GENERA

Canis
All types of dogs, wolves and jackals

Vulpes
All types of foxes

(Others)

SPECIES

Timber wolf

Coyote

(Others)

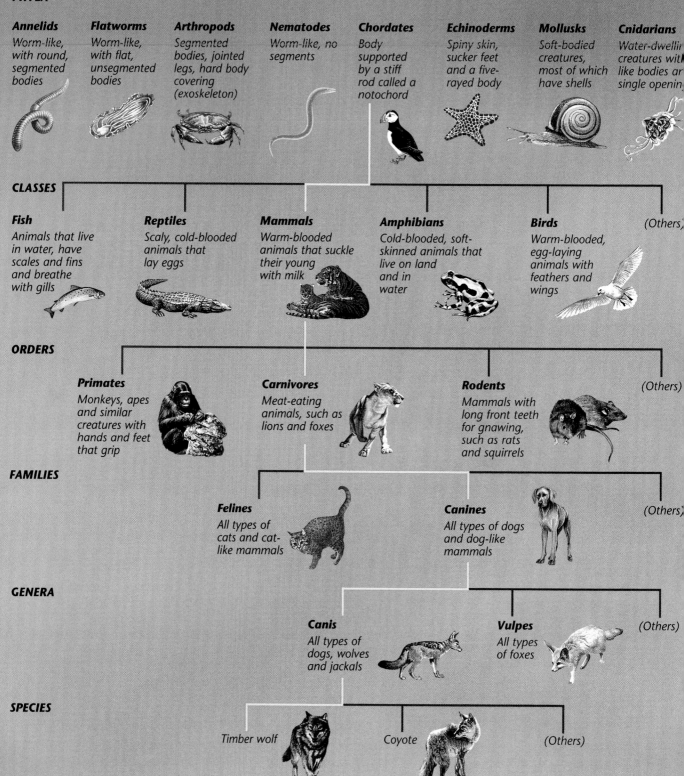

NAMING THINGS

Living things are generally given one or more common names and a biological name. The common name is the one used by most people, for example "tawny owl" or "red squirrel". A biological name is needed because an animal may have many common names, each one used in a different area. Biological names are usually in Latin. These names can be recognized by scientists all over the world.

These butterflies are so rare that they do not have common names, only biological names.

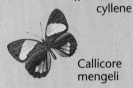

Callicore
cyllene

Agrias
claudina

Callicore
mengeli

The biological name is created using the binomial system, which means that it is made up of two parts. The first part, called the generic name, is based on the organism's genus. The second part, called the specific epithet, identifies its species.

In many cases, a biological name refers to the animal's appearance, habitat or body features. For instance, a giraffe's biological name is *Giraffa camelopardalis*. Giraffa means "swift walker," camel means "camel-like," and pardalis means "marked like a leopard." So a giraffe is a swift-moving, camel-like animal with a patterned coat like a leopard's.

SUBSPECIES

In some cases, there are also subspecies that have a third part added to their biological name. This can refer to the area in which the subspecies is found, or to a particular characteristic.

This tiger's name is Panthera tigris sumatrae. *The third part of its name tells you that it is a subspecies from Sumatra.*

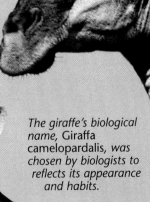

The giraffe's biological name, Giraffa camelopardalis, *was chosen by biologists to reflects its appearance and habits.*

Internet links

For a link to a website where you can find out more about the classification of living things, go to **www.usborne-quicklinks.com**

INFORMAL GROUPS

Species that share certain types of lifestyles can also be put together in informal groups, by using terms that describe this lifestyle. Social and nocturnal (night) animals are two such terms, and there are other examples below.

An animal or plant that lives and feeds on another organism (called the host) is known as a parasite. Some parasites are harmful to their hosts.

Fleas are common parasites that feed on the blood of their host.

Mutualists are animals or plants that live close together in a situation where both gain. For example, birds called oxpeckers eat parasites that live on the hides of larger animals, such as buffalo and zebra. The larger animals benefit in turn from having the pests removed.

Two species in a relationship where one gains without affecting the other are called commensals. House mice, for example, live where humans are found, and feed on their scraps.

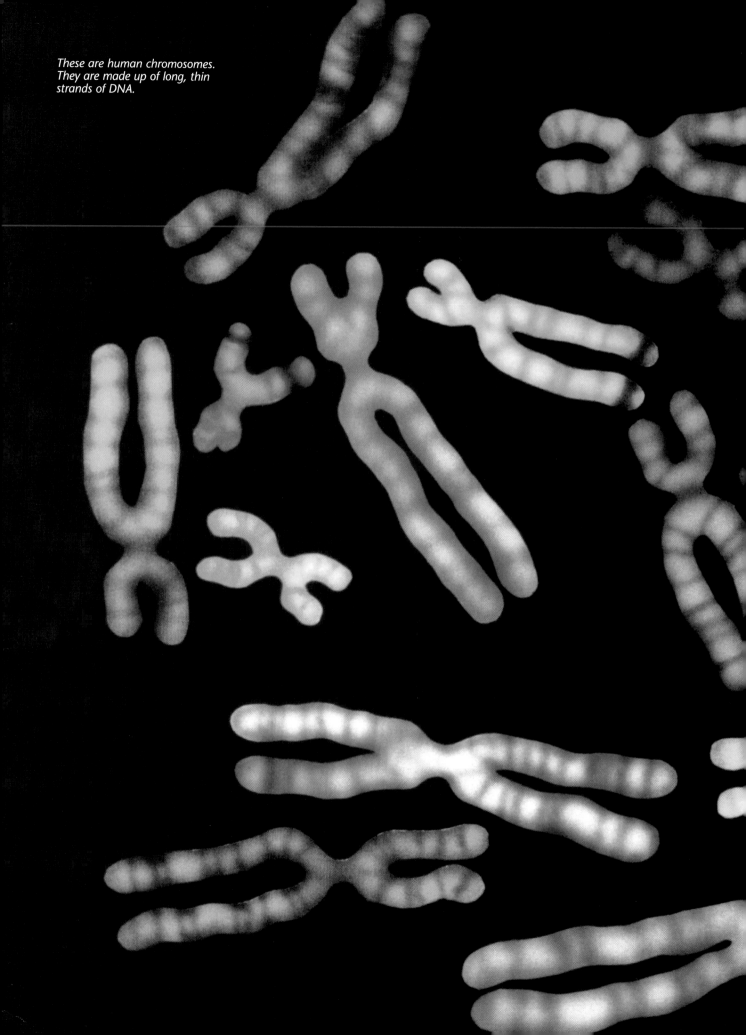

These are human chromosomes. They are made up of long, thin strands of DNA.

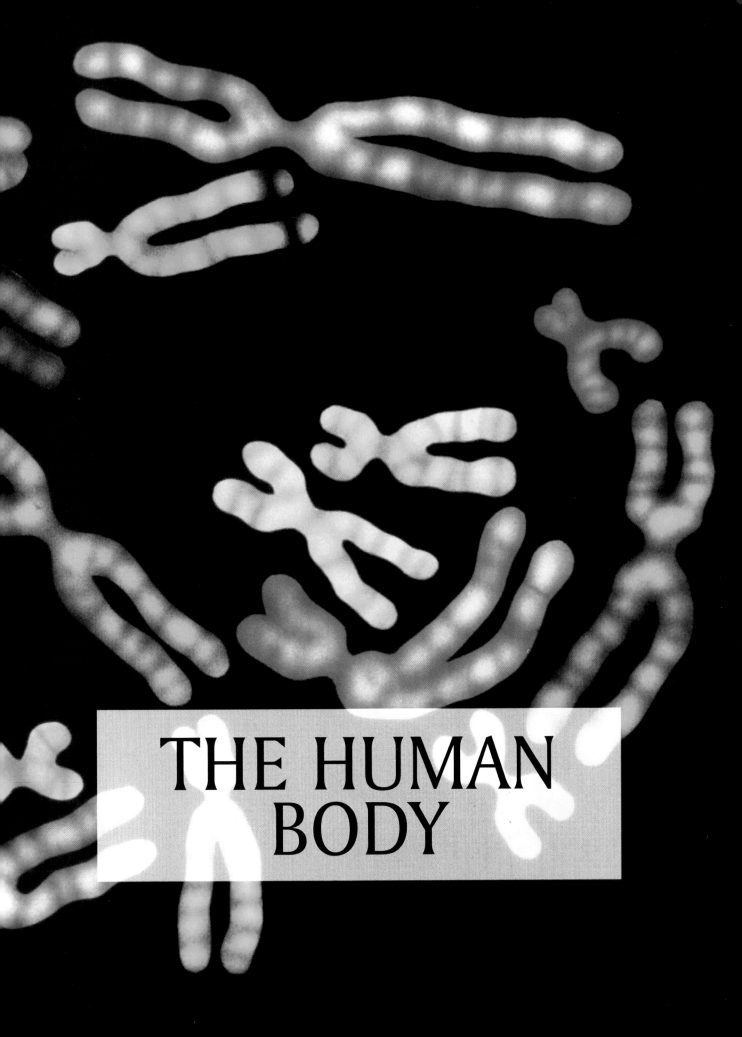

THE HUMAN
BODY

THE SKELETON

Your skeleton is a framework of bones that supports your body and gives it shape. It protects delicate parts, such as the heart, and muscles attach to its hard surfaces.

TYPES OF BONE

The bones in your body can be divided into four main types, depending on their shape.

Flat bones protect your organs, and muscles attach to the surfaces of the bones. Your ribs are flat bones.

Ribs

Short bones are knobbed nugget shapes, which are almost equal in length and width. The bones in your wrists and ankles are short bones.

Wrist bone

Long bones are longer than they are wide. They are slightly curved to make them stronger. The bones in your arms and fingers are long bones.

Finger bones

Irregular bones have complicated shapes. The bones that make up your spine are irregular bones.

Spine ★

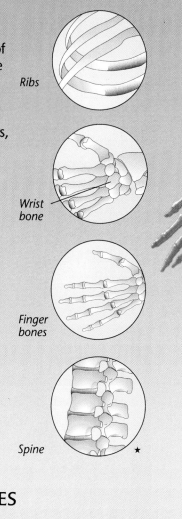

SKELETAL MUSCLES

There are 640 skeletal muscles. They are attached to your bones by tough bands of tissue called tendons. When a muscle contracts (squeezes together), the bone it is attached to moves with it.

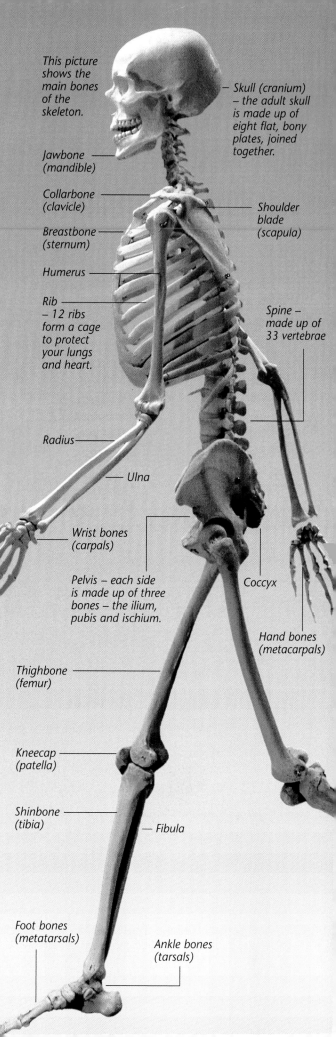

This picture shows the main bones of the skeleton.

Jawbone (mandible)

Collarbone (clavicle)

Breastbone (sternum)

Humerus

Rib – 12 ribs form a cage to protect your lungs and heart.

Radius

Ulna

Wrist bones (carpals)

Skull (cranium) – the adult skull is made up of eight flat, bony plates, joined together.

Shoulder blade (scapula)

Spine – made up of 33 vertebrae

Coccyx

Pelvis – each side is made up of three bones – the ilium, pubis and ischium.

Hand bones (metacarpals)

Thighbone (femur)

Kneecap (patella)

Shinbone (tibia)

Fibula

Foot bones (metatarsals)

Ankle bones (tarsals)

TYPES OF JOINTS

Joints are places where bones meet. Most help you to bend and move. At a joint, the bones are held in place by strong straps called ligaments. The ends of the bones are tough, to prevent wear and tear. Inside your joints is a liquid called synovial fluid, which helps the bones to move smoothly.

Your hip joint is a ball and socket joint. It has a round-ended bone which fits into a fixed, cup-like socket. This lets you swivel your leg in many directions.

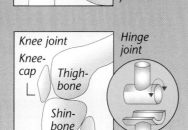

Hip joint — Pelvis — Thighbone — Ball and socket joint

Your knee joint allows you to bend your leg up and down. This type of joint is called a hinge joint. It works like a hinge on a door.

Knee joint — Knee-cap — Thigh-bone — Shin-bone — Hinge joint

The joints in your wrist are gliding or sliding joints. The surfaces that touch are flat, and the bones can move from side to side and back and forth.

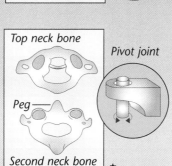

Gliding joint — Wrist joint — Wrist bones

The joint between the top two bones in your neck is a pivot joint. The rounded end of one bone (called the peg) twists around in a hole in the other. This allows you to turn your head from side to side.

Top neck bone — Pivot joint — Peg — Second neck bone ★

BABY SKELETONS

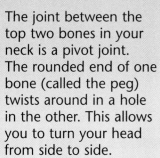

A newborn baby's skeleton has over 300 parts. Most are not made of bone, but of a tough, flexible material called cartilage. Over time, this slowly turns into bone. As the baby grows, some of the bones join together to make bigger bones. By the time it is an adult, its skeleton contains only 206 separate bones.

INSIDE YOUR BONES

Bones are living tissue. They can grow and repair themselves, and they will hurt if they are damaged. Bones are made up of blood vessels, nerves and bone cells, all held together within a hard framework. The inner part of a bone is called spongy bone and the outer part is called compact bone.

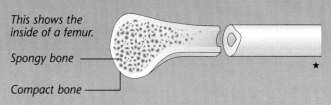

This shows the inside of a femur.

Spongy bone

Compact bone — ★

Spongy bone isn't spongy to touch, but it does look like a sponge. This strong, light tissue is found in short, flat bones, and in the ends of long bones.

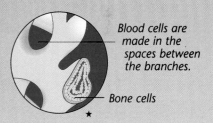

This shows spongy bone that has been highly magnified.

Spongy bone is made up of a mesh of branches called trabeculae.

Blood cells are made in the spaces between the branches.

Bone cells

Compact bone is the hard, strong part of your bones. It is made strong by a mineral called calcium, which is found in milk and some foods.

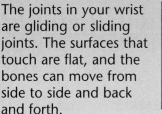

This shows compact bone that has been highly magnified.

Bone cells are found in these tiny spaces.

Blood vessels run through this channel.

Compact bone is made up of dense, circular layers of bone.

Channels like this one carry nerves and blood vessels to the bone cells.

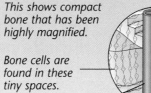

Internet links

Website 1 Discover some fascinating facts about bones.

Website 2 Watch a short movie to discover why bones are so strong.

Website 3 Find out how doctors mend broken bones.

Website 4 Learn about the foot bones and how they affect sports performance.

For links to these websites, go to **www.usborne-quicklinks.com**

THE CIRCULATORY SYSTEM

Your circulatory system transports substances such as food and oxygen around your body, and collects some waste substances. It has three main parts: blood, the liquid that carries the substances; tubes called blood vessels, which the blood travels along; and the heart, which pumps blood to all parts of your body.

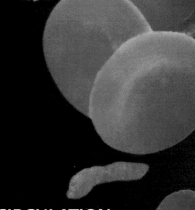

HEART

Your heart is a muscular organ that never gets tired. A muscular wall inside it divides it into two sides. Each side has an upper chamber, called an atrium, which leads to a lower chamber, called a ventricle. One-way valves between the chambers keep your blood

Position of heart

flowing in the right direction. The valves have flaps called cusps. As blood flows through the valves, it forces the cusps open. They then snap shut, to stop blood from flowing back. As the valves shut, they make the thumping "heartbeat" sound.

This diagram shows how blood circulates around your heart.

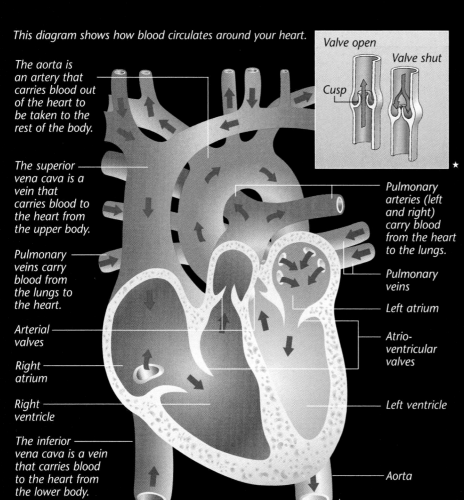

The aorta is an artery that carries blood out of the heart to be taken to the rest of the body.

The superior vena cava is a vein that carries blood to the heart from the upper body.

Pulmonary veins carry blood from the lungs to the heart.

Arterial valves

Right atrium

Right ventricle

The inferior vena cava is a vein that carries blood to the heart from the lower body.

Valve open

Valve shut

Cusp

Pulmonary arteries (left and right) carry blood from the heart to the lungs.

Pulmonary veins

Left atrium

Atrio-ventricular valves

Left ventricle

Aorta

CIRCULATION

Blood passes through the heart twice during one complete circulation of your body. First, it is pumped from the right side of the heart to the lungs, where it picks up fresh oxygen you have breathed in. It then returns to the left side of the heart, before being pumped to the rest of the body to deliver the oxygen. Blood needing oxygen returns to the heart to begin the cycle again.

This diagram shows how blood travels around your body.

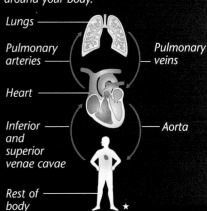

Lungs

Pulmonary arteries

Pulmonary veins

Heart

Inferior and superior venae cavae

Aorta

Rest of body

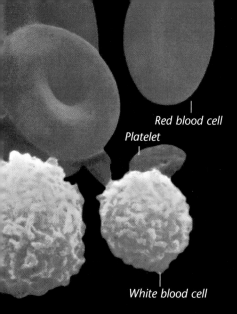

Red blood cell
Platelet
White blood cell

This is an electron microscope image showing three types of cells in a drop of blood.

BLOOD VESSELS

If all your blood vessels were joined end to end, they would stretch more than twice around the Earth. There are three types of blood vessels: arteries, veins and capillaries.

Arteries carry blood away from the heart. They lead to capillaries in your organs and body tissue such as your liver and muscles.

Capillaries have extremely thin walls, so that oxygen and food can pass through them from the blood into the body, and waste products can pass from the body into the blood. In each circulation of the body, some of the blood passes through the capillaries in your kidneys, where waste is filtered out. The waste is later flushed out of your body in your urine.

Once blood has traveled through the capillaries, it passes into veins, which lead back to the heart.

BLOOD

The average adult has 1.3 gallons of blood. As well as carrying substances around your body, it helps to fight germs, heal wounds and control your body temperature.

Blood is made up of red and white blood cells, and platelets, which help to stop the bleeding if you cut yourself. These three substances float in a pale yellow liquid called plasma.

Red blood cells are disc-shaped and contain a purple-red chemical called hemoglobin. As blood passes through the lungs, oxygen combines with the hemoglobin, to form oxyhemoglobin, which is bright red. As the cells deliver oxygen around the body, the oxyhemoglobin turns back into hemoglobin.

Red blood cell with oxygen   *Red blood cell without oxygen*

The cell's disc shape helps it to squeeze along inside tiny capillaries.

Red blood cells wear out about every four months and are replaced by new ones. They are made at a rate of two million per second.

White blood cells are larger than red ones. They help your body to fight disease.

This chart shows the composition of blood.

Plasma (55%) —————

White blood cells and platelets (0.45%) ———

Red blood cells (44.55%) ——

HEALING WOUNDS

Most minor cuts only bleed for a short time before a dry scab forms. The scab is produced when blood turns into a gel-like mass called a clot. This is triggered by a chemical reaction started by platelets.

The clot stops more blood from leaking out, and helps to prevent germs from entering the wound. A clot dissolves once the broken blood vessel is repaired.

Sticky threads forming a clot over a cut.

Skin

WORKING HARD

Your heart can easily pump the amount of oxygen your muscles need for everyday activities, such as walking and climbing stairs.

When you do strenuous exercise, such as running, your muscles have to work harder, so they need more oxygen. Your heart works harder, pumping blood around your body more quickly, so that more oxygen can reach them. If the blood can't get there quickly enough, your muscles don't get enough oxygen and they begin to ache. This is called muscle fatigue.

Internet links

Website 1 See pictures and watch short movies about how the heart works.

Website 2 Watch an animated slideshow showing how blood flows through the heart.

For links to these websites, go to **www.usborne-quicklinks.com**

DIGESTION

As food passes through your body, it is broken down into pieces small enough to be dissolved in your blood. This process is called digestion. Food travels along a tube called the digestive tract that runs from your mouth to a hole in your bottom called the anus. If your digestive tract was stretched out, it would be about four times as long as you.

STAGES OF DIGESTION

1. Food is chewed in the mouth and mixed with a digestive juice called saliva (or spit). Saliva makes food soft and mushy, so it slides down your throat easily. It also starts to break down starch in foods. Starch is a substance that is converted into energy once it has been digested.

2. Your throat muscles guide food through a cavity at the back of your throat called the pharynx and into a passage called the esophagus. As you swallow, a flap of skin called the epiglottis blocks off the top of your windpipe, so the food doesn't go down the wrong way.

The two diagrams below show what happens when you chew and swallow food.

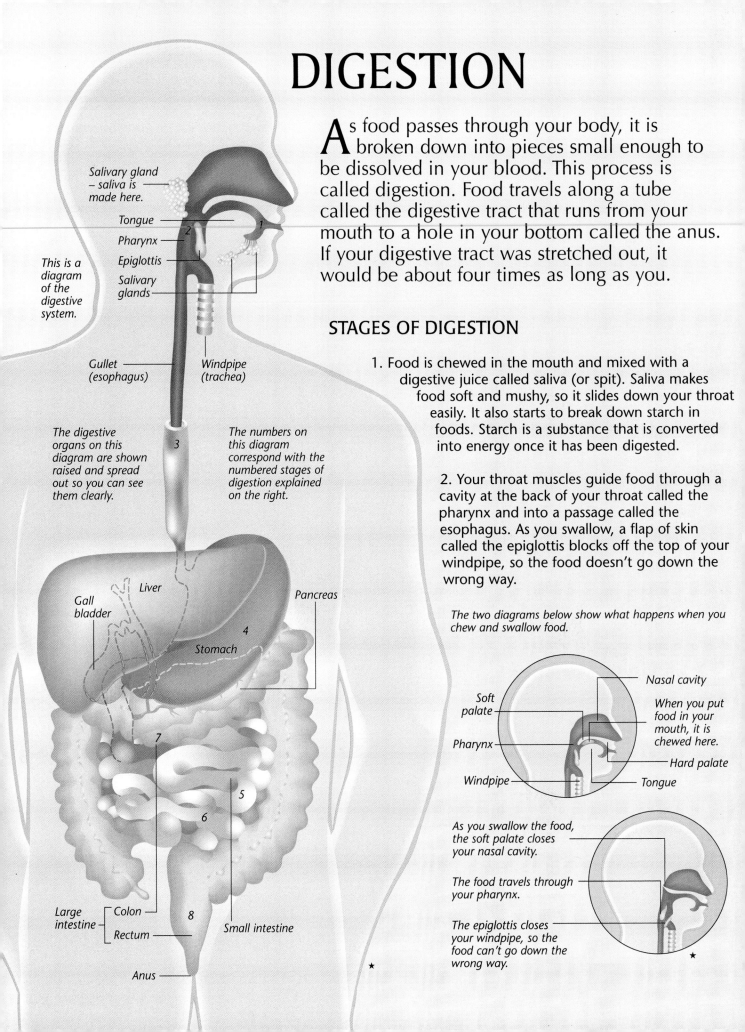

Salivary gland – saliva is made here.

Tongue

Pharynx

Epiglottis

Salivary glands

This is a diagram of the digestive system.

Gullet (esophagus)

Windpipe (trachea)

The digestive organs on this diagram are shown raised and spread out so you can see them clearly.

The numbers on this diagram correspond with the numbered stages of digestion explained on the right.

Liver

Gall bladder

Pancreas

Stomach

Large intestine — Colon

Rectum

Small intestine

Anus

Nasal cavity

When you put food in your mouth, it is chewed here.

Soft palate

Pharynx

Hard palate

Windpipe

Tongue

As you swallow the food, the soft palate closes your nasal cavity.

The food travels through your pharynx.

The epiglottis closes your windpipe, so the food can't go down the wrong way.

3. Food travels down the esophagus into your stomach. Muscles in the wall of your esophagus contract to push the food along. This action takes place all the way along your digestive tract.

4. In the stomach, food is churned up with more digestive juices, called gastric juices. These help to kill germs. They also start to break down and digest proteins in the food. Proteins are important for the growth and repair of your body.

5. The food moves into a tube called the small intestine. In the first part of the small intestine, digestive juices made by the liver and pancreas break down fats, proteins and starch in the food.

This is a diagram of the small and large intestine.

Colon

Small intestine

Rectum ★

Anus

6. The small intestine is lined with thousands of tiny lumps, called villi. (Each one is called a villus.) The villi help to increase the surface area of the small intestine. They are packed with blood vessels, which absorb the digested food and carry it to the liver for further processing, before it is carried around your body in your blood.

This is a cross section of a small intestine.

This shows a villus that has been highly magnified.

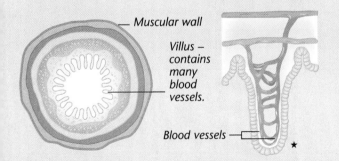

Muscular wall

Villus – contains many blood vessels.

Blood vessels ★

7. Water and any food that cannot be digested move into the first part of your large intestine, called the colon. Water is absorbed into your bloodstream there.

8. Anything left is waste. It passes into the second part of your large intestine, called the rectum. It is pushed out through the anus when you go to the toilet. It can take up to three days for food to travel all the way through your digestive tract.

DIGESTIVE GLANDS

Digestive juices contain chemicals called enzymes, which help to break down food. These juices are made inside your digestive glands. Some digestive glands are tiny, and set into the walls of digestive organs. For example, the wall of your stomach contains gastric glands. Other glands, such as your salivary glands, are separate organs.

This diagram shows the largest digestive glands.

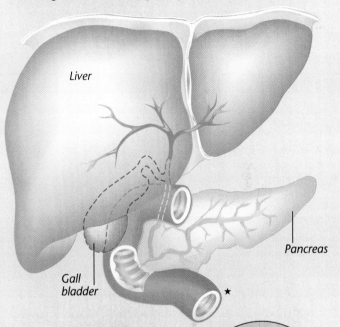

Liver

Pancreas

Gall bladder

★

Gall bladder

Bile is stored here. ★

The largest digestive glands are the liver and pancreas. Your liver makes a green liquid called bile. This breaks up fats into tiny drops so that enzymes can break them down more easily. Bile is stored in a sac called the gall bladder. Your pancreas makes pancreatic juice. This contains enzymes that break down fats, proteins and starch.

FOOD AND DIET

A healthy diet consists of a variety of foods, because different foods contain different things that your body needs. Carbohydrates, proteins and fats are vital for energy or growth. They are called nutrients. Vitamins, minerals and water are also important as they help your body to work properly.

CARBOHYDRATES

Carbohydrates give you energy. There are two types: sugars and starches.

Sugars are found in fruit, cake and other sweet foods. They give you a quick burst of energy. Starch is found in bread, potatoes and rice. The energy it produces lasts much longer.

Chocolate contains lots of sugar.

During digestion, carbohydrates are broken down into simple sugars, such as glucose. Your body uses most of these as fuel to produce energy, but some are stored in the liver, or turned into fat and stored under your skin.

Pasta is a healthy source of starch.

PROTEINS

Proteins are used for the growth and repair of body tissue. They are found in lean meat, fish, eggs, nuts, milk and beans. Teenagers need lots of protein because they are growing quickly. Pregnant women need protein for their unborn baby.

Proteins are like building blocks. During digestion, they are broken down and absorbed into the blood. Then they are carried to different parts of your body, where they are rearranged to make whichever protein is needed.

These are some examples of proteins in the body.

Hemoglobin is a protein found in red blood cells. It helps carry oxygen around the body.

Keratin is the protein from which hair and nails are made.

Actin and myosin are the proteins that enable muscles to contract.

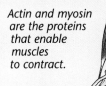

FATS

Fats are needed by your body for energy and warmth. Unused fats are stored in various areas of your body, such as under the skin. There are two types of fats: saturated and unsaturated.

Saturated fats are found mostly in animal products, such as butter, lard and fatty meat. These foods also contain cholesterol, a fat-like substance. Unsaturated fats are found in non-animal products, including vegetable oils and nuts.

Junk food is often high in fat. Eating too much saturated fat and cholesterol may cause heart disease.

See for yourself

Look at the labels on the packaging of some of the foods that you eat. They tell you how much carbohydrate, protein and fat the foods contain. Some labels also include information about the vitamins and minerals in a particular food.

VITAMINS

Vitamins are substances your body needs to remain healthy. They are found in a wide variety of foods. A balanced, healthy diet will give your body all the vitamins it needs. Your body needs tiny amounts of about 15 different vitamins for essential chemical processes to take place.

Vegetables and fruit are good sources of dietary fiber, vitamins and minerals.

The table explains the important sources and uses of some vitamins.

Vitamin	Good sources	Necessary for
A (retinol)	Milk, butter, eggs, fish oils, fresh green vegetables	Eyes (especially seeing in very dim light), skin
B (a group of several vitamins)	Whole wheat bread and rice, yeast, liver, soy beans	Energy production in all your cells, nerves, skin
C (ascorbic acid)	Oranges, lemons, blackcurrants, tomatoes, fresh green vegetables	Blood vessels, gums, healing wounds, preventing colds
D (calciferol)	Fish oils, milk, eggs, butter (and sunlight)	Bones, teeth
E (tocopherol)	Vegetable oils, whole wheat bread, rice, eggs, butter, fresh green vegetables	Blood vessels, heart, lungs, slowing ageing of cells
K (phylloquinone)	Fresh green vegetables, liver	Clotting blood

MINERALS

Minerals are another group of substances needed by your body. You need small amounts of about 20 different minerals in all. Trace minerals, such as iron, are needed in extremely small quantities.

This table explains the important sources and uses of some minerals.

Mineral	Good sources	Necessary for
Calcium and phosphorus	Milk, cheese, butter, water in some areas	Strong bones and teeth
Sodium	Salt, milk and spinach	Blood, digestion, nerves
Fluorine (trace mineral)	Milk, toothpaste, drinking water in some areas	Healthy teeth and bones
Iodine (trace mineral)	Seafood, table salt, drinking water in some areas	Hormone thyroxin (which controls your metabolism)
Iron (trace mineral)	Liver, apricots and green vegetables	Hemoglobin in red blood cells

DIETARY FIBER

Dietary fiber, also known as roughage, is a type of carbohydrate found in bran, whole wheat bread, fruit and vegetables. Fiber cannot be digested by humans, but it is bulky, so it helps the muscles of your intestines to move food efficiently through your digestive system.

WATER

Water is vital for life. Without it, you would only survive for a few days. You need to take in water to replace what you lose, for example in urine and sweat. There is water in what you drink, and also in some solid foods, such as lettuce, which is 90% water.

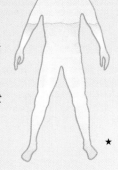

About 65% of your body weight is water. In very young children, up to 75% of their body weight is water.

Internet links

Website 1 Play games, try recipes and find out lots more about nutrition.

Website 2 Find out how to check if the foods you eat are healthy.

Website 3 Learn why too much fat and cholesterol can be bad for you.

Website 4 Try doing a quiz to see if you eat healthily.

For links to these websites, go to **www.usborne-quicklinks.com**

THE RESPIRATORY SYSTEM

The respiratory system is made up of your lungs and the passages that lead to them. When you breathe air into your lungs, oxygen from the air passes into your blood, which carries it around your body. The oxygen mixes with digested food to give you energy. Carbon dioxide is breathed out as waste.

HOW RESPIRATION WORKS

When you breathe in, air is sucked through your nose or mouth and down your windpipe. The lining of your nose and windpipe make a slippery liquid called mucus. This warms and moistens the air, so it can travel more easily along the passages. It also traps dirt and germs in the air. Tiny hairs called cilia waft the mucus away from your lungs toward your nose and throat.

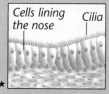

★ Cells lining the nose   Cilia

Your windpipe divides into two tubes (called bronchi), and one leads to each lung. Your lungs are made up of a network of tubes, called bronchioles. They get narrower as they branch off. At the end of these tubes are clusters of millions of tiny air sacs surrounded by many blood vessels. Oxygen passes through the thin walls of the sacs into the blood vessels, where it is absorbed into your blood.

The oxygen is carried to different parts of your body, where it is combined with nutrients that have been absorbed during digestion. This produces energy and carbon dioxide. The carbon dioxide is carried back to the lungs in your blood and you breathe it out.

Bronchi

Narrow tubes (bronchioles)

Tiny air sac

This is a pair of lungs. Each lung contains many tubes, the smallest of which end in tiny air sacs.

Air sac

Blood vessels

From heart

Air sac wall

Carbon dioxide

Oxygen

Blood vessel

★

To heart

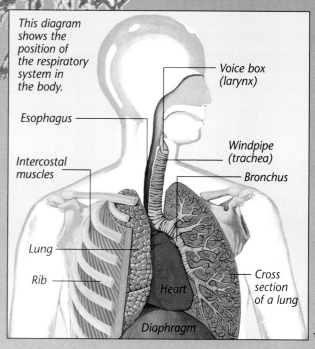

This diagram shows the position of the respiratory system in the body.

Voice box (larynx)

Esophagus

Windpipe (trachea)

Intercostal muscles

Bronchus

Lung

Rib

Heart

Cross section of a lung

Diaphragm

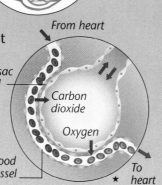

BREATHING

Breathing, or ventilation, is the movement of air in and out of the lungs. It is controlled by a group of muscles in your chest, called the intercostal muscles, and a flat sheet of muscle called the diaphragm, which lies under your lungs.

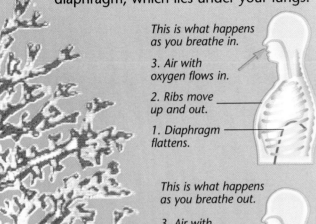

This is what happens as you breathe in.

3. Air with oxygen flows in.

2. Ribs move up and out.

1. Diaphragm flattens.

This is what happens as you breathe out.

3. Air with carbon dioxide flows out.

2. Ribs move down and in.

1. Diaphragm rises.

As you breathe in, your intercostal muscles pull your ribs up and out, and your diaphragm flattens. This leaves space for your lungs to expand and air rushes into them.

As you breathe out, your diaphragm relaxes, so it becomes arched again. Your intercostal muscles also relax, moving your ribs down and in. The space inside your chest gets smaller again, and air is squeezed out. This is called exhalation.

COUGHING AND SNEEZING

The normal rhythm of your breathing is sometimes interrupted. Sneezing clears dust, pollen or germs from your nose. Coughing helps to clear similar blockages from your windpipe. Yawning raises the level of oxygen in your blood, and helps to rid your body of large amounts of carbon dioxide.

VOICE BOX

Your voice box, or larynx, is at the top of your windpipe. Inside it are two bands of muscles called vocal cords. These open to let air past when you breathe, but when you speak or sing, the cords pull together. The air passing up through the cords makes them vibrate. These vibrations can be heard as sounds.

These are cross sections of the vocal cords.

Closed   Open

See for yourself

Place your fingers lightly on the front of your neck while you talk, shout and sing. You will be able to feel the vibrations in your vocal cords, and the movement of your muscles as they relax and tighten.

The louder and lower the sound is, the stronger the vibrations. Your muscles will tighten when you sing higher notes and relax as you sing lower ones.

The shorter your vocal cords are and the faster they vibrate, the higher the sound you will make. Women's vocal cords are short and vibrate about 220 times a second, so their voices are high. Men's vocal cords are longer and vibrate about 120 times a second, so their voices are deeper.

Internet links

Website 1 Find out what asthma is and what causes it.

Website 2 Find out what healthy and unhealthy lungs sound like. You'll find lots of information and quizzes too.

Website 3 Watch a short movie about respiration.

Website 4 Discover how mountaineers adapt to breathing air with less oxygen in it.

For links to these websites, go to **www.usborne-quicklinks.com**

THE NERVOUS SYSTEM

T he nervous system is a network of nerve cells, called neurons, stretching from your brain to the tips of your toes. Neurons send messages to the brain about what's happening to your body. The brain decides what should be done and then instructions are sent back down other neurons to muscles, organs or cells, which carry out the response.

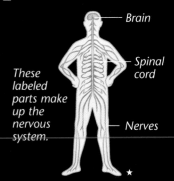

These labeled parts make up the nervous system.

Brain

Spinal cord

Nerves

★

USING YOUR SENSES

There are different neurons to perform different tasks. Sensory neurons in your skin, mouth, eyes, nose and ears collect information about things you touch, taste, see, smell or hear. There are sensory neurons inside your body too. They gather information about how the organs inside you are working.

Sensory neurons have sensitive nerve endings called receptors, which pick up information. They pass it on to neurons in your brain known as association neurons.

Once your brain has decided what to do, the association neurons pass the information on to motor neurons. Motor neurons carry the instructions to other parts of your body, such as your muscles, where the instructions are carried out.

PARTS OF A NEURON

Neurons have a cell body surrounded by long strands called nerve fibers. There are two types of nerve fibers – dendrites and axons. Messages pass from the end of an axon to the nearest dendrite of the next neuron. The messages are passed from one neuron to the next until the information reaches the part of the brain that responds to your senses.

This is a diagram of a chain of neurons.

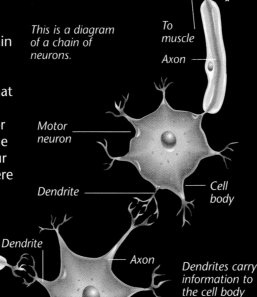

To muscle

★

Axon

Motor neuron

Dendrite

Cell body

Sensory neuron

Axon

Dendrite

Axon

Long dendrite, called a dendron

From receptor

Cell body

Association neuron

Cell body

NERVES

Nerve fibers are grouped together in bundles surrounded by a protective sheath. Each bundle is called a nerve. The biggest nerve in the body is the spinal cord. It runs from your brain down a tunnel of holes in your spine.

This is a diagram of a nerve.

Bundle of nerve fibers

Protective sheath

Messages from most parts of your body pass through the spinal cord on their way to your brain and on their way back again.

In this highly-magnified picture of nerve cells in the brain, the bright orange areas are cell bodies.

Dendrites carry information to the cell body and axons carry it away.

JUMPING THE GAP

Messages travel around your body as electrical impulses, but axons and dendrites are separated by tiny gaps that the impulses can't jump. When an impulse reaches the end of an axon, special chemicals are released. These spread across the gap, and when they reach the other side, the dendrite fires off an impulse.

A nerve impulse reaches the end of an axon.

This gap is called a synapse.

Chemicals known as neurotransmitters jump the gap.

★ *The dendrite fires off an impulse.*

TYPES OF ACTIONS

There are two main types of actions carried out by your body – voluntary and involuntary. Voluntary actions are consciously controlled by your brain, such as when you lift a cup. Nerve impulses are analyzed in the brain before you decide what action to take. Involuntary actions are those that your brain does not consciously control, such as digestion and breathing.

Sweating is an involuntary action.

Kicking a ball is a voluntary action.

REFLEX ACTIONS

Reflex actions are involuntary actions. They are usually sudden movements, designed to protect you from danger, such as pulling your hand away from something hot. To do this as quickly as possible, the nerves bypass your brain. In most cases, a response is triggered in the spinal cord and the instruction is sent immediately to your muscles.

PINS AND NEEDLES

If you lie on your arm or cross your legs for too long, they may go numb. One reason for this is that nerves get squashed and can't pass messages on properly. When you take the weight off again, you may get tingling pins and needles as the nerves slowly get back to normal and sensation returns to your limbs.

Internet links

For a link to a website where you can find lots more interesting information about the nervous system, go to **www.usborne-quicklinks.com**

The tangled threads on the left are nerve fibers.

THE BRAIN

Your brain controls almost all of your activities, from thinking and moving to breathing. It is constantly making sure that all the different parts of your body work properly together. Information about everything that happens to you is stored inside it. By the time you are eight years old, your brain holds more information than a million encyclopedias.

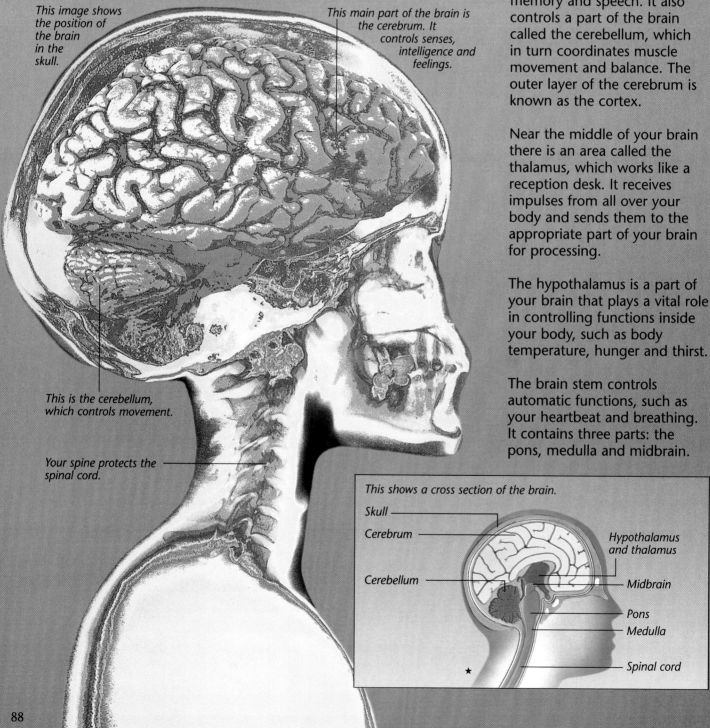

This image shows the position of the brain in the skull.

This main part of the brain is the cerebrum. It controls senses, intelligence and feelings.

This is the cerebellum, which controls movement.

Your spine protects the spinal cord.

INSIDE YOUR BRAIN

Your brain looks like a large, wrinkly walnut. It is made up of over 10,000 million neurons and is protected by your skull. The main parts of the brain are explained below.

The largest part of the brain is called the cerebrum. It controls most physical activities and many mental activities, such as memory and speech. It also controls a part of the brain called the cerebellum, which in turn coordinates muscle movement and balance. The outer layer of the cerebrum is known as the cortex.

Near the middle of your brain there is an area called the thalamus, which works like a reception desk. It receives impulses from all over your body and sends them to the appropriate part of your brain for processing.

The hypothalamus is a part of your brain that plays a vital role in controlling functions inside your body, such as body temperature, hunger and thirst.

The brain stem controls automatic functions, such as your heartbeat and breathing. It contains three parts: the pons, medulla and midbrain.

This shows a cross section of the brain.

Skull
Cerebrum
Cerebellum
Hypothalamus and thalamus
Midbrain
Pons
Medulla
Spinal cord

MAP OF YOUR SENSES

Information from your senses is sent to the cerebrum as impulses. Different areas of the cerebrum deal with different senses.

This is a diagram of the cerebrum. It has been numbered and shaded to show the different areas clearly.

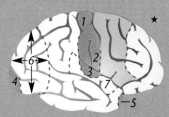

Sensory areas:
1. *Receives impulses from muscles, skin and inner organs.*
2. *Receives impulses from tongue.*
3. *Receives impulses from ears.*
4. *Receives impulses from eyes.*
5. *Receives impulses from nose.*

Association areas include:
6. *Produces sight.*
7. *Produces hearing.*

Motor areas. Each tiny part sends out impulses to a specific muscle.

TWO HALVES

The two sides of your brain are called the cerebral hemispheres. Each one looks after the opposite side of your body. They are joined by a thick band of nerve fibers, which lets each side know what the other is doing.

Both sides control different kinds of actions. In right-handed people, the left side is used for speech and language. It is also used for logical thought, for example when playing chess. The right side specializes in recognizing objects. It also controls emotions and creativity. In most left-handed people it is the other way round.

Cerebral hemispheres

Left ——— Right

MEMORY

There are two different types of memory. Motor-skill memory helps you to remember how to do actions, such as walking or riding a bicycle. Factual memory enables you to remember specific pieces of information.

There are also two levels of memory. Short-term memory stores information for only a few minutes. Anything that you can remember for longer is in your long-term memory. Information can be stored in your long-term memory for up to a lifetime.

See for yourself

Test your short-term memory by reading through the list of numbers below, then seeing how many you can write down in order. Most people cannot remember more than seven numbers.

3 0 9 7 1 2 8 5 4 1 6 9

BRAIN WAVES

Electrical impulses in your brain can be detected through your skull by sensor pads called electrodes. The patterns, or brain waves, are recorded on a chart called an EEG (or electroencephalogram). Doctors often use EEGs to find out if a person's brain is working normally and to study sleep.

The illustrations below show the main types of brain waves.

Alpha waves show when you are awake, but disappear during sleep.

Beta waves show when you are thinking, or receiving impulses from your senses.

Theta waves show in EEGs of children and adults suffering from stress or some brain disorders.

Delta waves show in EEGs of babies and sleeping adults. They can be a sign of brain disorder in an awake adult.

SLEEPING

There are two kinds of sleep – REM (rapid eye movement) and NREM (non rapid eye movement). Each night you switch between the two.

In REM sleep, the peaks and troughs (ups and downs) on an EEG chart are close together, showing that the brain is very active. People dream during REM sleep.

In NREM sleep, the peaks and troughs are farther apart, showing that the brain is less active. This is when you are deeply asleep.

Internet links

Website 1 Try some quizzes and games, or read facts about the brain.

Website 2 Probe a virtual brain to see which areas control different body parts.

For links to these websites, go to **www.usborne-quicklinks.com**

SKIN, NAILS AND HAIR

The skin is the largest organ in the body. It covers your body, protecting it against damage, infection and drying out. Your skin also helps to keep your body at a constant temperature, removes waste and makes vitamin D. Your hair helps to keep you warm and your nails support your fingertips and toes.

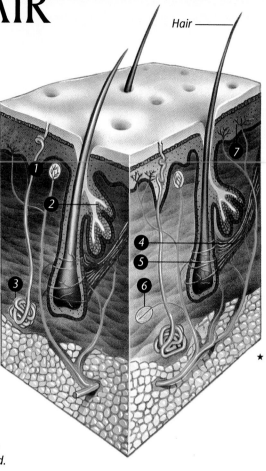

Hair

DIFFERENT LAYERS

Skin has two main layers. The outer layer is called the epidermis. It is made up of flat, dead skin cells, filled with a tough, waterproof protein called keratin. These cells are constantly being worn away and replaced by new cells from a layer lower down.

This illustration shows the different layers that make up your skin.

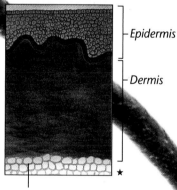

Epidermis

Dermis

★

Fat stores

Underneath the epidermis there is a thicker layer called the dermis. It contains blood vessels, which bring food and oxygen to the skin in your blood. Underneath the dermis there is a store of fat, which helps to keep your body warm.

INSIDE THE SKIN

As well as containing lots of blood vessels, skin also contains other structures, which perform many jobs.

The diagram on the right shows the different structures in skin. The key below explains the numbered parts.

1. Touch receptors are nerve endings that tell your brain if something feels hot, cold, rough, smooth, soft or hard.

2. Sebaceous glands produce an oil called sebum, which helps to keep your hair and skin waterproof and supple.

3. Sweat glands produce sweat, which helps you to cool down.

4. Hair erector muscles make hairs stand on end, for example when your body is cold.

5. Hair plexuses are nerve endings that let your brain know when your hair moves.

6. Pacinian corpuscles are pressure receptors that send impulses to the brain on receiving deep pressure.

7. Pain receptors are nerve endings that tell your brain if any stimulation, such as heat or pressure, becomes too much. Your brain interprets such impulses as pain.

See for yourself

Gently press a piece of clear tape onto the back of your hand, then pull it off and look at it carefully under a magnifying lens. You should be able to see tiny flakes of dead epidermal skin.

This picture shows hairs growing out of skin. It has been magnified over 1,000 times. The flakes you can see are dead skin cells from the top layer of the epidermis.

TEMPERATURE CONTROL

Your skin plays a vital part in keeping your body temperature constant, as shown below.

This shows how your skin cools you down.

Blood vessels widen, so more heat can be lost through the skin.

Hairs (only shown here at the surface) lie flat, so little warm air is trapped.

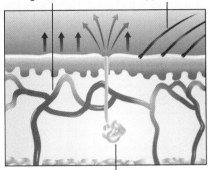

Sweat is produced. It escapes through holes called pores. As it dries, it uses heat from the skin, and cools you down.

This shows how your skin keeps you warm.

Blood vessels narrow, so less heat escapes through the skin.

Muscles contract and make hairs stand up, trapping warm air.

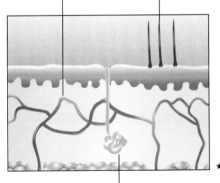

Sweat glands produce less sweat.

Your body also keeps warm by shivering. Your muscles jerk automatically, producing heat as they do so.

The outer surface of a hair is called the cuticle. It is made up of flat, overlapping scales of keratin.

NAILS

Nails are firm pads that support your sensitive fingertips. Like skin, they are mostly made of keratin. Without them, your fingertips would bend too much when you touched things.

This diagram shows a cross section of a finger.

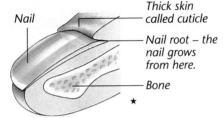

Nail

Thick skin called cuticle

Nail root – the nail grows from here.

Bone

HAIR

There are about 5 million hairs on your body. Each one grows out of a deep hole in your skin called a follicle. Cells at the base of each hair push the hair up through the follicle. The hair you can see, called the shaft, is made of dead cells. This is why cutting your hair does not hurt.

This diagram shows the structure of a hair.

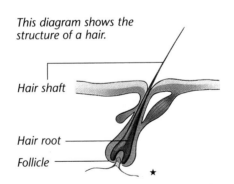

Hair shaft

Hair root

Follicle

Whether your hair is curly or straight depends on the shape of your follicles. These diagrams show which follicles produce different types of hair.

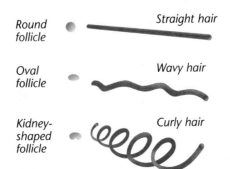

Round follicle *Straight hair*

Oval follicle *Wavy hair*

Kidney-shaped follicle *Curly hair*

DARK AND FAIR

Your skin contains cells called melanocytes, which produce a brown substance called melanin. This absorbs some of the Sun's harmful ultraviolet rays, and so helps to protect your skin. The amount of melanin produced affects the color of the skin.

Fair-skinned people only have melanin in the lower layers of the epidermis, but people with dark skin have larger amounts of it in all layers. Melanin mixed with an orange chemical called carotene gives skin a yellow tint. Freckles are small patches of skin that contain more melanin than the surrounding area.

The color of hair is also due to melanin. Dark hair, for example, contains mostly pure melanin. Fair hair contains a type of melanin with sulfur in it, and red hair results from a type of melanin with iron in it.

You can see some variations in the skin and hair color of these children.

Internet links

Website 1 Watch short movies about skin, hair and nails.

Website 2 Learn about fingerprints and how police use them to catch criminals.

Website 3 Learn about goosebumps.

Website 4 Read facts about hair and watch an animation of the growth cycle of a hair.

For links to these websites, go to **www.usborne-quicklinks.com**

The eyes are the organs of sight. You see things because light rays bounce off objects and enter your eyes. Light-sensitive nerve endings at the back of your eyes send information to the brain, which interprets it as an image. Each eye sees objects from a different angle and your brain joins the two images together to help you see in 3-D.

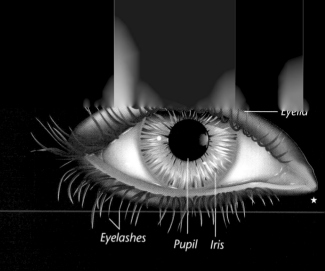

Eyelid

Eyelashes   Pupil   Iris

HOW EYES WORK

Light rays enter your eyes through a hole called the pupil. They travel through a clear layer called the cornea and a disc called the lens. These bend the light rays so that they form an upside down image on the back of your eye (the retina).

This shows a cross section of an eye.

The retina contains light-sensitive nerve endings called rods and cones. These change the image into nerve impulses, which travel along the optic nerve to the brain. Your brain interprets these impulses as an image, which it also turns the right side up again.

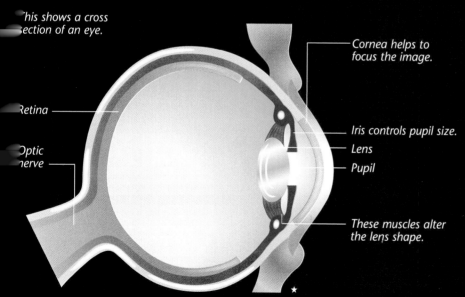

Retina

Optic nerve

Cornea helps to focus the image.

Iris controls pupil size.
Lens
Pupil

These muscles alter the lens shape.

See for yourself

There are no rods and cones in the area where the optic nerve leaves your eye. If an image falls here, you cannot see it, so this area is called the blind spot. Test to find your blind spot by holding this page at arm's length. Close your left eye and stare at the square with your right eye. Slowly bring the page closer to your face and notice the circle disappear.

RODS AND CONES

Each eye has about 125 million rods and 7 million cones. Rods only detect black and white, but they work well in dim light. Cones see colours but need bright light to work. At night, you see mainly in shades of gray because only your rods are working.

SEEING COLORS

You can produce any color in the spectrum by mixing the three basic colors of light: red, green and blue. Similarly, you have three types of cones in your eyes, sensitive to red, blue or green light. Each type responds by a different amount depending on the color you are looking at. If you look at a purple object, the blue and red cones respond more strongly than the green ones. Color-blind people can't tell the difference

DARK AND LIGHT

Your pupils change size as it gets lighter or darker around you. Muscles around your irises make your pupils smaller in bright light, so you are not dazzled. In dim light, the muscles make your pupils wider, so they can take in as much light as possible. If you suddenly go from a light room to a dark room, it takes your pupils a while to adjust.

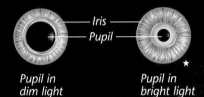

Pupil in dim light

Pupil in bright light

The fine threads you can see in the iris below are muscles that help to control the size of the pupil.

SEEING CLEARLY

The point at which light rays meet in your eye is called the focus. If they focus on the retina, everything you see looks sharp and clear. The lens changes shape when looking at objects at different distances. This bends the light rays by different amounts, and keeps the image in focus.

This diagram shows how a person with perfect sight focuses.

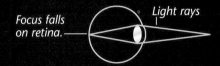

Focus falls on retina.

Light rays

Some people cannot focus light properly. Near-sighted people cannot see distant objects clearly. They have long eyeballs, and the lens bends the rays too much, so they focus in front of the retina.

This diagram shows how a near-sighted person focuses.

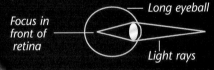

Focus in front of retina

Long eyeball

Light rays

Far-sighted people cannot see close objects clearly. They have short eyeballs, and the lens bends the rays too little, so the image reaches the retina before it is in focus.

This diagram shows how a far-sighted person focuses.

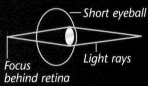

Short eyeball

Focus behind retina

Light rays

Glasses or contact lenses with concave lenses can correct near sight. People with far sight need convex lenses.

Concave lens

Convex lens

EYE PROTECTION

Eyes are very delicate. Most of the eyeball is protected by the bones of your skull. The front of the eye is protected by the thin layer of skin known as the eyelid.

This is a cross section of an eyeball. You can see how it is protected by other parts of the eye.

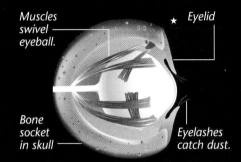

Muscles swivel eyeball.

★ Eyelid

Bone socket in skull

Eyelashes catch dust.

Eyelids keep dust and dirt out of your eyes. When you blink, your eyelids wipe tears over the eyes, keeping them moist and clean. Tears contain chemicals that help to kill germs. They are made in glands above each eye and are drained away through channels that lead into your nose.

Here you can see where tears are made.

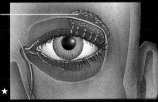

A gland here produces tears.

Internet links

Website 1 Learn more about the eye and eye disorders.

Website 2 Find out more about how your eyes see colors.

Website 3 Find out how glasses correct sight.

For links to these websites, go to **www.usborne-quicklinks.com**

EARS

The ears are the organs of hearing. They can pick up sounds as loud as the roar of a jet aircraft and as quiet as a whisper. The object making the sound causes the air around it to vibrate. Your ears are designed to pick up these vibrations, which are called sound waves.

As well as hearing sounds, your ears help you to keep your balance.

EARS AND HEARING

Your ear is divided into three areas: the outer ear, which is the part you can see, and the middle and inner ear, which are the main working parts.

The ear flap funnels sound waves into a passage called the ear canal. The waves travel along this passage until they hit a thin layer of tissue called the eardrum, making it vibrate. The vibrations pass through three tiny bones (the malleus, incus and stapes) and into a small hole called the oval window, which also vibrates. The vibrations then pass into a spiral-shaped tube called the cochlea.

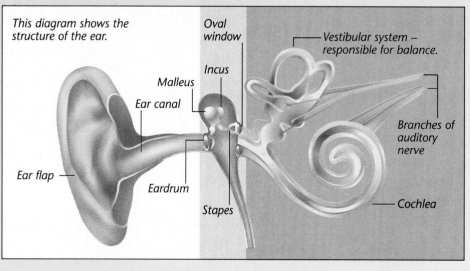

This diagram shows the structure of the ear.

Oval window

Incus

Malleus

Ear canal

Vestibular system – responsible for balance.

Branches of auditory nerve

Ear flap

Eardrum

Stapes

Cochlea

☐ Outer ear (filled with air)　☐ Middle ear (filled with air)　☐ Inner ear (filled with liquid)

The cochlea is filled with liquid. The vibrations make the liquid shake and this stimulates tiny hair cells that run along a thin piece of tissue inside the cochlea. These hair cells have sensitive nerve endings that change vibrations into nerve impulses. The impulses travel along the auditory nerve to the brain, where your brain interprets them as sounds. High sounds are caused by the air vibrating very quickly, while low sounds are caused by the air vibrating slowly. Your cochlea picks up these differences in vibrations.

KEEPING BALANCED

Many parts of your body help you to keep balanced. Your eyes tell you about the position of your body. So do sensitive cells in your muscles and tendons.

The vestibular system in your inner ear also has an important part to play in maintaining your balance. It has two main areas: three loops, called semicircular canals, and two sacs called the utricle and saccule.

This shows the vestibular system.

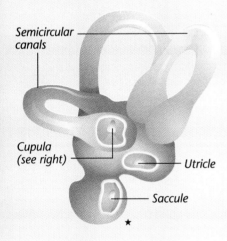

Semicircular canals

Cupula (see right)

Utricle

Saccule

★

See for yourself

If you spin around very quickly, you will probably feel dizzy when you stop. This is because the liquid in your semicircular canals keeps on spinning after your body stops.

You can see how this works by holding a glass of water in your hand and swirling it around. The water in the glass will continue swirling for a little while after you stop moving the glass.

The semicircular canals are tubes filled with liquid. At the end of each tube there is a structure called an ampulla, made up of a hard lump known as a cupula and tiny hairs at its base.

When you turn your head, the liquid moves more slowly than your head, bending the cupula back and triggering the hairs. Sensitive nerve endings in the hairs send your brain information about which way your head is moving.

This is an illustration of an ampulla.

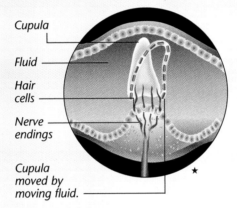

Cupula

Fluid

Hair cells

Nerve endings

Cupula moved by moving fluid.

The utricle and saccule send information to your brain about the angle of your head. They both contain a small, gel-like patch called a macula, and sensitive hair cells. When your head moves, the gel pulls the hairs to one side. This tells your brain whether the head is in a forward, backward, sideways or tilted position.

This diagram explains how a macula works.

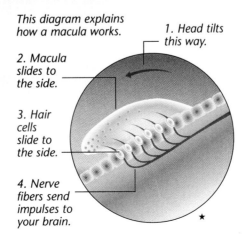

1. Head tilts this way.

2. Macula slides to the side.

3. Hair cells slide to the side.

4. Nerve fibers send impulses to your brain.

TWO EARS

Having two ears gives your brain two sources of information about sounds, movement and position. By combining this information, the brain finds out more than it would from one ear alone.

For instance, having two ears helps you to tell which direction a sound is coming from. A sound coming from the left will hit your left ear slightly earlier than your right and will produce stronger vibrations there. If the sound is directly in front or behind, the sound arrives at each ear at the same time and volume.

See for yourself

You can use this test to find out how your brain locates a sound. Sit on a chair, blindfolded. Ask someone to make a sound by tapping together two pencils, in different places around and above your body. Say where you think the sound is coming from.

You will probably find it hardest to pinpoint the sound when it is coming from directly behind, above or in front of you, in line with the center of your body. This is because the sound has reached both ears at the same time and volume.

Internet links

Website 1 Watch some animations about ears.

Website 2 Try a simple balance experiment.

Website 3 Find out how loud everyday sounds are and which ones can damage your hearing.

For links to these websites, go to **www.usborne-quicklinks.com**

THE NOSE AND TONGUE

The nose and tongue are the organs of smell and taste respectively. Smells and tastes are chemicals. Sensitive nerve endings in your nose and tongue detect these chemicals and send information to your brain, which identifies the smell or taste. Both organs also have other important jobs to do; for example, the nose is part of the respiratory system, and the tongue plays a role in digestion and speech.

INSIDE THE NOSE

The two holes in your nose, called nostrils, open into a hollow space called the nasal cavity. As you breathe in, air is sucked into the lower part of the nasal cavity. Here, short hairs filter out large dust particles from the air, and mucus in the cavity's lining warms and moistens the air before it travels into the lungs.

The roof of the nasal cavity is lined with many tiny sensitive threads. Chemicals in the air dissolve in the mucus and are absorbed by the threads.

This man is collecting rose petals to make into perfume. Your sense of smell can detect subtle variations in perfumes.

Sensitive nerve endings in the threads send impulses to your brain, which interprets them as a smell.

Normally, when you breathe in, only a small amount of air floats into your nasal cavity. When you sniff hard, you direct a stream of air toward the sensitive threads. This is why things smell stronger if you sniff their scent.

This is a diagram of the inside of the nose.

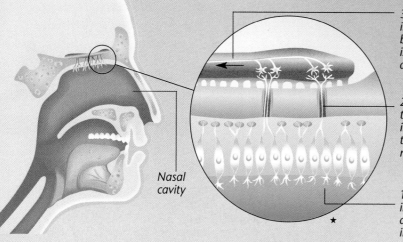

3. The impulse is carried to the brain, where it is interpreted as a smell.

2. The chemicals trigger an impulse, which travels along nerve cells.

Nasal cavity

1. Tiny threads in the nasal cavity absorb chemicals in smells.

DIFFERENT SMELLS

Most humans can tell the difference between thousands of different smells. For many years, scientists thought that all smells could be divided up into seven groups, called the seven basic scents. Recent research, however, suggests that there are many more groups – perhaps hundreds.

This table shows the seven basic scents.

Smell	Example
Camphor	Mothballs
Musk	Aftershave/Perfume
Floral	Roses
Peppermint	Mint toothpaste
Ether	Dry cleaning fluid
Pungent	Vinegar
Putrid	Rotten eggs

SMELLY MEMORIES

The sense of smell is strongly linked to memory. For example, the scent of mown grass might remind you of a sporting event. This is probably because nerve impulses from the nose are analyzed in the same part of the brain that deals with memory.

TONGUE AND TASTE

The main purpose of your sense of taste is to tell you whether or not something is safe to eat. For example, rotten food and most poisonous plants taste revolting, so your immediate reaction is to spit them out.

The surface of your tongue is covered with tiny bumps called papillae. Many of these are lined with taste buds containing sensitive nerve endings. When you eat, chemicals in the food dissolve in your saliva and are absorbed by your taste buds. The nerve endings in the taste buds send impulses to your brain, which interprets them as a taste.

The diagrams below shows the position of the tongue within the mouth, the papillae within the tongue and the taste buds within the papillae.

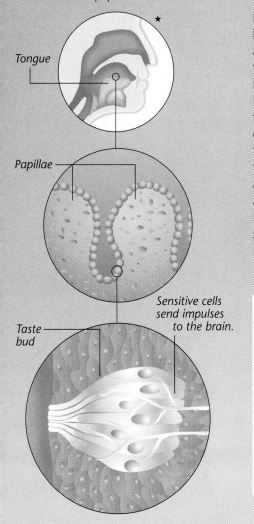

Tongue

Papillae

Taste bud

Sensitive cells send impulses to the brain.

This diagram shows the taste-sensitive areas of the tongue.

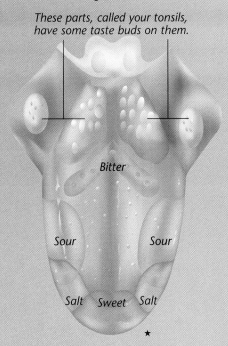

These parts, called your tonsils, have some taste buds on them.

Bitter

Sour

Sour

Salt   Sweet   Salt

FLAVORS

Most of your taste buds lie at the sides and back of your tongue, although you have a few in other places around your throat. Buds in different areas of your tongue respond more strongly to different tastes. Scientists think that there are four main tastes: salt, sweet, sour and bitter. All flavors are made up of these basic tastes, plus smells detected by the nose.

Lemons taste sour.

Toffees taste sweet.

See for yourself

Wash your hands, and use your fingertip to place drops of cold, black coffee in different places on your tongue. Notice where your tongue is most sensitive to the coffee's bitter taste. Repeat the test using salty water, sugary water and lemon juice. Rinse your mouth with water and dry it with a piece of bread between each test.

See for yourself

You can use this test to show that the senses of taste and smell are closely linked. Grate a small amount of apple, pear and carrot into different bowls. Then shut your eyes tightly and hold your nose. Ask someone to feed you a spoonful of each food, one at a time. Try to identify the food. Repeat the experiment without holding your nose. You will probably find it easier to identify the food correctly.

WORKING TOGETHER

Your senses of smell and taste are closely related. When you eat, food smells travel up your throat into your nasal cavity, where the smell is detected in the usual way.

If you have a cold, you often lose your sense of smell and taste. This is because the lining of your nose swells, and makes thicker mucus than normal. This makes it harder for smells to reach the sensitive threads in your nasal cavity. Your tongue can still detect the basic tastes, but you cannot identify the more subtle flavors.

Internet links

Website 1 Find out why your tongue is important for speech.

Website 2 Try some experiments to test your sense of smell.

Website 3 Find out how some animals use bad smells to defend themselves.

Website 4 Learn some gross but interesting facts about the nose.

For links to these websites, go to **www.usborne-quicklinks.com**

GENES AND DNA

There are up to 100 trillion cells in your body. Almost every single one of them contains a set of instructions that tells the cell how to grow and what to do. These instructions are called genes.

Chromosome

The four colors in this diagram show the four chemicals that make up DNA.

This is a strand of DNA.

DNA strands consist of two spirals, which are linked by pairs of the four DNA chemicals. This shape is called a double helix.

CHEMICAL CODES

Genes are made of a chemical called DNA (deoxyribonucleic acid), which is stored inside each cell, in an area called the nucleus. DNA forms long, thin strands, which often coil into short, thick "X" shapes, called chromosomes.

DNA contains four chemicals: adenine, cytosine, guanine and thymine (or A, C, G and T for short). The order of these chemicals in the DNA strand acts as a code. Cells follow a gene's instructions by reading this code.

FAMILY TRAITS

A complete set of genes is made up of 46 chromosomes. People inherit 23 chromosomes from their mother and 23 from their father, which is why children often look like their parents. As well as looks, you can also inherit abilities, diseases and maybe even parts of your personality in your genes. Something that is passed down from one generation to the next in genes is called a genetic trait.

DIFFERENT ALMOST EVERY TIME

Every sperm cell or egg cell produced has its own unique selection of half a parent's genes. This means that if the same two parents have more than one child, the children will not have exactly the same genes as each other. This is why brothers and sisters can look very different from one another.

Identical twins are the only people who have the same genes as each other. Identical twins are made when a fertilized egg cell splits after the sperm and egg have joined. The separate parts grow into two babies with exactly the same DNA.

These identical twins have exactly the same DNA as each other.

GIRL OR BOY?

The chromosomes that determine whether a baby develops as a male or a female are called sex chromosomes. There are two kinds: X and Y chromosomes.

Eggs and sperm have one sex chromosome each. All ova have an X chromosome, but half the sperm have an X chromosome and half have a Y chromosome.

If a sperm with an X chromosome joins an ovum, the baby will be a girl. If a sperm with a Y chromosome joins an ovum, the baby will be a boy.

This diagram shows how the sex chromosome of the sperm determines whether a baby will be a boy or a girl.

X + *X* = *Girl* **XX**

X + *Y* = *Boy* **XY**

This baby has inherited many traits from its parents, such as its blue eyes and pale skin.

DOMINANT GENES

It isn't possible for a child to develop all the genetic traits it inherits from both parents, so some genes overrule others. A gene that overrules another is called a dominant gene. The weaker one is called a recessive gene.

For example, if one parent has freckles, but the other doesn't, their children will all have freckles. This is because the freckles gene is dominant, while the "no-freckles" gene is recessive.

Recessive genes will only give a person their genetic trait if that person inherits the gene from both parents. For example, if neither parent has freckles, their children won't have them either.

NATURE OR NURTURE?

Genes are important, but they aren't the only things that make you who you are. People are also affected by environmental factors, such as their surroundings and diet.

For example, everyone has a genetically-determined height, but they won't reach that height unless they eat a well-balanced diet. It is thought that some people inherit genes that make them gifted at playing a musical instrument, but they still have to learn how to play. Many qualities like this are a mixture of "nature" (genes) and "nurture" (education and upbringing).

Internet links

For a link to a website where you can explore an interactive introduction to genes and DNA, go to **www.usborne-quicklinks.com**

99

GENE SCIENCE

In the 21st century, genetics has become one of the most important of all sciences. Scientists are finding the genes that contribute to diseases, making new medicines and redesigning living things. The different branches of gene science are changing all our lives.

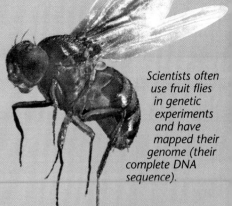
Scientists often use fruit flies in genetic experiments and have mapped their genome (their complete DNA sequence).

DNA TESTING

It's now possible to read the patterns in a person's DNA. This will enable scientists to do many things they weren't able to do previously, such as:
• see if you have genes that carry genetic diseases;
• see whether two people belong to the same family;
• trace a criminal using a sample of hair or skin from a crime scene;
• find out more about mummies and preserved prehistoric animal and plant life.

Internet links

For a link to a website where you can find out more about gene science and its potential uses, go to
www.usborne-quicklinks.com

GENOME MAPPING

Genome mapping means figuring out the genome, or the complete DNA sequence, of a living thing. Humans, fruit flies and many other species have now had their genomes mapped.

Genome mapping doesn't show how genes work. It just provides a long sequence of DNA code. This raw data can then be used to find out what particular genes do and how they work.

To map a genome, cells are taken from a living thing, such as a worm or fruit fly.

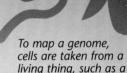

The chromosomes containing the DNA are extracted from the cells.

The DNA is analyzed and powerful computers figure out its sequence.

GENETIC ENGINEERING

Genetic engineering means making changes to DNA in order to change the way living things work. It is used to create new types of crops and farm animals, and to make bacteria that can make medicines. In theory, humans can be genetically engineered too.

These chickens have been genetically engineered to have no feathers. They are bred by farmers in hot countries because they stay cooler, and they don't need to be plucked if they are sold for meat.

GM FOODS

Many farmers now grow crops that have been genetically modified. They are usually more hardy than natural, unmodified plants, so they produce bigger crops and make more profits for farmers.

For example, scientists have produced strawberries that can withstand frost. To do this, they transferred a gene from a fish that lives in freezing conditions into the strawberry's DNA.

CHANGING OURSELVES

Soon, scientists may begin to alter human genes. This could have all kinds of medical uses. For example, it could help to eliminate genetic diseases or enable people to live for much longer. It might also be possible to change people's appearance or improve their memory, intelligence and strength.

Scientists have created genetically engineered salmon that grow much faster than normal salmon. They could make big profits for fish farmers.

CLONING

Cloning means making exact copies of living things by copying their DNA. Some types of cloning occur naturally. For example, identical twins are natural clones, as they have exactly the same DNA, and you can clone a plant by taking a cutting from it.

Deliberate scientific cloning of animals only began recently. It could have many uses, such as helping scientists to breed identical animals for research. Although it is possible to clone human babies, this is banned in most countries.

CLONING BABIES

Cloning a human would involve copying the DNA of just one person and implanting it inside the empty egg cell of a woman. The diagrams below show how this could be done.

1 *Scientists would take an egg cell from a woman and remove its DNA.* ★

Egg cell with DNA removed

DNA

2 *Then they would take a complete cell, such as a skin cell, from another person's body.*

Skin cell containing a complete set of DNA

3 *The empty egg cell and the complete skin cell would be placed close together and given an electric shock to make them fuse together.*

4 *The new cell would be implanted into a woman's womb, where it would begin to grow.*

5 *Nine months later, the cloned baby would be born.*

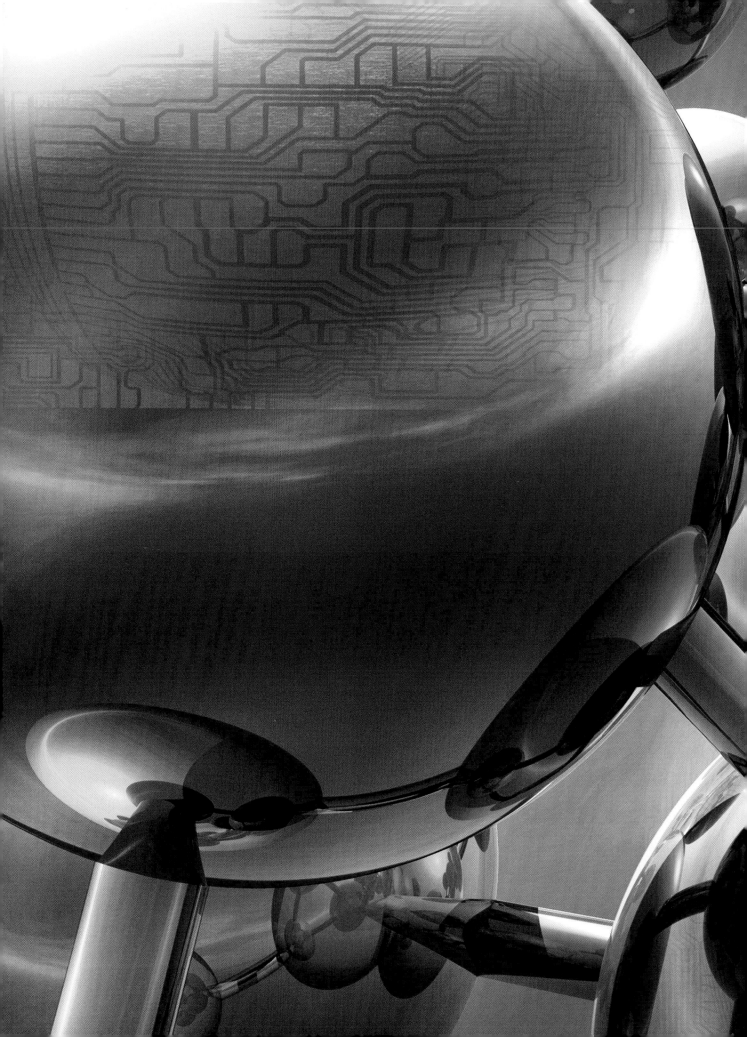

SCIENCE AND TECHNOLOGY

This is part of a model showing the structure of a molecule.

SOLIDS, LIQUIDS AND GASES

Everything is made of tiny units called atoms, which can join together to make bigger units called molecules. Most materials can exist in three different forms: as a solid, a liquid and a gas. In solids, molecules are packed together tightly. In liquids and gases, they are more spread out.

The molecules in solids are strongly attracted to each other and don't move around much. Because of this, most solids stay the same shape.

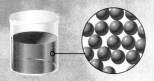

The molecules in liquids have more energy and are not as strongly attracted to each other. They can move around more, which is why they flow into every part of a container.

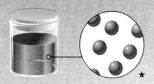

The molecules in gases have even more energy and are hardly attracted to each other at all. Gases spread out quickly to fill the space they are in. They have no shape of their own.

CHANGING STATE

Materials can change from a solid to a liquid or from a liquid to a gas, and vice versa. These changes are called changes of state. They often happen when materials heat up or cool down.

When you heat water, it turns from a liquid into a gas (known as water vapor or steam). This process is called evaporation. When water vapor cools, it turns back into a liquid. This process is known as condensation.

When water becomes very cold, it turns from a liquid into a solid (ice). Water gets bigger, or expands, when it freezes, but most other materials shrink as they get colder and expand as they get hotter.

This is a hot spring, or geyser. The water is heated up underground. When it reaches boiling point, it turns from a liquid into a gas and shoots out of a crack in the ground.

MEASURING VOLUME

Volume is the amount of space occupied by a solid, liquid or gas. It is measured in cubic meters (m³). You can calculate the volume of a rectangular solid using this formula:

$$Volume = Length \times Width \times Height$$

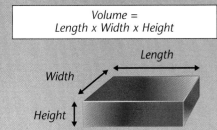

The volume of a liquid can be found by pouring the liquid into a measuring cylinder marked with a scale. The volume of an irregularly shaped solid is measured by finding how much liquid it displaces, using a kind of beaker called a Eureka can.

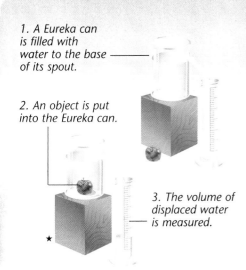

1. A Eureka can is filled with water to the base of its spout.

2. An object is put into the Eureka can.

3. The volume of displaced water is measured.

WEIGHT AND MASS

Many people confuse mass with weight, but they are two very different things. The mass of a solid, liquid or gas is the amount of matter (atoms and molecules) it contains. Weight is a measure of the pull, or force, of gravity on an object's mass.

An object would weigh less on the Moon than it does on Earth because the Moon has weaker gravity than Earth. The mass of the object would be the same wherever it was measured.

Mass is measured in kilograms (kg). You can measure the mass of an object by comparing it with a known mass, using scales.

Unknown mass   Known mass

As weight is actually a force, it is measured in newtons (N), the unit of measurement of all forces. You can calculate the weight of an object using the formula below:

$$Weight = Mass \times Strength\ of\ Gravity$$

The strength of gravity on Earth is 10 N/kg, so you can calculate the weight of an object by multiplying its mass by 10.

MEASURING DENSITY

Density is a measurement that compares the mass of objects of the same size. For example, a piece of cork that is the same size as a piece of iron has less mass. It is lighter because it is less dense.

Density is calculated by dividing the mass of an object by its volume, using the formula below. It is measured in kilograms per cubic meter (kg/m³).

$$Density = \frac{Mass}{Volume}$$

Objects that are denser than water sink in water, while objects that are less dense float. People are almost the same density as water, and just barely float.

Internet links

Website 1 Watch animations of the molecules of a solid, a liquid and a gas.

Website 2 Make a substance that is halfway between a solid and a liquid.

Website 3 Watch a short movie about mass, volume and density.

For links to these websites, go to **www.usborne-quicklinks.com**

THE ELEMENTS

An element is a substance that contains only one kind of atom. For example, sulfur, helium and iron are elements: they contain only sulfur, helium or iron atoms, and they cannot be broken down into simpler substances.

GROUPING ELEMENTS

So far, 115 elements have been discovered, but there may be more that we don't yet know about. Only 90 occur naturally on Earth. The rest have been artificially created by scientists. Elements can be grouped into metals, nonmetals and semimetals. The elements in each group share certain characteristics, or properties. For example, most metals are shiny.

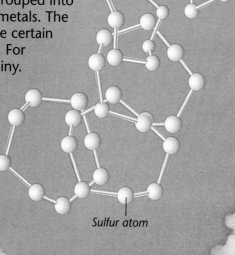

This diagram shows a group of sulfur molecules. Each molecule forms an irregular ring shape consisting of eight sulfur atoms. Sulfur is one of the 90 elements that occur naturally on Earth. It is a nonmetal.

Sulfur atom

The Space Shuttle burns elements to blast it into space. The red-brown fuel tank stores the nonmetals hydrogen and oxygen, which burn in the shuttle's engines. The white rockets give an extra boost by burning powdered aluminum metal in their own engines.

METAL ELEMENTS

Over three-quarters of all known elements are metals. Most of these are dense and shiny. They have many uses, as they are strong, but can easily be shaped. They are also good conductors of heat and electricity, which means heat and electricity flow through them easily. Metals are usually found combined with other elements in the Earth's crust.

These chocolate eggs are wrapped in thin aluminum foil to keep them fresh. Aluminum is the most common metal on Earth.

Aluminum can be reshaped easily. Here, it is being rolled into a long, thin sheet.

NONMETALS

There are 16 nonmetal elements. They all occur naturally on Earth. All (apart from graphite, a form of carbon) are insulators – poor conductors of heat and electricity.

At room temperature, four nonmetals (phosphorus, carbon, sulfur and iodine) are solids, and bromine is a liquid. The other 11 nonmetals are gases.

SEMIMETALS

Semimetals, also called metalloids, are usually poor conductors, just like nonmetals. But they can also be made to conduct well, like metals. Because of this, semimetal elements are called semiconductors. There are nine semimetals and they are all solids at room temperature.

Nonmetals	
Hydrogen	Sulfur
Helium	Chlorine
Carbon	Argon
Nitrogen	Bromine
Oxygen	Krypton
Fluorine	Iodine
Neon	Xenon
Phosphorus	Radon

Internet links

For a link to a website where you can find out more about what is inside an element, go to
www.usborne-quicklinks.com

Semimetals	
Boron	Antimony
Silicon	Tellurium
Germanium	Polonium
Arsenic	Astatine
Selenium	

The semimetal germanium is used to make transistors like this one. They are used in radios.

Silicon is used to make integrated circuits like this one. Integrated circuits are used inside many electronic devices, such as computers, cameras and CD players.

COMPOUNDS

Elements can combine to make substances called compounds. For example, water is a compound that is made up of the elements hydrogen and oxygen. In a compound, the atoms of the different elements are joined, or bonded, together and cannot be separated easily.

Compounds don't keep the same properties as their combined elements. For example, iron sulfide is a compound of iron and sulfur. Iron is magnetic and sulfur floats in water, but iron sulfide is not magnetic and it sinks in water.

MIXTURES

When some substances are combined, their atoms don't bond, so they can be separated easily. These combinations are called mixtures.

For example, if you mix salt, which is a compound of sodium and chlorine, with water, it forms a mixture of the two compounds. The salt water mixture can easily be separated into the two substances again by boiling it. This makes the water evaporate, leaving the salt behind.

ENERGY

Energy makes things happen. Heat, light, electricity and sound are all forms of energy, and there are many others too. The different types of energy can be divided up into two groups: moving and stored energy.

The energy from the Sun is equal to that supplied by about one trillion large power stations.

POTENTIAL ENERGY

Potential energy is energy that is stored, ready to use. Anything that could fall, such as an apple on a tree, has gravitational potential energy. The higher the thing is, the farther it could fall, so the more gravitational potential energy it has. Objects that can be stretched or squashed, such as elastic bands and springs, have elastic potential energy or strain energy.

The energy used to move this hammer comes from food eaten and stored in the body of the person using the hammer. Chemical energy is released from the food by reactions in the body cells.

The higher the hammer, the greater its gravitational potential energy.

CHEMICAL ENERGY

Chemical energy is a type of potential energy that is released during chemical reactions. A chemical reaction is when the atoms of two or more substances rearrange to form new substances. Batteries, food and fuels such as coal, oil and gasoline are all stores of chemical energy.

KINETIC ENERGY

Moving objects have kinetic energy, the energy of movement. The faster something moves, the more kinetic energy it has. As it slows down, it loses kinetic energy.

The moving hammer transfers kinetic energy to the nail, which moves into the wood.

ENERGY CONVERSION

You can't create or destroy energy. This means the amount of energy in the Universe is always the same. Whenever anything happens, energy is just converted into a different form. This is what happens, for example, when plants use energy from sunlight to make food, which animals then eat.

This plant uses energy from sunlight to make food, which it stores as chemical energy.

★

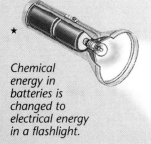

Chemical energy in batteries is changed to electrical energy in a flashlight.

Electrical energy is changed to light and heat energy in the bulb.

When the hummingbird feeds on the plant, the chemical energy becomes stored inside the bird. When the bird moves, the chemical energy is converted to kinetic and heat energy.

ENERGY CHAINS

An energy chain is a way of showing how energy is converted from one form to another. The pictures on the right show the energy changes that take place in a power station, where the chemical energy in coal is converted into electrical energy.

This is a coal-fired power station.

The final forms in most energy chains are heat and light. Even this energy is not lost, but it spreads out into the environment and is very difficult to harness for any useful purpose.

Coal is the fossilized remains of plants that grew long ago. It is a store of chemical energy that came originally from the Sun.

When the coal is burned, the chemical energy is converted to heat energy, which is used to heat water to make steam.

The steam turns turbines. This produces kinetic energy.

The kinetic energy is converted to electrical energy in a device called a generator.

Appliances such as lamps, televisions, heaters and audio equipment convert electrical energy into light, heat and sound.

★

MEASURING ENERGY

Energy is measured using units called joules (J), named after J. P. Joule, who discovered that heat was a type of energy. One thousand joules is called a kilojoule (kJ). The food that you eat gives you varying amounts of energy. A 3.5oz apple contains around 150kJ of chemical energy. The same amount of chocolate contains 2,335kJ.

Power is a measurement of the energy used over a period of time. It is measured in units called watts (W). One watt is equal to one joule per second. The more energy a machine uses in a certain period of time, the more powerful it is.

Internet links

Website 1 Find out about the Earth's energy resources.

Website 2 See how energy is converted from one form to another.

For links to these websites, go to **www.usborne-quicklinks.com**

SOUND

Asound is made when something vibrates, making the air around it vibrate too. The sound you hear is carried by the vibrating air as a sound wave.

The sound of falling leaves measures 10dB.

SOUND WAVES

Inside a loudspeaker, a paper cone vibrates, sending sound energy into the air. As the cone moves forward, it presses together air particles in front of it. As it moves back, it leaves an area where the particles are more spaced out.

Cone of loudspeaker (not moving)

Air particles

Cone moves forward.

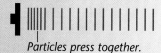

Particles press together.

Cone moves backward.

Particles spread out.

Sound waves can be shown as a wavy line of ups and downs, or peaks and troughs. The peaks show where particles have been squashed. The troughs show where particles are spread out.

This is a graph of a sound wave.

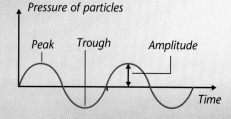

Pressure of particles

Peak   Trough   Amplitude

Time

PITCH AND FREQUENCY

The faster something vibrates, the higher the sound it makes. The slower it vibrates, the lower the sound. The number of vibrations something makes per second is called the frequency, or pitch, of the sound. Frequency is measured in hertz (Hz).

Bees beat their wings 200 times a second, so the sound you hear has a frequency of 200Hz. Mosquitoes make a higher-pitched sound than bees because they beat their wings faster, about 500 times per second. Humans can only hear sounds that are between 20Hz and 20,000Hz.

High-pitched sounds, such as birdsong, have high-frequency waves.

Low-pitched sounds, such as the rumble made by the engine of a heavy truck, have low-frequency waves.

LOUDNESS

A loud sound makes big vibrations. The size of a vibration is called its amplitude, so the louder the sound, the bigger the amplitude.

Loudness is measured in units called decibels (dB), named after A. G. Bell, the inventor of the telephone. The blue whale is the loudest animal in the world. It makes sounds of up to 188dB, which can be picked up over 530 miles away.

Aircraft make such loud sounds that the ground crew wear ear protectors to avoid hearing damage.

SPEED OF SOUND

Sound waves travel at a speed of 1,080ft per second through air at 32°F. This speed increases if the air temperature goes up, and decreases if the temperature goes down.

Sound waves travel at different speeds through different substances. They travel more quickly through solids than liquids, and more quickly through liquids than gases.

A speed that is faster than the speed of sound is known as a supersonic speed. One that is slower is a subsonic speed.

As it reaches supersonic speed, an aircraft makes a deafening bang called a sonic boom. In this photo, the sound waves can be seen as they disturb the misty air.

The sound of an aircraft landing measures about 120dB.

ECHOES

Echoes are sound waves that have been reflected off a surface and are heard shortly after the original sound. They can be used to find the position of objects by timing how long the sound waves take to return to their source. This is called echolocation. Animals such as bats and dolphins use echolocation to find their way around or to locate prey.

Echoes can also be used to see inside the body – for example to check on the growth of an unborn baby inside its mother. Very high-pitched sounds known as ultrasound (measuring over 20,000Hz) pass through the body. Bone, muscle and fat all reflect ultrasound differently. A computer uses this information to make a picture.

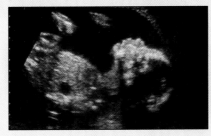

This is an ultrasound scan of an unborn baby.

Dolphins send out streams of high-pitched clicking sounds. The time the sounds take to return can tell them how far away they are from a school of fish.

SONAR

Echoes can be used to measure the depth of the seabed from a boat, or to detect things underwater, such as the wreck of a ship or a school of fish. This method of using echoes is called sonar, which stands for Sound Navigation and Ranging.

Ultrasound waves sent from a ship bounce off a wreck. A computer times the echoes to find the wreck's position.

Internet links

For a link to a website where you can try some sound experiments, go to
www.usborne-quicklinks.com

LIGHT

M ost of the light on our planet comes from the Sun, but light also comes from other things, including lightbulbs, candles, televisions and even some kinds of animals. It travels incredibly quickly – about 186,000 miles per second, which is faster than anything else in the Universe.

Here you can see light rays shining through gaps in the trees. This shows that light travels in straight lines.

LIGHT RAYS

Light travels in straight lines called rays. You can see this when you look at sunlight pouring in through a window or at the beam of a flashlight.

When light rays hit an object straight on, they are bounced back, or reflected, in the direction they came from. If the rays hit an object at an angle, they are reflected at the same angle. When light rays hit a smooth, shiny surface, such as a mirror, they are all reflected in the same direction, but if they hit a rough surface, they are reflected in many directions.

These two diagrams show how light rays are reflected off smooth and rough surfaces.

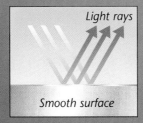

Light rays

Smooth surface

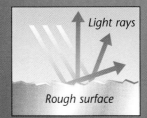

Light rays

Rough surface

BRIGHTNESS

Any object that gives off light is described as luminous. The level of brightness of the light is called its intensity.

The farther you are from a source of light, the less intense the light is. This is because light rays spread out as they travel away from their source.

Most objects aren't luminous. We can only see them because they are reflecting light from something that is luminous, such as the Sun or a light bulb.

This photograph of a train speeding along a track at night shows how light becomes less intense as it gets farther away from its source. You can see how the light fades as the rays spread out.

SHINING THROUGH

Some things allow light to shine through them and others don't. Substances that allow lots of light to shine through them, such as clear glass, are described as transparent. Those that only allow a little light through, such as frosted glass, are said to be translucent.

Substances that won't allow any light to shine through them are described as opaque. Most substances are opaque. Light rays bounce off them instead of traveling through them. When light shines on an opaque object, a shadow forms on the other side of the object.

BENDING LIGHT

If you look at a straw in a glass of water, the straw looks bent. This is because light rays travel at different speeds through different materials. They travel faster through air than through water, but faster through water than through glass. The change in speed makes the light rays bend, or refract.

In this photograph, you can see how the straw looks distorted at the point where it meets the liquid. This is caused by refraction.

Internet links

For a link to a website where you can see pictures of animals that can light up their bodies, go to
www.usborne-quicklinks.com

LIGHT MESSAGES

Some animals are able to create their own light, through chemical reactions in their bodies. This is called bioluminescence. They use it to communicate with each other, to find mates, to catch prey or to defend themselves. For example, glow-worms light up their bodies to attract a mate.

Many deep-sea fish are also able to produce light. This is very useful for defense. Comb jellyfish release clouds of brightly glowing particles when they are being attacked by a predator. The particles temporarily blind the attacker, providing a chance for escape.

This is a black dragonfish. It has two spots near its eyes which light up. They help the fish to find food.

Female black dragonfish have a long bristle hanging from their chin, which lights up. Many scientists think they use it to attract prey, such as these shrimp. When the shrimp swim too close, they get eaten.

MIRROR IMAGES

If you look at an object in a mirror, it is reversed. You can see this if you write on a piece of paper and then hold it up in front of a mirror. The words will look reversed. The light rays are reflected off the object and then off the mirror before entering your eyes, so you are only seeing an image of the object, not the object itself. In an image, the left and the right sides are flipped.

COLOR

Light from the Sun and from lightbulbs is called white light. White light is made up of seven different colors: red, orange, yellow, green, blue, indigo and violet, which are the colors of a rainbow.

SEPARATING COLORS

The colors that make up white light are called the spectrum. In 1666, scientist Isaac Newton discovered that white light could be divided into its separate colors. This process is called dispersion.

He dispersed light using a piece of shaped glass called a prism. When light travels through one, it is bent, or refracted, because the prism slows it down. The colors travel at different speeds through the prism, so they are bent by different amounts, which separates them.

RAINBOWS

When the Sun comes out after a shower of rain, you sometimes see a rainbow. This is because the air is still full of tiny drops of water. Each drop works like a tiny prism, splitting the light up into all its colors.

This picture shows how light shines through a prism.

SKY COLORS

The color of the sky is a result of sunlight being scattered by the Earth's atmosphere. Some of the colors in sunlight are scattered more than others. The atmosphere scatters blue light most, so during the day, the sky looks blue.

The different colors of this evening sky are caused by light scattering.

At sunrise and sunset, the position of the Sun means that sunlight has to travel through more of the atmosphere than it does when the Sun is directly overhead. The blue light is scattered so much that you can't see it. Instead, you can see the red light.

MIXING LIGHT

Almost any color of light can be made by using different combinations of red, green and blue light. For this reason, these three colors are known as the primary colors of light.

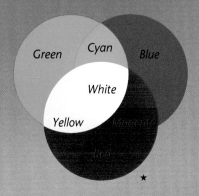

Cyan, magenta and yellow are the secondary colors of light.

When two primary colors are added together, the color they make is called a secondary color. Any two colors opposite each other in the diagram above, such as red and cyan, can be added together to make white light. They are called complementary colors.

Rainbows, like this one, form when light hits tiny drops of water in the air and splits up into separate colors.

SEEING IN COLOR

You can see colors when light reflecting off objects is detected by color-sensitive cells in your eyes.

All colored objects and paints contain pigments. These are substances that absorb certain colors and reflect others. You can see the color of an object because it reflects only light of that color. For example, a red flower reflects red light and absorbs all the other colors of the spectrum.

This bottle looks blue because it reflects blue light and absorbs all the other colors.

White objects appear white because they reflect all the colors of light equally. Black objects absorb all the colors, so hardly any light is reflected, making the object look black.

The white feathers on this penguin reflect all the light that hits them. The black feathers absorb all the light that hits them.

MIXING PAINTS

The three primary colors used in painting are magenta, yellow and cyan. They are not the same as the primary colors of light. By mixing them, you can make almost any color, apart from white. Mixing all three colors together makes black.

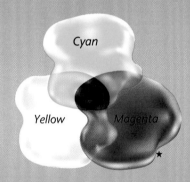

Cyan

Yellow

Magenta

In painting, green, blue and red are the secondary colors.

See for yourself

You can see the colors of the spectrum form white light by making a color spinner. Draw around the bottom of a jar on some stiff cardboard. Cut out the circle, divide it into seven sections and paint them with the colors of the rainbow. Push a pencil through the middle and spin it on a table. As it spins, the colored light reflecting off it merges to make white.

COLOR PRINTING

Color printing in books and magazines uses dots of magenta, yellow and cyan ink, along with black ink to make the pictures look sharper. This process is called four-color printing.

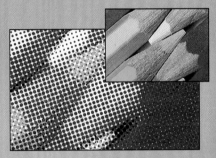

This magnified picture shows how all the colors are made up of tiny dots of magenta, yellow, cyan and black.

If you look through a magnifying glass at any picture in this book, you will see the dots that make up the image.

Colors used in four-color printing

Cyan   Magenta   Yellow   Black

Internet links

Website 1 Learn more about how rainbows are made.

Website 2 Try some experiments that play tricks with light and color.

For links to these websites, go to **www.usborne-quicklinks.com**

ELECTRICITY

Electricity is a useful form of energy that can easily be converted to other forms, such as heat or light. It can flow along cables, making it easy to transport, and is used to power many devices, from kettles to computers.

Lightning is a form of electricity.

ELECTRIC CHARGES

An atom is made up of three kinds of tiny particles: protons, neutrons and electrons. Protons and neutrons are tightly packed together in a tiny space called the nucleus, while the electrons whizz around the outside of the nucleus.

Protons have a positive electrical charge, electrons have a negative electrical charge and neutrons have no charge. An atom is usually electrically neutral, which means that it contains an equal number of protons and electrons, so the positive and negative charges cancel each other out. But some electrons can move from atom to atom.

If an atom gains electrons, it becomes negatively charged (–). If it loses electrons, it becomes positively charged (+). Electricity is caused by the presence or movement of charged particles.

This is a diagram of an atom.

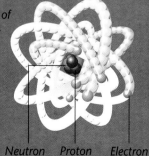

Neutron Proton Electron

FORCES AND FIELDS

When charged particles are close together, they have an effect on each other known as an electric force. The area this force affects is called an electric field.

ELECTRIC CURRENTS

In certain substances, such as metals, electrons can move fairly easily from atom to atom. When they move, there is a flow of electric charge called an electric current. Substances that electric currents can flow through easily are called conductors.

The electrons of some substances are not able to move from atom to atom easily, which means electric currents can't flow easily through them. These substances, which include wood, plastic and rubber, are called insulators.

These diagrams show what effect charged particles have on each other.

Particles with opposite charges pull toward, or attract, each other.

Particles with the same charge push apart, or repel each other.

SENDING ELECTRICITY

Most electricity comes from power stations. Machines called generators turn energy from fuel, such as coal or gas, into electricity. The electricity travels along underground cables, or wires attached to high towers, into people's homes.

Electricity is carried to different parts of the home along wires, which are usually made of copper and covered with a layer of plastic to insulate them.

Internet links

For a link to a website where you can find out more about electricity, go to **www.usborne-quicklinks.com**

STATIC ELECTRICITY

Some insulating materials can become charged when rubbed. This happens because electrons are rubbed off one material onto another. The charge cannot flow away because there is no conductor, so it builds up on the surface of the material. Electrical charge that is held by a material is called static electricity.

You can see how static electricity works by rubbing a balloon against your sweater. Some of the electrons are rubbed off your sweater onto the balloon. The balloon becomes negatively charged and your sweater become positively charged. They cling together because their opposite charges attract each other.

The diagrams below show how static electricity builds up if you rub a balloon on a sweater.

Before they are rubbed, the balloon and the sweater are electrically neutral.

After they are rubbed, the sweater has a positive charge and the balloon has a negative charge, so they cling together because their opposite charges attract.

LIGHTNING

Lightning is caused by static electricity that builds up when falling water droplets and rising ice crystals rub against each other in storm clouds.

Water droplets and ice crystals become charged as they rub against each other and the air.

Positive charges gather at the top of the cloud and negative charges in the base. As this happens, positive charges collect together on the ground beneath the cloud.

A giant spark flashes out from the cloud, seeking a point with the opposite charge on the ground. When it finds it, it makes a path, which is then followed by a powerful stroke of lightning.

A build-up of negative charge at the base of a storm cloud causes a build-up of positive charge in the ground below.

When lightning strikes, an electric current flows between the cloud and the ground, leaving them both electrically neutral.

The air heated by the lightning expands very rapidly. This makes the noise of thunder. Light travels faster than sound, so unless the storm cloud is directly overhead, you see the lightning before you hear the thunder.

Lightning contains a vast amount of electrical energy, which is changed into light, heat and sound (thunder).

MAGNETISM

A magnet is a piece of metal that can pull some other types of metal toward it. Magnetism is a force. The area around a magnet where the force acts is called a magnetic field. It is strongest at the ends of the magnet, which are called poles.

NORTH AND SOUTH

If you tie a thread around a magnet and then let it hang freely, the magnet will always point in a north–south direction. The end of the magnet that points north is called the north pole. The other end is called the south pole.

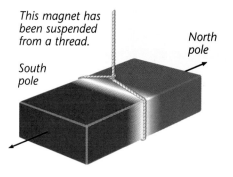

This magnet has been suspended from a thread.

South pole

North pole

If you put the north pole of a magnet close to the south pole of another magnet, they will attract each other. If you try to put two north poles or two south poles together, they will repel each other.

Unlike poles attract each other.

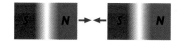

Like poles repel each other.

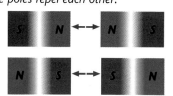

This horseshoe-shaped magnet has attracted tiny pieces of metal called iron filings.

MAGNETIC METALS

Magnets strongly attract iron, cobalt, nickel and several alloys, which are a mixture of two or more metals or a metal and another substance. Steel is the most common magnetic alloy. These metals are all described as ferromagnetic, which means that when they are near a magnet, they become magnetic.

Some ferromagnetic metals only remain magnetic while they are close to a magnet. These are known as soft ferromagnetic metals. The moment the magnet is removed, they lose their magnetic properties. Hard ferromagnetic metals retain their magnetic properties long after the magnet has been removed.

Each iron paper clip in this chain has become magnetized by contact with the magnet.

If the magnet is removed, the clips will lose their magnetism.

MAGNETIC FIELDS

Magnetic fields are invisible, but scientists often draw lines around magnets to illustrate their magnetic fields. These are called magnetic flux lines. They are usually marked with arrows, which show the direction of the field. The lines are closest near the magnet's poles, where the magnetic field is strongest.

This diagram shows the magnetic field around a bar magnet.

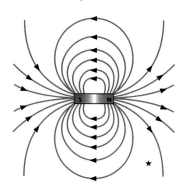

USEFUL MAGNETS

Magnets are used in many everyday devices, such as compasses, watches and DVD players. They can also be used to separate different kinds of metals. For example, drink cans are often made from aluminum or steel. When the cans are collected for recycling, they are all mixed up together. If a powerful magnet is held above the cans, it attracts the steel cans and leaves the aluminum cans behind.

ELECTROMAGNETISM

When an electric current flows through a metal wire wrapped around a piece of soft ferromagnetic metal, a magnetic field is created. This kind of magnet is called an electromagnet. If the electric current is switched off, the magnetic field disappears.

Huge electromagnets are used to lift heavy loads at steelworks. When a current flows through the metal, it attracts steel, which can then be moved from one place to another. When the current is switched off, the load is released.

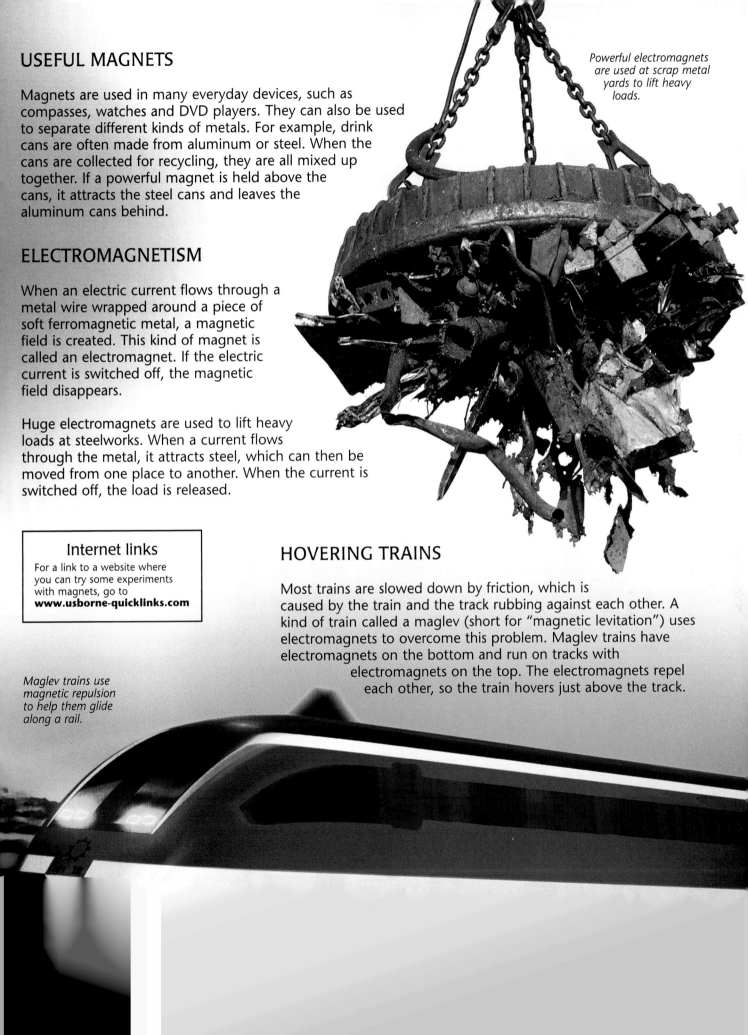

Powerful electromagnets are used at scrap metal yards to lift heavy loads.

Internet links

For a link to a website where you can try some experiments with magnets, go to
www.usborne-quicklinks.com

Maglev trains use magnetic repulsion to help them glide along a rail.

HOVERING TRAINS

Most trains are slowed down by friction, which is caused by the train and the track rubbing against each other. A kind of train called a maglev (short for "magnetic levitation") uses electromagnets to overcome this problem. Maglev trains have electromagnets on the bottom and run on tracks with electromagnets on the top. The electromagnets repel each other, so the train hovers just above the track.

FLIGHT

The first powered flight took place a century ago and lasted only twelve seconds. Now planes can travel faster than the speed of sound and helicopters can hover in the air.

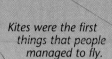

Kites were the first things that people managed to fly.

THE FORCES OF FLIGHT

When a plane is in flight, there are four forces acting on it: lift, thrust, gravity and drag. Lift and thrust help the plane to fly. The force of lift is powerful enough to keep birds and very light planes called gliders in the air. Heavier aircraft have to use thrust as well.

CREATING LIFT

The wings on planes are designed to work in the same way as birds' wings. Both are curved on top and flatter underneath. This shape is called an airfoil. It causes air to flow faster over the tops of the wings than underneath them. The air under the wings pushes up more than the air on top of them pushes down. This creates lift.

This shows how the shape of a bird's wings help it to fly.

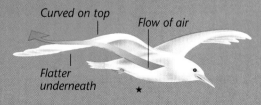

Curved on top

Flow of air

Flatter underneath

Internet links

For a link to a website where you can find out how to make a paper plane, and learn about the forces acting on it, go to **www.usborne-quicklinks.com**

USING THRUST

Thrust is the force that makes a plane move forward. It is provided by a plane's engines and its propeller. The more thrust there is, the faster the plane goes, which in turn improves the lift of the plane. This is because as the plane travels faster, the air pressure pushing up on the wings increases.

Jet engines force hot gases backward out of the plane, which pushes the plane forward.

Propellers at the front of the plane push air backward, pulling the plane forward.

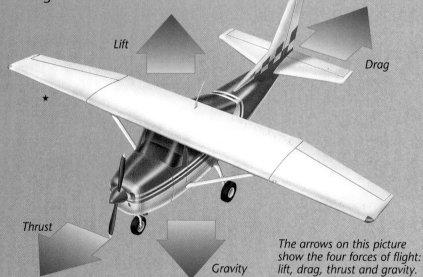

Lift

Drag

Thrust

Gravity

The arrows on this picture show the four forces of flight: lift, drag, thrust and gravity.

REDUCING DRAG

As a plane moves forward, a type of friction known as drag slows it down. This is caused by air rubbing against the body of the plane. Drag can be reduced if the plane's shape is designed so that it is streamlined. This means that air can move around it easily.

FIGHTING GRAVITY

While a plane is in the air, the Earth's gravity is constantly trying to pull it toward the ground. For this reason, planes are built using the lightest, but strongest materials possible.

CONTROLLING A PLANE

A plane needs to be able to move up and down, and to turn and tip to each side. To enable it to do this, the wings, tail and tail fin are fitted with hinged flaps, known as control surfaces. The flaps on the wings are called ailerons, the ones on the tail are called elevators and the one on the tail fin is called a rudder. By using a particular control surface, a pilot increases the drag on that part of the plane. This pushes the plane into a new position, as shown in the diagrams below.

This shows how control surfaces work.

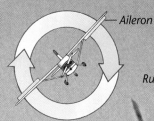
— Aileron

Rudder

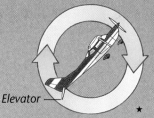
Elevator
★

When turning, a plane also tips. This is called rolling. It is controlled by the ailerons on the wings.

Turning to the left or right is called yawing. It is controlled by the rudder on the tail fin.

Moving up and down is called pitching. Elevators on the tail control this.

This Airbus is just about to land. As the pilot controls the jet's descent, its ailerons, elevators and rudder are constantly twitching up and down or back and forth.

Big passenger jets have three or four engines.

The engine's thrust is reduced little by little so that the plane loses lift. Gradually, it comes down to the ground.

Big jets like this one have their wheels, or undercarriage, tucked away during flights. This reduces the drag on the plane.

This is an aileron. The next time you fly, look for these moving on the backs of the wings.

TV AND RADIO

The first radio transmissions were made about a hundred years ago. Television was invented in 1926. The first signals could only be sent over very short distances; but today, satellites can instantly broadcast clear signals all around the world.

This early radio was invented by Marconi. It was called a marconiphone.

RADIO WAVES

There are radio waves all around you, but you can't see or hear them. They travel at the speed of light and can carry signals. There are several kinds of radio waves, which travel in different ways and can be used for different purposes.

Long waves (LW) curve around the Earth's surface. They are used for ship navigation, military communications and to transmit some radio programs.

Medium waves (MW) usually travel close to the ground, but some travel higher and bounce back when they reach a layer in the Earth's atmosphere called the ionosphere. They are used to transmit radio programs.

Short waves (SW) can travel long distances because they are able to bounce off the ionosphere. Police and taxi drivers use them to communicate.

Very high frequency (VHF) and ultra high frequency (UHF) waves travel in straight lines. Some travel close to the ground, but others are able to pass through the ionosphere and can be deflected back to Earth by satellites. VHF and UHF waves are used for ship navigation, aircraft communications, and for transmitting television and radio programs.

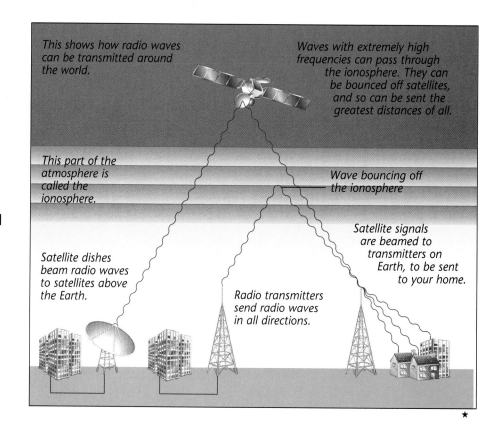

This shows how radio waves can be transmitted around the world.

Waves with extremely high frequencies can pass through the ionosphere. They can be bounced off satellites, and so can be sent the greatest distances of all.

This part of the atmosphere is called the ionosphere.

Wave bouncing off the ionosphere

Satellite dishes beam radio waves to satellites above the Earth.

Radio transmitters send radio waves in all directions.

Satellite signals are beamed to transmitters on Earth, to be sent to your home.

RADIO BROADCASTING

In a radio station, sound is picked up by microphones. These change the sound waves into signals called analog waves, which are carried by electricity. A special device called a transmitter is used to change the electrical signals carrying the analog waves into radio waves. The radio waves are beamed into the atmosphere by a large antenna, or aerial. The small antenna on your radio picks up the radio signals and changes them back into analog waves. By turning the tuning control on your radio, you can tune in to one of the radio stations that are picked up by the antenna. A loud speaker changes the analog waves into sound waves that you can hear.

— Antenna

— Tuner

TELEVISION BROADCASTING

Traditional television broadcasting works in a similar way to radio broadcasting. Television cameras pick up light from things in the studio. They divide the light into the three primary colors – red, green and blue – and then change it into analog waves, which are carried by electricity. The analog waves are changed into radio waves and transmitted by an antenna.

The radio waves are picked up by an antenna on top of your home, which turns them back into analog waves. These travel along a cable that leads into the back of your television. A device inside the television, called a cathode ray tube, turns the analog waves into the pictures you see on screen.

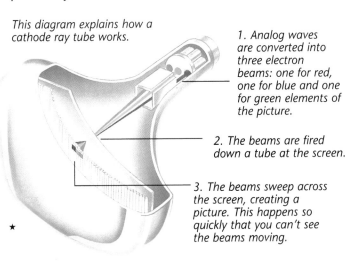

This diagram explains how a cathode ray tube works.

1. Analog waves are converted into three electron beams: one for red, one for blue and one for green elements of the picture.

2. The beams are fired down a tube at the screen.

3. The beams sweep across the screen, creating a picture. This happens so quickly that you can't see the beams moving.

The picture on your screen is made up of about 350,000 red, green and blue shapes called pixels. This is what they would look like if they were greatly magnified.

CABLE BROADCASTING

Once television signals have been changed into analog waves, they can be transmitted by a cable network. This is made up of a huge number of underground cables, which lead into people's homes. The cables can carry more signals than radio waves, so cable broadcasting companies are able to provide many more channels.

SATELLITE SIGNALS

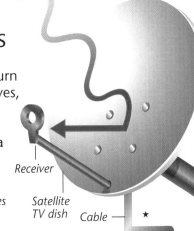

Satellite TV companies turn TV signals into radio waves, which they bounce off satellites in space. These are received directly by a small dish attached to the side of your home.

The dish focuses the radio waves onto a receiver.

Receiver

Satellite TV dish

Cable

DIGITAL BROADCASTING

By 2010, most television and radio broadcasting will be done digitally. In digital broadcasting, television and radio signals are changed into a code called binary code, which is also used by computers. These digital signals are carried by cable networks along fiber optic cables, made of glass or plastic, or they can be changed into radio waves and transmitted by an antenna or satellite.

When digital signals reach your television, a device called a decoder reads the binary code and turns it into pictures and sounds. New televisions have decoders fitted inside, but you can buy them to adapt older televisions. Digital radio signals can be picked up through a digital radio and also through new or adapted televisions or the Internet.

Digital signals transmit clearer sound and pictures than analog waves. Digital signals can also be compressed, so more information can be sent. This enables broadcasters to transmit more channels.

INTERACTIVE TV

Digital broadcasting also makes it possible to communicate in two directions. As a result, you can send information back through your television. For example, you can order programs to watch whenever you want, buy things, or even take part in competitions. This is called interactive TV.

This television shows an interactive game to play during a soccer game.

TELEPHONES

Since the invention of the telephone in 1876, there have been many improvements to telephone systems. As well as being used to make calls, telephone systems are also used to send information between computers. This technology is called telecommunications, or telecoms.

Many older phone handsets are attached by a cord to their base unit. Most modern phones are cordless. They communicate with their base unit using radio waves.

MAKING CALLS

Most telephone calls are carried by electrical cables made of copper, which are either buried underground or attached to high poles. If you make a long-distance call, your message may be bounced off a satellite in space, beamed between transmitter masts, or it may be routed through huge lengths of cabling. Whichever route it takes, your call will reach its destination in a matter of seconds.

This diagram shows what happens when you make a telephone call.

ANALOG AND DIGITAL

All telephone messages used to be sent as analog waves. Now analog waves are gradually being replaced with digital signals.

Some modern phones can make and receive calls digitally, but many still only work with analog waves, so most calls start off as analog waves and are changed into digital signals at a telephone exchange. They are changed back into analog waves at another exchange before reaching the receiver.

Satellite

Radio-signal transmitter masts

Main exchange

Main exchange

5. A computer at the main exchange reads the number you dialed. This tells it where to send the digital signals.

4. The digital signals travel along fiber optic cables to a larger telephone exchange.

6. The digital signals are then sent on in the quickest way possible. This is often along more fiber optic cables.

Local exchange

Local exchange

2. The wires join onto a cable, which runs underground.

3. The cables lead to a local telephone exchange. When the analog waves reach it, they are translated into digital signals.

7. When the digital signals reach a local telephone exchange near the receiver's home, the call is turned back into analog waves.

8. The analog waves travel along an underground cable toward the receiver's home.

Local switch box

Local switch box

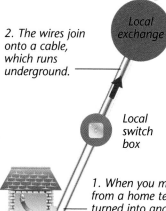

1. When you make a call from a home telephone, it is turned into analog waves, which travel out of your home along copper wires.

9. Copper wires lead from the cable into the receiver's home. When the waves reach the phone, it rings. When someone picks up the phone, your phone becomes connected to theirs. ★

MODEMS

A modem (or modulator demodulator) is a device that enables a computer or fax to send and receive digital information along analog telephone lines. Most computers and faxes have one fitted inside.

A modem changes, or modulates, the digital signals into analog waves, which travel along telephone lines to another modem attached to the receiver's phone or fax. When the other modem receives the analog waves, it turns them back into digital signals, which the computer or fax can understand. When all telephone networks become digital, modems will no longer be needed.

TRANSMISSION SPEED

The amount of information that can be sent by a modem is limited by the speed at which it can process information. Data compression can speed this up by cutting out any information that is not vital. For example, music can be compressed using MP3 software. This removes parts of sound that your ears can't detect, leaving a smaller version, which is quicker to send.

Amount of digital information on a music CD

Amount of digital information after MP3 compression

MP3 software cuts out any very high or very low frequency sound waves that are out of the range of sounds you can hear. It also cuts out sounds that are masked by other sounds.

Here you can see light shining out of the ends of a bundle of fiber optic cables. Fiber optic cables carry digital information.

BANDWIDTH

The amount of information that can be processed each second by a telephone line is called its bandwidth. Copper cabling has a limited bandwidth. Fiber optic cables have a much greater bandwidth. However, they are expensive to install.

Internet links

For a link to a website where you can find out how technology, including the telephone, changed during the 20th century, go to
www.usborne-quicklinks.com

MOBILE PHONES

Mobile phones send digital radio signals through the air to nearby transmitter masts called base stations. The signals are then sent along fiber optic cables to a mobile switching center, which forward the signals to the receiver's nearest base station. Finally, the signals are transmitted through the air to the receiver's mobile phone.

See for yourself

Dial a fax number from a telephone. When the fax answers, you will hear a high-pitched sound. This is its internal modem sending a message to establish whether a fax is calling it, and if so, to tell the other fax to start transmitting its information.

The diagrams below show how a mobile phone connects to another mobile phone.

1. You dial a number and press the call key.

2. Your phone chooses an available radio channel and sends a digital radio signal to the nearest base station.

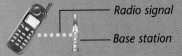

Radio signal

Base station

3. The base station sends the digital signal along fiber optic cables to a mobile switching center, which sends the message on to the base station nearest to the receiver. The base station contacts the receiver's phone along another radio channel.

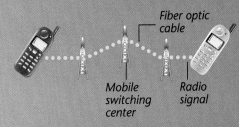

Fiber optic cable

Mobile switching center

Radio signal

4. A connection is made between the receiver's phone and your phone and you hear the ringing tone.

COMPUTERS

At their most basic, computers are machines that do calculations and sort information. When they were invented in the late 1940s, computers were so big they filled whole rooms. Since then, they have been improved continuously and made smaller. Today, computers with more power than the early ones are no bigger than this book.

The Analytical Engine, a forerunner of the computer, was built over a hundred years ago.

HARDWARE

The pieces that make up a computer are called hardware. The computer's main electronic circuits are stored inside a hard case. Items of hardware that are connected to the outside of the case are called peripherals. The mouse, keyboard and screen, or monitor, are all peripherals.

Portable computers, called laptops, and handheld computers, called PDAs (personal digital assistants) or Palm Pilot, have flat screens. These screens contain a thin layer of liquid crystal solution, which darkens to form an image when an electric current passes through it.

The keyboard is laid out like an old-fashioned typewriter, but it has some extra keys, called function keys. These make the computer do certain tasks.

With the mouse, you move a pointer around the screen and click on instructions. This can be quicker than using the keyboard.

Monitor

This type of computer is called a personal computer, or PC.

Mouse

This is a keyboard. The function keys are lined up across the top.

In this PC, the main circuits are stored inside a case attached to the back of the monitor.

Internet links

For a link to a website where you can watch short movies about computers, floppy disks and binary code, go to **www.usborne-quicklinks.com**

SOFTWARE

A computer won't work unless it has a set of instructions called a program, or software, stored inside it. Software that controls how a computer works is called an operating system. Most computers use an operating system called Microsoft® Windows®.

There are all kinds of other programs available too, which enable you to write letters, play games, listen to music, connect to the Internet and do many other things.

See for yourself

When you switch on, or start up, a PC, you will see lines of information flash up on your screen. This is the computer checking through its hardware and software, making sure that everything is working correctly.

This stream of 0s and 1s gives an artist's impression of how digital information flows through a computer.

COMPUTER TALK

Computers do all their calculations using binary code, which only uses two numbers: 0 and 1. Each 0 or 1 is called a bit (short for binary digit). A sequence of eight bits, called a byte, is used to represent a small piece of information, such as a letter of the alphabet, number, symbol or punctuation mark.

Long strings of bytes can be used to represent more complex things, such as pictures. A thousand bytes is called a kilobyte (KB), a thousand kilobytes is called a megabyte (MB) and a thousand megabytes is called a gigabyte (GB).

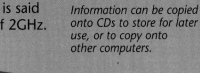

This sequence of the numbers 0 and 1 is the binary code for the letter "B."

PROCESSING

Calculations in a computer are done by devices called microprocessors. In a personal computer, the most important microprocessor is called the central processing unit, or CPU. It is like the computer's brain. CPUs can deal with several billion calculations per second. Bytes travel around a computer along tiny electronic pathways, called buses. These take information between the CPU and other parts of the computer.

PROCESSING SPEED

How quickly a microprocessor can deal with information depends on two things:

- the number of bytes that it can process at once, called bandwidth;

- the number of calculations it can deal with in one second, called clock speed. Depending on how fast the microprocessor is, this is either measured in millions per second, known as megahertz (MHz), or billions per second, known as gigahertz (GHz). A CPU that can process 2,000,000,000 calculations per second is said to have a clock speed of 2GHz.

This is a CPU microprocessor made by Intel.

STORING DATA

Information, or data, that a computer needs long-term is stored in its memory on a set of disks called the hard disk.

Any information that the computer is currently using, such as a computer program, is moved into the random access memory (RAM). This allows the computer to work very quickly because it doesn't have to keep checking through the entire hard disk to find the information it needs.

Information can be copied onto CDs to store for later use, or to copy onto other computers.

THE INTERNET

The Internet is a vast network linking together millions of computers all over the world. It can be used to exchange information, send messages, buy things and much more.

These are some web pages on the Internet.

GETTING CONNECTED

Most computers on the Internet are linked together by telephone systems. Computer information is translated into telephone signals and sent along telephone lines from one computer to another in seconds.

Most people connect to the Internet through a company called an Internet Service Provider (ISP). ISPs run very powerful computers, called servers, which work like electronic post offices, automatically sorting, storing and sending information. Home users connect to ISPs and the ISPs connect them to the Internet. When someone is connected to the Internet, they are said to be "online."

WORLD WIDE WEB

The main part of the Internet is called the World Wide Web (or Web). Information is stored on the Web as web pages, which you can look at using a program called a web browser.

Opening a page on the Internet is called downloading, because the information travels from the server computer onto your computer and loads on your screen. If a web page has a lot of text and pictures, it can sometimes take a while for it to download.

INTERNET LANGUAGE

To make sure that web pages can be downloaded by any computer in the world, they are written in a special computer language called HyperText Markup Language (HTML). If you are looking at a web page in a web browser, you can see the HTML language by clicking on "View" at the top of your web browser, and then "Source" from the list that appears.

This is the HTML code for a web page.

People can connect their computers at home to the Internet.

Cables and telephone lines link one part of the network to another.

This server computer, run by an ISP, provides people at home or in offices with Internet access.

At school, children can use the Internet to learn and to communicate with children in other countries.

Universities use the Internet to share their research.

Some people use computers at Internet cafes to connect to the Internet.

Businesses use the Internet to exchange information and to sell products.

FINDING WEB PAGES

Each web page on the Internet has a unique address, called a URL (Uniform Resource Locator). To find a web page on the Internet, you can type its URL into a web browser and then press the "Return" button.

Most organizations have many web pages that are linked together. This is called a website. You can jump to the other pages in a website by clicking on certain pieces of text or pictures. These are called hyperlinks, or links.

You can tell whether a piece of text or picture is a link by resting your mouse pointer over it. If it is a link, the pointer will change into a hand symbol. Some links will take you to new websites altogether.

This is an example of a URL.

http://www.usborne.com/home.html

This part tells your computer that the page is a web page.

This tells you the filename of the web page.

This is called the domain name. It tells you which server the page is stored on. For example, this page is stored on the Usborne server.

USING EMAIL

Email (electronic mail) is a way of sending messages across the Internet. You write and read emails using an email program, such as Microsoft® Outlook® Express.

When you send an email, it travels down the phone line to your ISP's server. Your ISP sends the message to the receiver's ISP, via the Internet. The next time the receiver connects to the Internet, their ISP delivers the message to them.

Every email user has a unique email address. Each email address has three parts: the username, which you choose, followed by the "@" (at) symbol. The third part is the domain name. It is the name of the server that directs messages to you. For home users, this is usually their ISP's name. Many businesses have their own servers, so work email addresses often have the company name as the domain name.

This is an example of an email address.

emma@usborne.com

This is the username.

This is the domain name.

This symbol means "at."

DOT COM

The last part of a domain name is called the top-level domain. It tells you more about what sort of organization it is. Here are some examples and what they mean:

.com or **.co**	a business
.edu or **.ac**	a school, college or university
.gov	a government agency
.org	a non-profit organization (e.g. a charity)

Some domain names have an extra two letters to identify which country they are based in. For example:

.es	Spain
.th	Thailand
.uk	United Kingdom
.au	Australia
.ca	Canada

This is a web browser called Microsoft® Internet Explorer.

You type the URL of the web page you want to visit in here.

The symbols along this bar are tools that you can click on to help you browse the Internet.

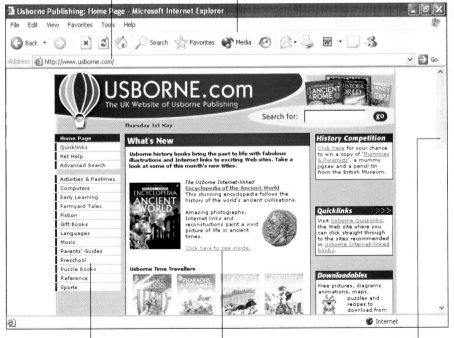

Web pages are displayed here, in the middle of the web browser.

You click on some of the words and pictures on a web page to jump to another page. These are called links.

You can slide this bar down to see more of the web page.

This satellite image shows the southern part of the Florida peninsula, in the U.S.A.

MAPS

160° 140° 120° 100° 80° 60° 40° 20° W

80°

GREENLAND
(Denmark)

Arctic Circle

ALASKA
(U.S.A.)

ICELAND

60°

C A N A D A

UNIT
KINGD
IRELAND

40°

**UNITED STATES
OF AMERICA**

Azores
(Portugal)

PORTUGAL

SPAIN

MOROCCO

Canary Islands
(Spain)

A L

Tropic of Cancer

WESTERN SAHARA
(Morocco)

20°
N

*Hawaiian
Islands*
(U.S.A.)

THE BAHAMAS

MEXICO

CUBA

DOMINICAN
REPUBLIC

HAITI

MAURITANIA

MAL

JAMAICA

BELIZE

CAPE VERDE

SENEGAL

THE GAMBIA

BURKIN
FASO

HONDURAS

GUATEMALA

Caribbean Sea

DOMINICA

GUINEA-BISSAU

EL SALVADOR

NICARAGUA

GUINEA

SIERRA LEONE

IVORY
COAST

GHA

COSTA RICA

TRINIDAD AND TOBAGO

LIBERIA

0°

Equator

PANAMA

VENEZUELA

GUYANA

SURINAM

SAO TOME
PRINCI

Galapagos Islands
(Ecuador)

COLOMBIA

FRENCH GUIANA
(France)

KIRIBATI

P A C I F I C

ECUADOR

O C E A N

A T L A N T I C

PERU

B R A Z I L

O C E A N

*Cook
Islands*
(New Zealand)

*French
Polynesia*
(France)

20°
S

BOLIVIA

Tropic of Capricorn

*Pitcairn
Islands*
(U.K.)

PARAGUAY

1:80,000,000

0   1,000   2,000   3,000   4,000 5,000km

CHILE

URUGUAY

0   1,000   2,000   3,000 miles

ARGENTINA

40°

Falkland Islands
(U.K.)

South Georgia
(U.K.)

60°

Antarctic Circle

*Weddell
Sea*

80°

160° 140° 120° 100° 80° 60° 40° 20° W

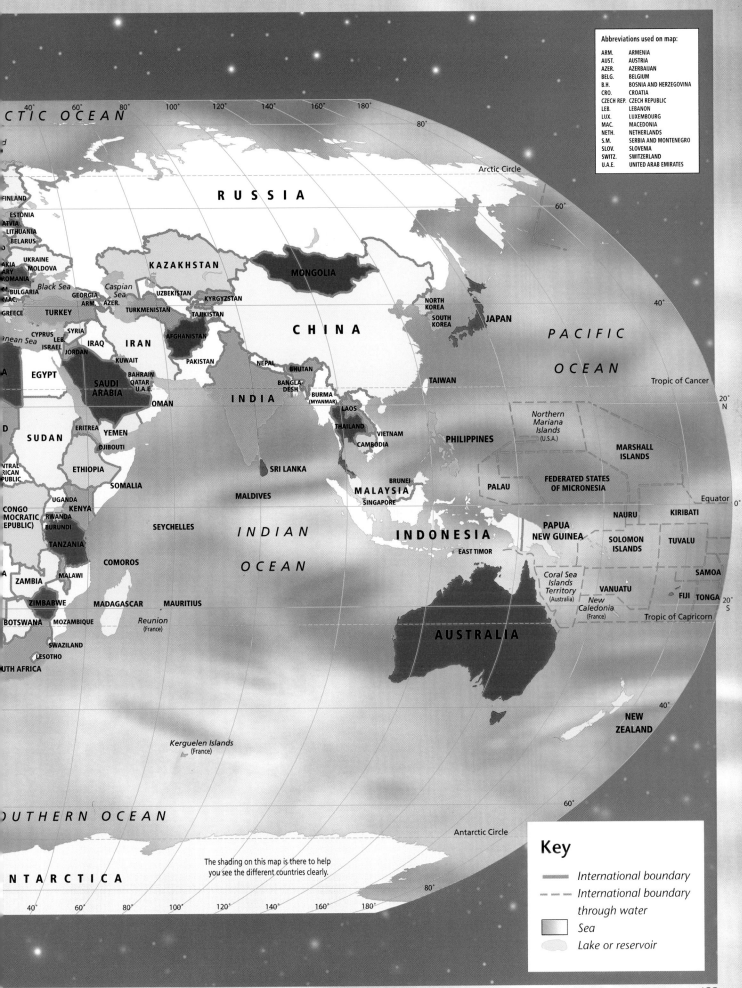

ARCTIC OCEAN

40°   60°   80°   100°   120°   140°   160°   180°

Arctic Circle

80°

FINLAND
ESTONIA
ATVIA
LITHUANIA
BELARUS

RUSSIA

60°

AKIA
ARY
ROMANIA
BULGARIA
MAC.
GREECE
TURKEY

UKRAINE
MOLDOVA

Black Sea

GEORGIA
ARM.   AZER.

KAZAKHSTAN

Caspian
Sea

UZBEKISTAN

MONGOLIA

KYRGYZSTAN

40°

CYPRUS
nean Sea   LEB
ISRAEL

SYRIA

IRAQ

JORDAN

TURKMENISTAN

TAJIKISTAN

IRAN

AFGHANISTAN

CHINA

NORTH
KOREA

SOUTH
KOREA

JAPAN

PACIFIC

KUWAIT

EGYPT

SAUDI
ARABIA

BAHRAIN
QATAR
U.A.E.

PAKISTAN

OMAN

INDIA

NEPAL

BHUTAN

BANGLA-
DESH

BURMA
(MYANMAR)

TAIWAN

OCEAN

Tropic of Cancer

20°
N

LAOS

SUDAN

ERITREA

YEMEN

DJIBOUTI

THAILAND

VIETNAM

CAMBODIA

Northern
Mariana
Islands
(U.S.A.)

PHILIPPINES

MARSHALL
ISLANDS

ETHIOPIA

SOMALIA

SRI LANKA

NTRAL
RICAN
PUBLIC

UGANDA

MALDIVES

MALAYSIA

SINGAPORE

BRUNEI

PALAU

FEDERATED STATES
OF MICRONESIA

Equator   0°

CONGO
MOCRATIC
EPUBLIC)

RWANDA
KENYA
BURUNDI

SEYCHELLES

INDIAN

INDONESIA

PAPUA
NEW GUINEA

NAURU

KIRIBATI

TANZANIA

OCEAN

EAST TIMOR

SOLOMON
ISLANDS

TUVALU

ZAMBIA

COMOROS

MALAWI

Coral Sea
Islands
Territory
(Australia)

SAMOA

ZIMBABWE

MADAGASCAR

MAURITIUS

VANUATU

New
Caledonia
(France)

FIJI   TONGA

20°
S

BOTSWANA

MOZAMBIQUE

Reunion
(France)

AUSTRALIA

Tropic of Capricorn

SWAZILAND

LESOTHO

UTH AFRICA

40°

NEW
ZEALAND

Kerguelen Islands
(France)

60°

OUTHERN OCEAN

Antarctic Circle

NTARCTICA

The shading on this map is there to help
you see the different countries clearly.

80°

40°   60°   80°   100°   120°   140°   160°   180°

Key

International boundary

International boundary
through water

Sea

Lake or reservoir

WORLD PHYSICAL

Beaufort
Sea

80°

Victori
a

Queen
Elizabeth
Islands

Ellesmere
Island

Baffin
Bay

Greenland

Greenla
Sea

Iceland

Arctic Circle

Alaska
Mount McKinley
▲

Yukon

Baffin
Island

Hudson
Bay

Labrador
Sea

Newfoundland

British
Isles

60°

6,194m
(20,321ft)

Aleutian Islands

Gulf of Alaska

Rocky Mountains

Great Plains

NORTH
AMERICA

Great
Lakes

Appalachian Mountains

Azores

40°

Mississippi

Canary
Islands

Atlas M

Tropic of Cancer

Hawaiian
Islands

Gulf of
Mexico

Cuba
Greater Antilles

West

Cape Verde
Islands

20°
N

Caribbean
Sea

Lesser
Antilles

Guiana
Highlands

Galapagos
Islands

Amazon
Basin

Amazon

ATLANTIC

Equator

0°

PACIFIC

Selvas

OCEAN

Polynesia

OCEAN

SOUTH
AMERICA

Andes

20°
S

Tahiti

Atacama Desert

Acontagua
▲

Tropic of Capricorn

Easter Island

6,959m
(22,831ft)

Pampas

Patagonia

Falkland Islands

Cape Horn

South Georgia

Antarctic Circle

Antarctic
Peninsula

Weddell
Sea

80°

160°   140°   120°   100°   80°   60°   40°   20° W

Key

- Boreal forest
- Temperate forest
- Tropical forest
- Temperate grassland
- Savanna
- Semi-desert and scrub
- Hot desert
- Wetland
- Mountain (Only high mountains are marked)
- Tundra
- Ice
- Cultivation
- Sea
- Lake or reservoir
- River
- ▲ Height above or below sea level

160° 140° 120° 100° 80° 60° 40° 20° W

CTIC OCEAN

Novaya
Zemlya
Barents Sea
Kara Sea
Severnaya
Zemlya
Laptev Sea
New Siberia
Islands
East Siberian Sea

Arctic Circle

60°

navia
lbard
ape

European Plain

ROPE

Danube

Black Sea

erranean Sea

Nile
Red Sea

RICA

I

Ethiopian
Highlands

Lake
Victoria

Congo
Basin

Kilimanjaro
5,895m
(19,340ft)

Comoro
Islands

Rift Valley

Madagascar
Mauritius
Reunion

Kalahari
Desert

Drakensberg

Good Hope

Ural Mountains

Volga

Mount
Elbrus
5,642m
(18,510ft)

Caspian
Sea

Aral
Sea

Zagros Mountains

Arabian
Peninsula

Arabian
Sea

Deccan
Plateau

Seychelles

ASIA

Altai Mountains

Gobi
Desert

Himalayas

Ganges

Mount Everest
8,850m
(29,035ft)

Bay
of
Bengal

Sri Lanka

INDIAN

OCEAN

Siberia

Yenisey

Ob

Lake
Baikal

Huang He

Chang Jiang

Yellow

Mekong

South
China
Sea

Sumatra

Borneo

Celebes
Sea

Verkhoyansk Range

Sea
of
Okhotsk

Kamchatka
Peninsula

Sea
of
Japan

Hokkaido

Honshu

East
China
Sea

Taiwan

Philippine
Islands

Micronesia

PACIFIC

OCEAN

80°

60°

40°

Tropic of Cancer

20°
N

Equator

0

New Guinea
Mount Wilhelm
4,509m
(14,793ft)

Greater Sunda Islands

Java

Lesser Sunda Islands

Arafura
Sea

Melanesia

Solomon
Islands

Grea

Coral
Sea

New
Caledonia

Fiji
Islands

20°
S

Kerguelen
Islands

Scale 1:80,000,000

0   1,000   2,000   3,000   4,000   5,000km

0   1,000   2,000   3,000 miles

Great Sandy
Desert

AUSTRALASIA   AND   OCEANIA

Great Victoria
Desert

Gre

Tasman
Sea

Tasmania

North
Island

South
Island

Tropic of Capricorn

40°

OUTHERN OCEAN

60°

Antarctic Circle

ANTARCTICA

40°   60°   80°   100°   120°   140°   160°   180°

80°

135

NORTH AMERICA

In this book, North America includes Canada, the U.S.A., the Caribbean, and the countries of Central America, which run along the narrow strip of land between the U.S.A. and South America. This large continent contains over 20 countries, ranging from Canada, the world's second-largest country, to tiny islands such as Grenada and Saint Lucia.

These are columns of rock called hoodoos in Bryce Canyon National Park, U.S.A.

Arctic Circle

ARCTIC OCEAN

Beaufort Sea

Bering Sea

Yukon

ALASKA
(U.S.A.)

Victoria Island

⊙ Anchorage

CANAD

Vancouver ⊙

Columbia

PACIFIC

OCEAN

UNITED STA

Colorado

Hawaiian Islands
(U.S.A.)

Los Angeles ⊙

Rio Grande

Tropic of Cancer

MEXIC

Mexico

Key

- ■ National capital
- ⊙ Major city or town
- ── International boundary
- ─ ─ International boundary through water
- ▢ Sea
- Lake or reservoir
- River

The shading on this map is there to help you see clearly the different countries that make up the continent.

GREENLAND
(Denmark)

Arctic Circle

Baffin Island

Godthab ■

Hudson Bay

Newfoundland

St. Lawrence

Great Lakes

Montreal ⊙
Ottawa ■

Chicago ⊙

New York ⊙

Washington D.C. ■

AMERICA

Mississippi

ATLANTIC

OCEAN

Tropic of Cancer

Houston

THE BAHAMAS

Gulf of Mexico

Havana ■ **CUBA**

Puerto Rico (U.S.A.)

Guadeloupe (France)

HAITI **DOMINICAN REPUBLIC**

DOMINICA
Martinique (France)

BARBADOS

JAMAICA

TRINIDAD AND TOBAGO

BELIZE

Caribbean Sea

HONDURAS

GUATEMALA

NICARAGUA

EL SALVADOR

COSTA RICA **PANAMA**

FACTS

Total land area 8,745,289 sq miles
Total population 487 million
Biggest city Mexico City, Mexico
Biggest country Canada 3,849,653 sq miles
Smallest country Saint Kitts and Nevis 104 sq miles

Highest mountain Mount McKinley, Alaska, U.S.A. 20,321ft
Longest river Mississippi/Missouri, U.S.A. 3,741 miles
Biggest lake Lake Superior, between the U.S.A. and Canada 31,820 sq miles
Highest waterfall Yosemite Falls, on the Yosemite Creek, California, U.S.A. 2,425ft
Biggest desert Great Basin Desert, U.S.A. 190,000 sq miles
Biggest island Greenland 840,000 sq miles

Main mineral deposits Silver, gold, copper, lead, zinc, graphite, molybdenum, nickel
Main fuel deposits Oil, coal, natural gas, uranium

The bald eagle is the national bird of the U.S.A. It is not really bald, but has white feathers on its head.

SOUTH AMERICA

Triangle-shaped South America is made up of only 12 independent countries, along with French Guiana, which belongs to France. A huge part of this continent is taken up with the Amazon Rainforest, which covers the Amazon Basin with over a third of the world's trees. South America also has dusty deserts, towering mountains and, in Venezuela, the world's highest waterfall – Angel Falls.

This is a guanaco. Guanacos are members of the camel family that live in South America. Guanaco hair is used to make textiles.

Caribbean Sea

Caraca

VENEZUEL

Medellin○ ●Bogota

Orinoco

COLOMBIA

Equator

Quito●

Galapagos
Islands
(Ecuador)

ECUADOR

Guayaquil○

M

PERU

Lima■

BOLIV

La Paz■

■Su

Tropic of Capricorn

CHILE

PACIFIC

OCEAN

Santiago■   ○Mendoza

ARGEN

Cape H

Drake Pa

The shading on this map is there to help you see clearly the different countries that make up the continent. For a key to the features on this map, see page 139.

Equator

Tropic of Capricorn

ATLANTIC

OCEAN

rgetown
Paramaribo
Cayenne
NAM **FRENCH GUIANA**
(France)

°Recife

B R A Z I L

■**Brasilia**

°Belo Horizonte

Parana

GUAY   Sao Paulo° ○ °Rio de Janeiro

uncion

°Porto Alegre

GUAY
Montevideo
os Aires

land Islands
(U.K.)

This is a red-eyed tree frog. These frogs live in rainforests in South and Central America.

FACTS

Total land area 6,898,113 sq miles
Total population 346 million
Biggest city Sao Paulo, Brazil
Biggest country Brazil 3,300,151 sq miles
Smallest country Surinam 63,039 sq miles

Highest mountain Aconcagua, Argentina 22,831ft
Longest river Amazon, mainly in Brazil 4,000 miles
Biggest lake Lake Maracaibo, Venezuela 5,140 sq miles
Highest waterfall Angel Falls, on the Churun River, Venezuela 3,212ft
Biggest desert Patagonian Desert, Argentina 260,000 sq miles
Biggest island Tierra del Fuego 17,900 sq miles

Main mineral deposits Copper, tin, molybdenum, bauxite, emeralds
Main fuel deposits Oil, coal

AUSTRALASIA AND OCEANIA

Australasia and Oceania are made up of Australia, New Zealand, Papua New Guinea and thousands of other islands stretching out into the Pacific Ocean. This is one of the world's least populated areas. Some of its countries are made up of hundreds of islands.

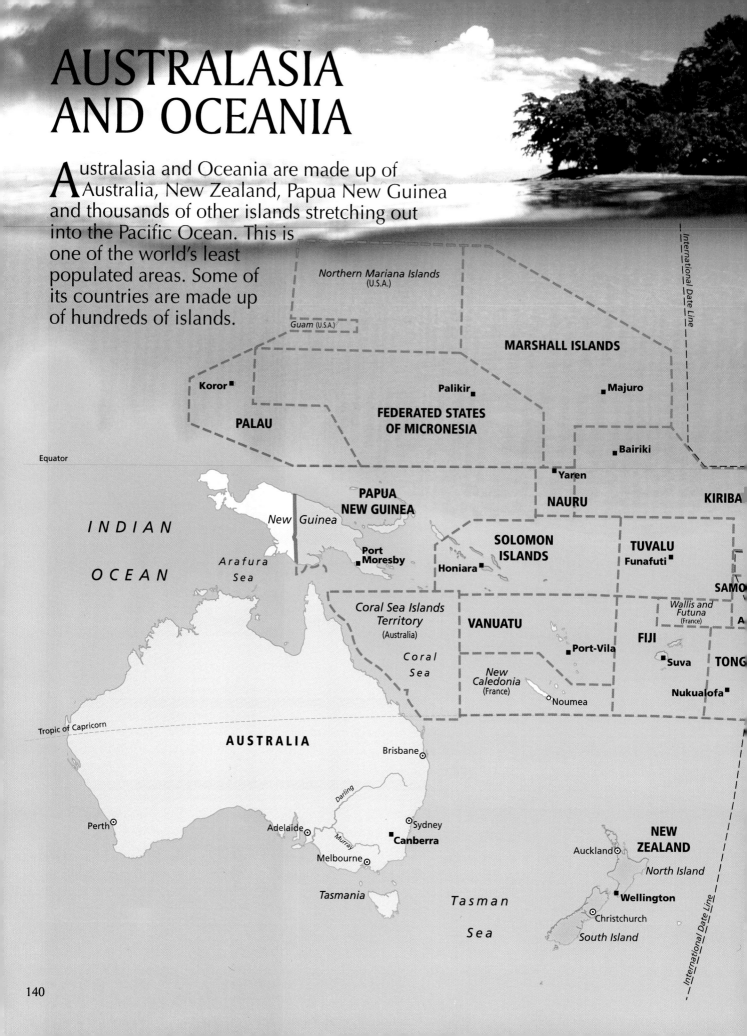

International Date Line

Northern Mariana Islands (U.S.A.)

Guam (U.S.A.)

MARSHALL ISLANDS

Koror ■

Palikir ■

■ Majuro

PALAU

FEDERATED STATES OF MICRONESIA

■ Bairiki

Equator

■ Yaren

KIRIBA

PAPUA NEW GUINEA

New Guinea

NAURU

INDIAN

Arafura Sea

SOLOMON ISLANDS

TUVALU

Funafuti ■

OCEAN

Port Moresby ■

Honiara ■

SAMO

Coral Sea Islands Territory (Australia)

Wallis and Futuna (France)

A

VANUATU

Coral Sea

Port-Vila ■

FIJI

TONG

New Caledonia (France)

Noumea ○

Suva ■

Nukualofa ■

Tropic of Capricorn

AUSTRALIA

Brisbane ○

Darling

Perth ○

Sydney ○

Adelaide ○

Murray

Canberra ■

NEW ZEALAND

Melbourne ○

Auckland ○

North Island

Tasmania

Tasman Sea

Wellington ■

Christchurch ○

South Island

International Date Line

140

This small island is part of Papua New Guinea.

PACIFIC OCEAN

The shading on this map is there to help you see clearly the different countries that make up the continent. For a key to the features on this map, see page 139.

Line Islands

Equator

au (land)

an

Marquesas Islands

e aland)

French Polynesia (France)

Society Islands

Cook Islands (New Zealand)

Pitcairn Islands (U.K.)

Tropic of Capricorn

FACTS

Total land area 3,306,715 sq miles
Total population 31 million
Biggest city Sydney, Australia
Biggest country Australia 2,967,124 sq miles
Smallest country Nauru 8 sq miles

Highest mountain Mount Wilhelm, Papua New Guinea 14,793ft
Longest river Murray/Darling River, Australia 2,310 miles
Biggest lake Lake Eyre, Australia 3,470 sq miles
Highest waterfall Sutherland Falls, on the Arthur River, New Zealand 1,904ft
Biggest desert Great Victoria Desert, Australia 150,000 sq miles
Biggest island New Guinea 309,000 sq miles
(Australia is counted as a continental land mass and not as an island.)

Main mineral deposits Iron, nickel, precious stones, lead, bauxite
Main fuel deposits Oil, coal, uranium

The Moorish idol fish is found in shallow waters throughout the Pacific. It has a long, distinctive dorsal fin.

141

ASIA

Asia is the world's largest continent and has over 40 countries, including Russia, the biggest country in the world. As well as large land masses, it has thousands of islands and inlets, giving it over 100,000 miles of coastline. Asia also contains the Himalayas, the world's highest mountain range. Turkey and Russia are part in Europe and part in Asia, but both are shown in full on this map.

The shading on this map is there to help you see clearly the different countries that make up the continent. For a key to the features on this map, see page 139.

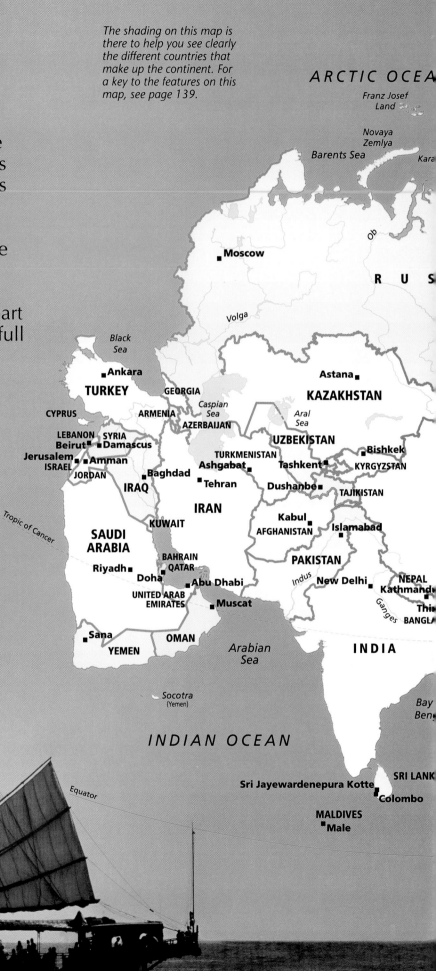

ARCTIC OCEAN

Franz Josef Land

Novaya Zemlya

Barents Sea

Kara

Ob

Moscow

RUSS

Volga

Black Sea

Ankara

TURKEY

GEORGIA

Astana

KAZAKHSTAN

CYPRUS

ARMENIA

Caspian Sea

Aral Sea

LEBANON

SYRIA

AZERBAIJAN

UZBEKISTAN

Beirut

Damascus

TURKMENISTAN

Bishkek

Jerusalem

Amman

Ashgabat

Tashkent

KYRGYZSTAN

ISRAEL

JORDAN

Baghdad

Dushanbe

TAJIKISTAN

IRAQ

Tehran

IRAN

Tropic of Cancer

KUWAIT

Kabul

Islamabad

SAUDI ARABIA

AFGHANISTAN

BAHRAIN

PAKISTAN

Riyadh

QATAR

Doha

Abu Dhabi

Indus

New Delhi

NEPAL

Kathmand

UNITED ARAB EMIRATES

Muscat

Ganges

Thi

BANGLA

Sana

OMAN

Arabian Sea

INDIA

YEMEN

Socotra (Yemen)

Bay Ben

INDIAN OCEAN

Equator

SRI LANK

Sri Jayewardenepura Kotte

Colombo

MALDIVES

Male

A type of Chinese sailing boat called a junk in the port at Singapore

Wrangel
Island

Bering Sea

*East
Siberian
Sea*

*New Siberia
Islands*

*naya
lya*

*Laptev
Sea*

Lena

*Sea of
Okhotsk*

Lake
Baikal

Hokkaido

Ulan Bator ■

*Sea of
Japan*

JAPAN

MONGOLIA

**NORTH
KOREA**

■**Tokyo**

Pyongyang■

Honshu

Beijing ■

■**Seoul**

**SOUTH
KOREA**

C H I N A

Huang He (Yellow)

*East China
Sea*

Tropic of Cancer

Chang Jiang (Yangtze)

■ **Taipei**

TAIWAN

PACIFIC

OCEAN

rrawaddy)

**URMA
YANMAR)**

■**Hanoi**

LAOS

PHILIPPINES

Vientiane ■

*South China
Sea*

Mekong

■**Manila**

THAILAND

VIETNAM

*Philippine
Sea*

■**Bangkok**

CAMBODIA

*aman
ands
ndia)*

**Phnom
Penh** ■

Equator

*icobar
lands
(India)*

BRUNEI

MALAYSIA

New Guinea

■**Kuala Lumpur**

SINGAPORE

Borneo

Celebes

Sumatra

INDONESIA

Dili■

Arafura Sea

■**Jakarta**

■**EAST
TIMOR**

Java

FACTS

Total land area 17,196,090
sq miles
Total population 3.8 billion
(including all of Russia)
Biggest city Tokyo, Japan
Biggest country Russia *Total
area: 6,592,735 sq miles
Area of Asiatic Russia: 14,934,667
sq miles*
Smallest country Maldives
3116 sq miles

Highest mountain Mount
Everest, Nepal/China border
29,035ft
Longest river Chang Jiang
(Yangtze), China *3,964 miles*
Biggest lake Caspian Sea,
western Asia *143,243 sq miles*
Highest waterfall Jog Falls, on
the Sharavati River, India *830ft*
Biggest desert Arabian Desert,
in and around Saudi Arabia
900,000 sq miles
Biggest island Borneo *290,000
sq miles*

Main mineral deposits Zinc,
mica, tin, chromium, iron, nickel
Main fuel deposits Oil, coal,
uranium, natural gas

*These are lotus flowers, a type of
water lily. In China they are
associated with purity and for
Buddhists they are sacred.*

EUROPE

Europe is a small continent, packed with over 40 countries and more than 700 million people. It has no deserts, but its geography ranges from high mountain ranges to icy tundra, rocky islands and lush farmland. With dozens of islands and peninsulas, many of Europe's countries are largely surrounded by sea.

The shading on this map is there to help you see clearly the different countries that make up the continent. For a key to the features on this map, see page 137.

Arctic Circle

ARCTIC OCEAN

Reykjavik
ICELAND

Norwegian Sea

SWED

*Faroe Islands
(Denmark)*

NORWAY

Oslo ■

Stockho

Shetland Islands

Orkney Islands

North Sea

DENMARK
Copenhagen ■

IRELAND
Dublin ■

UNITED KINGDOM

London ■

The Hague ■ Amsterdam
■ **NETHERLANDS**

Berlin ■

■ Brussels
BELGIUM

GERMANY

PO

LUXEMBOURG
■ Luxembourg

Prague
CZECH REPUBLIC

■ Paris

Rhine

Vienna
LIECHTENSTEIN Bratislava

■ Bern ■ Vaduz **AUSTRIA** Buda

Bay of Biscay

FRANCE **SWITZERLAND**

HU

SLOVENIA
Ljubljana ■

Zag
CRO

ATLANTIC

OCEAN

MONACO

ANDORRA ■
■ Andorra
la Vella

SAN MARINO

BOSNIA HERZEGO
Sarajev

ITALY

PORTUGAL

Lisbon ■

■ Madrid

SPAIN

Corsica

■ **VATICAN CITY**
Rome ■

A

Balearic Islands

Sardinia

Mediterranean Sea

Sicily

■ **MALTA**
Valletta

Barents Sea

Arctic Circle

Murmansk

Arkhangelsk

FINLAND

St. Petersburg

Tallinn
ESTONIA

RUSSIA

Nizhniy Novgorod
Kazan

LATVIA

Moscow

HUANIA
Vilnius

Minsk

BELARUS

Volga

rsaw

Kiev

Volgograd

UKRAINE

Dnieper

AKIA

MOLDOVA

Chisinau

ROMANIA

Bucharest

Black Sea

A AND
ENEGRO

BULGARIA

Sofia

opje

DONIA

TURKEY

ECE

Athens

Crete

FACTS

Total land area 3,940,428 sq miles (including European Russia)
Total population 727 million (including all of Russia)
Biggest city Paris, France
Biggest country Russia *Total area: 6,592,735 sq miles Area of European Russia: 1,658,068 sq miles*
Smallest country Vatican City *0.17 sq miles*

Highest mountain Elbrus, Russia *18,510ft*
Longest river Volga *2,298 miles*
Biggest lake Lake Ladoga, Russia *6,834 sq miles*
Highest waterfall Utigard, on the Jostedal Glacier, Norway *2,625ft*
Biggest desert No deserts in Europe
Biggest island Great Britain *88,753 sq miles*

Main mineral deposits Bauxite, zinc, iron, potash, fluorspar
Main fuel deposits Oil, coal, natural gas, peat, uranium

A dairy cow in Devon, in the south of England

AFRICA

Africa is the second-biggest continent and has 53 countries altogether. More than a quarter of them are landlocked, with no access to the sea except through other countries. Africa is home to the world's longest river, the Nile, and its largest desert, the Sahara. It also has vast amounts of natural resources, such as gold, copper and diamonds. Many of them have not yet begun to be used.

A group of Masai people from East Africa silhouetted against a sunset over the flat grasslands

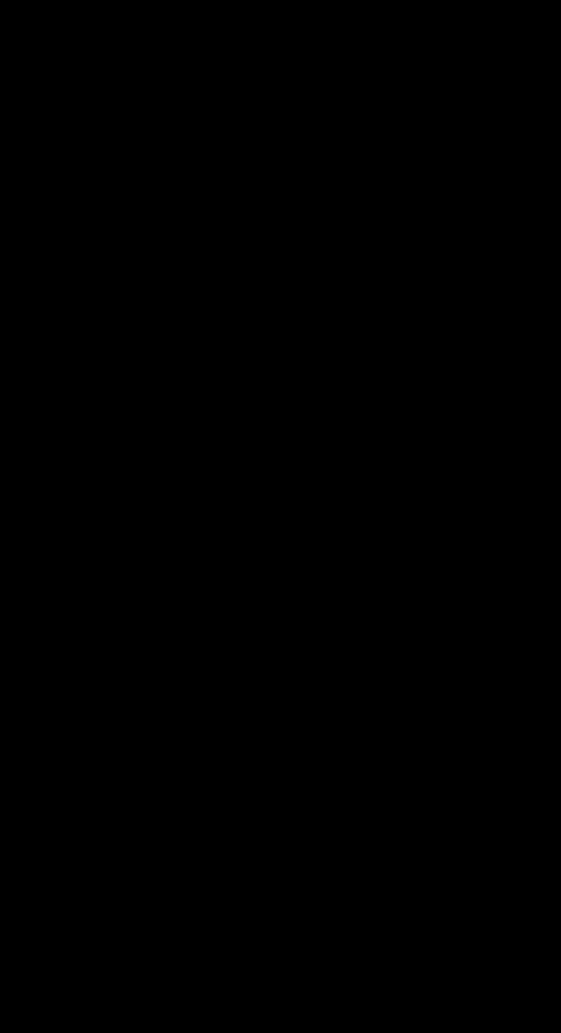

Algiers Tunis
Madeira
(Portugal) Rabat TUNISIA
MOROCCO Tripoli

Canary Islands
(Spain)

Laayoune ALGERIA LIBYA

Tropic of Cancer WESTERN
SAHARA
(Morocco)

MAURITANIA MALI NIGER
Nouakchott Niger CHAD

CAPE VERDE Dakar Niamey
Praia SENEGAL Bamako
THE GAMBIA Banjul Ouagadougou Ndjam
Bissau BURKINA FASO
GUINEA-BISSAU GUINEA BENIN NIGERIA
Conakry TOGO Abuja
Freetown IVORY CEN
SIERRA LEONE COAST GHANA Porto-Novo AFR
Monrovia Yamoussoukro Lome CAMEROON REP
LIBERIA Accra Bangui
Malabo Yaounde
EQUATORIAL
GUINEA
Equator Libreville CONGO
SAO TOME GABON
AND PRINCIPE

Brazzaville
Kinsha

ATLANTIC

OCEAN Luanda

ANGOLA

NAMIBI

Tropic of Capricorn Windhoek

Or

Cape Town

The shading on this map is there to help you see clearly the different countries that make up the continent. For a key to the features on this map, see page 139.

FACTS

Total land area 11,703,343 sq miles
Total population 794 million
Biggest city Cairo, Egypt
Biggest country Sudan 967,493 sq miles
Smallest country Seychelles 176 sq miles

Highest mountain Kilimanjaro, Tanzania *19,340ft*
Longest river Nile, running from Burundi to Egypt *4,145 miles*
Biggest lake Lake Victoria, between Tanzania, Kenya and Uganda *26,724 sq miles*
Highest waterfall Tugela Falls, on the Tugela River, South Africa *2,000ft*
Biggest desert Sahara, North Africa *3,500,000 sq miles*
Biggest island Madagascar *226,656 sq miles*

Main mineral deposits Gold, copper, diamonds, iron ore, manganese, bauxite
Main fuel deposits Coal, uranium, natural gas

Cairo

EGYPT

Tropic of Cancer

Nile

Khartoum

ERITREA
Asmara

SUDAN

DJIBOUTI Djibouti

Addis Ababa

SOMALIA

ETHIOPIA

UGANDA
Kampala

KENYA

Mogadishu

Equator

Kigali

Nairobi

RWANDA
BURUNDI
Bujumbura

Dodoma

Victoria
SEYCHELLES

TANZANIA Dar es Salaam

INDIAN

MALAWI

Moroni
COMOROS

Lilongwe

OCEAN

BIA

aka

ezi

Harare

MOZAMBIQUE

Antananarivo

ZIMBABWE

MAURITIUS
Port Louis

ANA

MADAGASCAR

Reunion
(France)

ne

Tropic of Capricorn

Pretoria Maputo

babane SWAZILAND
Lobamba

ontein

Maseru

LESOTHO

A

This greater flamingo lives in the Transvaal National Park, South Africa.

Each country has its own national flag. Here are just a few of them. The flag with the yellow stars on a blue background is the European Union flag.

COUNTRIES
AND FLAGS

GAZETTEER OF STATES

Afghanistan

This gazetteer lists the world's 193 independent states, along with key facts about each one. In the lists of languages, the language that is most widely spoken is given first, even if it is not the official language. In the lists of religions, the one followed by the most people is also placed first.

Armenia

Every state has a national flag, which is usually used to represent the country abroad. A few states also have a state flag which they prefer to use instead. The state flags appear here with a dot • beside them.

Australia

Albania

Algeria

Andorra

Angola

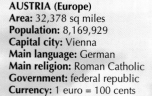
Antigua and Barbuda

• Argentina

AFGHANISTAN (Asia)
Area: 249,935 sq miles
Population: 27,755,775
Capital city: Kabul
Main languages: Dari, Pashto
Main religion: Muslim
Government: transitional
Currency: 1 afghani = 100 puls

ALBANIA (Europe)
Area: 11,100 sq miles
Population: 3,544,841
Capital city: Tirana
Main language: Albanian
Main religions: Muslim, Albanian Orthodox
Government: emerging democracy
Currency: 1 lek = 100 qintars

ALGERIA (Africa)
Area: 919,589 sq miles
Population: 32,277,942
Capital city: Algiers
Main languages: Arabic, French, Berber dialects
Main religion: Sunni Muslim
Government: republic
Currency: 1 Algerian dinar = 100 centimes

ANDORRA (Europe)
Area: 181 sq miles
Population: 68,403
Capital city: Andorra la Vella
Main languages: Catalan, Spanish
Main religion: Roman Catholic
Government: parliamentary democracy
Currency: 1 euro = 100 cents

ANGOLA (Africa)
Area: 481,351 sq miles
Population: 10,593,171
Capital city: Luanda
Main languages: Kilongo, Kimbundu, other Bantu languages, Portuguese
Main religions: indigenous, Roman Catholic, Protestant
Government: transitional
Currency: 1 kwanza = 100 lwei

ANTIGUA AND BARBUDA (North America)
Area: 171 sq miles
Population: 67,448
Capital city: Saint John's
Main languages: Caribbean Creole, English
Main religion: Protestant
Government: constitutional monarchy
Currency: 1 East Caribbean dollar = 100 cents

ARGENTINA (South America)
Area: 1,068,305 sq miles
Population: 37,812,817
Capital city: Buenos Aires
Main language: Spanish
Main religion: Roman Catholic
Government: republic
Currency: 1 peso = 100 centavos

ARMENIA (Asia)
Area: 11,506 sq miles
Population: 3,336,100
Capital city: Yerevan
Main language: Armenian
Main religion: Armenian Orthodox
Government: republic
Currency: 1 dram = 100 luma

AUSTRALIA (Australasia/Oceania)
Area: 2,967,124 sq miles
Population: 19,546,792
Capital city: Canberra
Main language: English
Main religion: Christian
Government: federal democratic monarchy
Currency: 1 Australian dollar = 100 cents

AUSTRIA (Europe)
Area: 32,378 sq miles
Population: 8,169,929
Capital city: Vienna
Main language: German
Main religion: Roman Catholic
Government: federal republic
Currency: 1 euro = 100 cents

Austria

Azerbaijan

Bahamas, The

Bahrain

Bangladesh

Barbados

Belarus

Belgium

Belize

Benin

Bhutan

• Bolivia

AZERBAIJAN (Asia)
Area: 33,436 sq miles
Population: 7,798,497
Capital city: Baku
Main language: Azeri
Main religion: Muslim
Government: republic
Currency: 1 manat = 100 gopiks

BAHAMAS, THE (North America)
Area: 5,382 sq miles
Population: 300,529
Capital city: Nassau
Main languages: Bahamian Creole, English
Main religion: Christian
Government: parliamentary democracy
Currency: 1 Bahamian dollar = 100 cents

BAHRAIN (Asia)
Area: 257 sq miles
Population: 656,397
Capital city: Manama
Main languages: Arabic, English
Main religion: Muslim
Government: traditional monarchy
Currency: 1 Bahraini dinar = 1,000 fils

BANGLADESH (Asia)
Area: 55,598 sq miles
Population: 133,376,684
Capital city: Dhaka
Main languages: Bengali, English
Main religions: Muslim, Hindu
Government: republic
Currency: 1 taka = 100 poisha

BARBADOS (North America)
Area: 166 sq miles
Population: 276,607
Capital city: Bridgetown
Main languages: Bajan, English
Main religion: Christian
Government: parliamentary democracy
Currency: 1 Barbadian dollar = 100 cents

BELARUS (Europe)
Area: 80,154 sq miles
Population: 10,335,382
Capital city: Minsk
Main language: Belarusian
Main religion: Eastern Orthodox
Government: republic
Currency: 1 Belarusian ruble = 100 kopecks

BELGIUM (Europe)
Area: 11,780 sq miles
Population: 10,274,595
Capital city: Brussels
Main languages: Dutch, French
Main religions: Roman Catholic, Protestant
Government: constitutional monarchy
Currency: 1 euro = 100 cents

BELIZE (North America)
Area: 8,865 sq miles
Population: 262,999
Capital city: Belmopan
Main languages: Spanish, Belize Creole,
English, Garifuna, Maya

Main religions: Roman Catholic, Protestant
Government: parliamentary democracy
Currency: 1 Belizean dollar = 100 cents

BENIN (Africa)
Area: 43,483 sq miles
Population: 6,787,625
Capital city: Porto-Novo
Main languages: Fon, French, Yoruba
Main religions: indigenous, Christian, Muslim
Government: republic
Currency: 1 CFA* franc = 100 centimes

BHUTAN (Asia)
Area: 18,146 sq miles
Population: 2,094,176
Capital city: Thimphu
Main languages: Dzongkha, Nepali
Main religions: Buddhist, Hindu
Government: monarchy
Currency: 1 ngultrum = 100 chetrum

BOLIVIA (South America)
Area: 424,162 sq miles
Population: 8,445,134
Capital cities: La Paz, Sucre
Main languages: Spanish, Quechua, Aymara
Main religion: Roman Catholic
Government: republic
Currency: 1 boliviano = 100 centavos

BOSNIA AND HERZEGOVINA (Europe)
Area: 19,741 sq miles
Population: 3,964,388
Capital city: Sarajevo
Main languages: Bosnian, Serbian, Croatian
Main religions: Muslim, Orthodox, Roman
Catholic
Government: emerging federal democracy
Currency: 1 marka = 100 pfenninga

BOTSWANA (Africa)
Area: 231,743 sq miles
Population: 1,591,232
Capital city: Gaborone
Main languages: Setswana, Kalanga,
English
Main religions: indigenous, Christian
Government: parliamentary republic
Currency: 1 pula = 100 thebe

BRAZIL (South America)
Area: 3,300,151 sq miles
Population: 176,029,560
Capital city: Brasilia
Main language: Portuguese
Main religion: Roman Catholic
Government: federal republic
Currency: 1 real = 100 centavos

BRUNEI (Asia)
Area: 2,228 sq miles
Population: 350,898
Capital city: Bandar Seri Begawan
Main languages: Malay, English, Chinese
Main religions: Muslim, Buddhist
Government: constitutional sultanate (a type
of monarchy)
Currency: 1 Bruneian dollar = 100 cents

Bosnia and Herzegovina

Botswana

Brazil

Brunei

Bulgaria

Burkina Faso

Burma (Myanmar)

Burundi

Cambodia

Cameroon

Canada

Cape Verde

**Central African
Republic**

Chad

BULGARIA (Europe)
Area: 42,822 sq miles
Population: 7,621,337
Capital city: Sofia
Main language: Bulgarian
Main religions: Bulgarian Orthodox, Muslim
Government: parliamentary democracy
Currency: 1 lev = 100 stotinki

BURKINA FASO (Africa)
Area: 105,869 sq miles
Population: 12,603,185
Capital city: Ouagadougou
Main languages: Moore, Jula, French
Main religions: Muslim, indigenous
Government: republic
Currency: 1 CFA* franc = 100 centimes

BURMA (MYANMAR) (Asia)
Area: 261,969 sq miles
Population: 42,238,224
Capital city: Rangoon
Main language: Burmese
Main religion: Buddhist
Government: military dictatorship
Currency: 1 kyat = 100 pyas

BURUNDI (Africa)
Area: 10,745 sq miles
Population: 6,373,002
Capital city: Bujumbura
Main languages: Kirundi, French, Swahili
Main religions: Christian, indigenous
Government: republic
Currency: 1 Burundi franc = 100 centimes

CAMBODIA (Asia)
Area: 69,900 sq miles
Population: 12,775,324
Capital city: Phnom Penh
Main language: Khmer
Main religion: Buddhist
Government: constitutional monarchy
Currency: 1 new riel = 100 sen

CAMEROON (Africa)
Area: 183,567 sq miles
Population: 16,184,748
Capital city: Yaounde
Main languages: Cameroon Pidgin English, Ewondo, Fula, French, English
Main religions: indigenous, Christian, Muslim
Government: republic
Currency: 1 CFA* franc = 100 centimes

CANADA (North America)
Area: 3,849,653 sq miles
Population: 31,902,268
Capital city: Ottawa
Main languages: English, French
Main religions: Roman Catholic, Protestant
Government: federal democracy
Currency: 1 Canadian dollar = 100 cents

CAPE VERDE (Africa)
Area: 1,557 sq miles
Population: 408,760
Capital city: Praia
Main languages: Crioulo*, Portuguese

Main religions: Roman Catholic, Protestant
Government: republic
Currency: 1 Cape Verdean escudo = 100 centavos

CENTRAL AFRICAN REPUBLIC (Africa)
Area: 240,536 sq miles
Population: 3,642,739
Capital city: Bangui
Main languages: Sangho, French
Main religions: indigenous, Christian, Muslim
Government: republic
Currency: 1 CFA* franc = 100 centimes

CHAD (Africa)
Area: 495,752 sq miles
Population: 8,997,237
Capital city: Ndjamena
Main languages: Arabic, Sara, French
Main religions: Muslim, Christian, indigenous
Government: republic
Currency: 1 CFA* franc = 100 centimes

CHILE (South America)
Area: 292,133 sq miles
Population: 15,498,930
Capital city: Santiago
Main language: Spanish
Main religions: Roman Catholic, Protestant
Government: republic
Currency: 1 Chilean peso = 100 centavos

CHINA (Asia)
Area: 3,705,386 sq miles
Population: 1,284,303,705
Capital city: Beijing
Main languages: Mandarin Chinese, Yue, Wu
Main religions: Taoist, Buddhist
Government: Communist state
Currency: 1 yuan = 10 jiao

COLOMBIA (South America)
Area: 439,733 sq miles
Population: 41,008,227
Capital city: Bogota
Main language: Spanish
Main religion: Roman Catholic
Government: republic
Currency: 1 Colombian peso = 100 centavos

COMOROS (Africa)
Area: 838 sq miles
Population: 614,382
Capital city: Moroni
Main languages: Comorian*, French, Arabic
Main religion: Sunni Muslim
Government: republic
Currency: 1 Comoran franc = 100 centimes

CONGO (Africa)
Area: 132,046 sq miles
Population: 2,958,448
Capital city: Brazzaville
Main languages: Munukutuba, Lingala, French
Main religions: Christian, animist
Government: republic
Currency: 1 CFA* franc = 100 centimes

China

Colombia

Comoros

Congo

Congo (Democratic Republic)

Costa Rica

*CFA = Communaute Financiere Africaine; Comorian = a blend of Swahili and Arabic; Crioulo = a blend of Portuguese and West African

Croatia

Cuba

Cyprus

Czech Republic

Denmark

Djibouti

Dominica

CONGO (DEMOCRATIC REPUBLIC) (Africa)
Area: 905,563 sq miles
Population: 55,225,478
Capital city: Kinshasa
Main languages: Lingala, Swahili, Kikongo, Tshiluba, French
Main religions: Roman Catholic, Protestant, Kimbanguist, Muslim
Government: transitional
Currency: 1 Congolese franc = 100 centimes

COSTA RICA (North America)
Area: 19,730 sq miles
Population: 3,834,934
Capital city: San Jose
Main language: Spanish
Main religions: Roman Catholic, Evangelical
Government: democratic republic
Currency: 1 Costa Rican colon = 100 centimos

CROATIA (Europe)
Area: 21,829 sq miles
Population: 4,390,751
Capital city: Zagreb
Main language: Croatian
Main religions: Roman Catholic, Orthodox
Government: parliamentary democracy
Currency: 1 kuna = 100 lipas

CUBA (North America)
Area: 42,803 sq miles
Population: 11,224,321
Capital city: Havana
Main language: Spanish
Main religion: Roman Catholic
Government: Communist state
Currency: 1 Cuban peso = 100 centavos

CYPRUS (Europe)
Area: 3,571 sq miles
Population: 767,314
Capital city: Nicosia
Main languages: Greek, Turkish
Main religions: Greek Orthodox, Muslim
Government: republic with a self-proclaimed independent Turkish area
Currency: Greek Cypriot area: 1 Cypriot pound = 100 cents; Turkish Cypriot area: 1 Turkish lira = 100 kurus

CZECH REPUBLIC (Europe)
Area: 30,450 sq miles
Population: 10,256,760
Capital city: Prague
Main language: Czech
Main religion: Roman Catholic
Government: parliamentary democracy
Currency: 1 koruna = 100 haleru

DENMARK (Europe)
Area: 16,639 sq miles
Population: 5,368,854
Capital city: Copenhagen
Main language: Danish
Main religion: Evangelical Lutheran
Government: constitutional monarchy
Currency: 1 Danish krone = 100 oere

DJIBOUTI (Africa)
Area: 8,957 sq miles
Population: 472,810
Capital city: Djibouti
Main languages: Afar, Somali, Arabic, French
Main religion: Muslim
Government: republic
Currency: 1 Djiboutian franc = 100 centimes

DOMINICA (North America)
Area: 290 sq miles
Population: 70,158
Capital city: Roseau
Main languages: English, French patois
Main religions: Roman Catholic, Protestant
Government: democratic republic
Currency: 1 East Caribbean dollar = 100 cents

DOMINICAN REPUBLIC (North America)
Area: 18,815 sq miles
Population: 8,721,594
Capital city: Santo Domingo
Main language: Spanish
Main religion: Roman Catholic
Government: democratic republic
Currency: 1 Dominican peso = 100 centavos

EAST TIMOR (Asia)
Area: 5,794 sq miles
Population: 952,618
Capital city: Dili
Main languages: Tetum, Portuguese, Indonesian
Main religions: Roman Catholic, animist
Government: republic
Currency: 1 U.S. dollar = 100 cents

ECUADOR (South America)
Area: 109,483 sq miles
Population: 13,447,494
Capital city: Quito
Main languages: Spanish, Quechua
Main religion: Roman Catholic
Government: republic
Currency: 1 sucre = 100 centavos

EGYPT (Africa)
Area: 386,660 sq miles
Population: 70,712,345
Capital city: Cairo
Main language: Arabic
Main religion: Sunni Muslim
Government: republic
Currency: 1 Egyptian pound = 100 piasters

EL SALVADOR (North America)
Area: 8,124 sq miles
Population: 6,353,681
Capital city: San Salvador
Main language: Spanish
Main religion: Roman Catholic
Government: republic
Currency: 1 Salvadoran colon = 100 centavos

EQUATORIAL GUINEA (Africa)
Area: 10,830 sq miles
Population: 498,144
Capital city: Malabo

• Dominican Republic

East Timor

• Ecuador

Egypt

• El Salvador

Equatorial Guinea

Eritrea

GAZETTEER OF STATES CONTINUED

Estonia

Main languages: Fang, Bubi, other Bantu languages, Spanish, French, Pidgin English
Main religion: Christian
Government: republic
Currency: 1 CFA* franc = 100 centimes

ERITREA (Africa)
Area: 46,842 sq miles
Population: 4,465,651
Capital city: Asmara
Main languages: Tigrinya, Afar, Arabic
Main religions: Muslim, Coptic Christian, Roman Catholic, Protestant
Government: transitional
Currency: 1 nafka = 100 cents

Ethiopia

ESTONIA (Europe)
Area: 17,462 sq miles
Population: 1,415,681
Capital city: Tallinn
Main languages: Estonian, Russian
Main religions: Evangelical Lutheran, Russian and Estonian Orthodox, other Christian
Government: parliamentary democracy
Currency: 1 Estonian kroon = 100 senti

ETHIOPIA (Africa)
Area: 435,184 sq miles
Population: 67,673,031
Capital city: Addis Ababa
Main languages: Amharic, Tigrinya, Arabic
Main religions: Muslim, Ethiopian Orthodox, animist
Government: federal republic
Currency: 1 birr = 100 cents

Federated States of Micronesia

FEDERATED STATES OF MICRONESIA (Australasia/Oceania)
Area: 271 sq miles
Population: 135,869
Capital city: Palikir
Main languages: Chuuk, Ponapean, English
Main religions: Roman Catholic, Protestant
Government: democracy
Currency: 1 U.S. dollar = 100 cents

Fiji

FIJI (Australasia/Oceania)
Area: 7,054 sq miles
Population: 856,346
Capital city: Suva
Main languages: Fijian, Hindustani, English
Main religions: Christian, Hindu
Government: republic
Currency: 1 Fijian dollar = 100 cents

Finland

FINLAND (Europe)
Area: 130,127 sq miles
Population: 5,183,545
Capital city: Helsinki
Main language: Finnish
Main religion: Evangelical Lutheran
Government: republic
Currency: 1 euro = 100 cents

France

FRANCE (Europe)
Area: 211,208 sq miles
Population: 59,765,983
Capital city: Paris
Main language: French

Gabon

Main religion: Roman Catholic
Government: republic
Currency: 1 euro = 100 cents

GABON (Africa)
Area: 103,347 sq miles
Population: 1,233,353
Capital city: Libreville
Main languages: Fang, Myene, French
Main religions: Christian, animist
Government: republic
Currency: 1 CFA* franc = 100 centimes

GAMBIA, THE (Africa)
Area: 4,363 sq miles
Population: 1,455,842
Capital city: Banjul
Main languages: Mandinka, Fula, Wolof, English
Main religion: Muslim
Government: democratic republic
Currency: 1 dalasi = 100 butut

GEORGIA (Asia)
Area: 26,911 sq miles
Population: 4,960,951
Capital city: Tbilisi
Main languages: Georgian, Russian
Main religions: Georgian Orthodox, Muslim, Russian Orthodox
Government: republic
Currency: 1 lari = 100 tetri

GERMANY (Europe)
Area: 137,846 sq miles
Population: 83,251,851
Capital city: Berlin
Main language: German
Main religions: Protestant, Roman Catholic
Government: federal republic
Currency: 1 euro = 100 cents

GHANA (Africa)
Area: 92,456 sq miles
Population: 20,244,154
Capital city: Accra
Main languages: Twi, Fante, Ga, Hausa, Dagbani, Ewe, Nzemi, English
Main religions: indigenous, Muslim, Christian
Government: democratic republic
Currency: 1 new cedi = 100 pesewas

GREECE (Europe)
Area: 50,942 sq miles
Population: 10,645,343
Capital city: Athens
Main language: Greek
Main religion: Greek Orthodox
Government: parliamentary republic
Currency: 1 euro = 100 cents

GRENADA (North America)
Area: 131 sq miles
Population: 89,211
Capital city: Saint George's
Main languages: English, French patois
Main religions: Roman Catholic, Protestant
Government: constitutional monarchy
Currency: 1 East Caribbean dollar = 100 cents

Gambia, The

Georgia

Germany

Ghana

Greece

Grenada

Guatemala

*CFA = Communaute Financiere Africaine

Guinea

Guinea-Bissau

Guyana

• **Haiti**

Honduras

Hungary

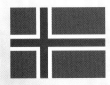

Iceland

GUATEMALA (North America)
Area: 42,042 sq miles
Population: 13,314,079
Capital city: Guatemala City
Main languages: Spanish, Amerindian languages including Quiche, Kekchi, Cakchiquel, Mam
Main religions: Roman Catholic, Protestant, indigenous Mayan beliefs
Government: democratic republic
Currency: 1 quetzal = 100 centavos

GUINEA (Africa)
Area: 94,927 sq miles
Population: 7,775,065
Capital city: Conakry
Main languages: Fuuta Jalon, Mallinke, Susu, French
Main religion: Muslim
Government: republic
Currency: 1 Guinean franc = 100 centimes

GUINEA-BISSAU (Africa)
Area: 13,946 sq miles
Population: 1,345,479
Capital city: Bissau
Main languages: Crioulo*, Balante, Pulaar, Mandjak, Mandinka, Portuguese
Main religions: indigenous, Muslim
Government: republic
Currency: 1 CFA* franc = 100 centimes

GUYANA (South America)
Area: 83,000 sq miles
Population: 698,209
Capital city: Georgetown
Main languages: Guyanese Creole, English, Amerindian languages, Caribbean Hindi
Main religions: Christian, Hindu
Government: republic
Currency: 1 Guyanese dollar = 100 cents

HAITI (North America)
Area: 10,714 sq miles
Population: 7,063,722
Capital city: Port-au-Prince
Main languages: Haitian Creole, French
Main religions: Roman Catholic, Protestant, Voodoo
Government: republic
Currency: 1 gourde = 100 centimes

HONDURAS (North America)
Area: 43,278 sq miles
Population: 6,560,608
Capital city: Tegucigalpa
Main language: Spanish
Main religion: Roman Catholic
Government: republic
Currency: 1 lempira = 100 centavos

HUNGARY (Europe)
Area: 35,919 sq miles
Population: 10,075,034
Capital city: Budapest
Main language: Hungarian
Main religions: Roman Catholic, Calvinist
Government: parliamentary democracy
Currency: 1 forint = 100 filler

ICELAND (Europe)
Area: 39,768 sq miles
Population: 279,384
Capital city: Reykjavik
Main language: Icelandic
Main religion: Evangelical Lutheran
Government: republic
Currency: 1 Icelandic krona = 100 aurar

INDIA (Asia)
Area: 1,269,339 sq miles
Population: 1,045,845,226
Capital city: New Delhi
Main languages: Hindi, English, Bengali, Urdu, over 1,600 other languages and dialects
Main religions: Hindu, Muslim
Government: federal republic
Currency: 1 Indian rupee = 100 paise

INDONESIA (Asia)
Area: 741,096 sq miles
Population: 231,328,092
Capital city: Jakarta
Main languages: Bahasa Indonesia, English, Dutch, Javanese
Main religion: Muslim
Government: republic
Currency: 1 Indonesian rupiah = 100 sen

IRAN (Asia)
Area: 636,293 sq miles
Population: 66,622,704
Capital city: Tehran
Main languages: Farsi and other Persian dialects, Azeri
Main religions: Shi'a Muslim, Sunni Muslim
Government: Islamic republic
Currency: 1 toman = 10 Iranian rials

IRAQ (Asia)
Area: 168,754 sq miles
Population: 24,001,816
Capital city: Baghdad
Main languages: Arabic, Kurdish
Main religion: Muslim
Government: transitional
Currency: 1 Iraqi dinar = 1,000 fils

IRELAND (Europe)
Area: 27,135 sq miles
Population: 3,883,159
Capital city: Dublin
Main languages: English, Irish (Gaelic)
Main religion: Roman Catholic
Government: republic
Currency: 1 euro = 100 cents

ISRAEL (Asia)
Area: 8,019 sq miles
Population: 6,029,529
Capital city: Jerusalem
Main languages: Hebrew, Arabic
Main religions: Jewish, Muslim
Government: parliamentary democracy
Currency: 1 Israeli shekel = 100 agorot

India

Indonesia

Iran

Iraq

Ireland

Israel

Italy

CFA = Communaute Financiere Africaine; Crioulo = a blend of Portuguese and West African **155**

Ivory Coast

ITALY (Europe)
Area: 116,305 sq miles
Population: 57,715,625
Capital city: Rome
Main language: Italian
Main religion: Roman Catholic
Government: republic
Currency: 1 euro = 100 cents

Jamaica

IVORY COAST (Africa)
Area: 124,502 sq miles
Population: 16,804,784
Capital city: Yamoussoukro
Main languages: Baoule, Dioula, French
Main religions: Christian, Muslim, animist
Government: republic
Currency: 1 CFA* = 100 centimes

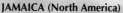

Japan

JAMAICA (North America)
Area: 4,243 sq miles
Population: 2,680,029
Capital city: Kingston
Main languages: Southwestern Caribbean Creole, English
Main religion: Protestant
Government: parliamentary democracy
Currency: 1 Jamaican dollar = 100 cents

Jordan

JAPAN (Asia)
Area: 145,882 sq miles
Population: 126,974,628
Capital city: Tokyo
Main language: Japanese
Main religions: Shinto, Buddhist
Government: constitutional monarchy
Currency: 1 yen = 100 sen

JORDAN (Asia)
Area: 35,637 sq miles
Population: 5,307,470
Capital city: Amman
Main languages: Arabic, English
Main religion: Sunni Muslim
Government: constitutional monarchy
Currency: 1 Jordanian dinar = 1,000 fils

Kazakhstan

KAZAKHSTAN (Asia)
Area: 1,049,150 sq miles
Population: 16,741,519
Capital city: Astana
Main languages: Kazakh, Russian
Main religions: Muslim, Russian Orthodox
Government: republic
Currency: 1 Kazakhstani tenge = 100 tiyn

Kenya

KENYA (Africa)
Area: 224,961 sq miles
Population: 31,138,735
Capital city: Nairobi
Main languages: Swahili, English, Bantu languages
Main religions: Christian, indigenous
Government: republic
Currency: 1 Kenyan shilling = 100 cents

Kiribati

KIRIBATI (Australasia/Oceania)
Area: 313 sq miles
Population: 96,335
Capital city: Bairiki (on Tarawa island)

Main languages: Gilbertese, English
Main religions: Roman Catholic, Protestant
Government: republic
Currency: 1 Australian dollar = 100 cents

KUWAIT (Asia)
Area: 6,880 sq miles
Population: 2,111,561
Capital city: Kuwait City
Main languages: Arabic, English
Main religion: Muslim
Government: monarchy
Currency: 1 Kuwaiti dinar = 1,000 fils

KYRGYZSTAN (Asia)
Area: 76,641 sq miles
Population: 4,822,166
Capital city: Bishkek
Main languages: Kyrgyz, Russian
Main religions: Muslim, Russian Orthodox
Government: republic
Currency: 1 Kyrgyzstani som = 100 tyiyn

LAOS (Asia)
Area: 91,428 sq miles
Population: 5,777,180
Capital city: Vientiane
Main languages: Lao, French, English
Main religions: Buddhist, animist
Government: Communist state
Currency: 1 new kip = 100 at

LATVIA (Europe)
Area: 24,938 sq miles
Population: 2,366,515
Capital city: Riga
Main languages: Latvian, Russian
Main religions: Lutheran, Roman Catholic, Russian Orthodox
Government: parliamentary democracy
Currency: 1 Latvian lat = 100 santims

LEBANON (Asia)
Area: 4,015 sq miles
Population: 3,677,780
Capital city: Beirut
Main languages: Arabic, French, English
Main religions: Muslim, Christian
Government: republic
Currency: 1 Lebanese pound = 100 piasters

LESOTHO (Africa)
Area: 11,718 sq miles
Population: 2,207,954
Capital cities: Maseru, Lobamba
Main languages: Sesotho, English, Zulu, Xhosa
Main religions: Christian, indigenous
Government: constitutional monarchy
Currency: 1 loti = 100 lisente

LIBERIA (Africa)
Area: 43,000 sq miles
Population: 3,288,198
Capital city: Monrovia
Main languages: Kpelle, English, Bassa
Main religions: indigenous, Christian, Muslim
Government: republic
Currency: 1 Liberian dollar = 100 cents

Kuwait

Kyrgyzstan

Laos

Latvia

Lebanon

Lesotho

Liberia

Libya

Liechtenstein

Lithuania

Luxembourg

Macedonia

Madagascar

Malawi

LIBYA (Africa)
Area: 679,358 sq miles
Population: 5,368,585
Capital city: Tripoli
Main languages: Arabic, Italian, English
Main religion: Sunni Muslim
Government: military rule
Currency: 1 Libyan dinar = 1,000 dirhams

LIECHTENSTEIN (Europe)
Area: 62 sq miles
Population: 32,842
Capital city: Vaduz
Main languages: German, Alemannic
Main religion: Roman Catholic
Government: constitutional monarchy
Currency: 1 Swiss franc = 100 centimes

LITHUANIA (Europe)
Area: 25,174 sq miles
Population: 3,601,138
Capital city: Vilnius
Main languages: Lithuanian, Polish, Russian
Main religions: Roman Catholic, Lutheran, Russian Orthodox
Government: democracy
Currency: 1 Lithuanian litas = 100 centas

LUXEMBOURG (Europe)
Area: 998 sq miles
Population: 448,569
Capital city: Luxembourg
Main languages: Luxemburgish, German, French
Main religion: Roman Catholic
Government: constitutional monarchy
Currency: 1 euro = 100 cents

MACEDONIA (Europe)
Area: 9,781 sq miles
Population: 2,054,800
Capital city: Skopje
Main languages: Macedonian, Albanian
Main religions: Macedonian Orthodox, Muslim
Government: emerging democracy
Currency: 1 Macedonian denar = 100 deni

MADAGASCAR (Africa)
Area: 226,656 sq miles
Population: 16,473,477
Capital city: Antananarivo
Main languages: Malagasy, French
Main religions: indigenous beliefs, Christian
Government: republic
Currency: 1 Malagasy franc = 100 centimes

MALAWI (Africa)
Area: 45,745 sq miles
Population: 10,701,824
Capital city: Lilongwe
Main languages: Chichewa, English
Main religions: Protestant, Roman Catholic, Muslim
Government: parliamentary democracy
Currency: 1 Malawian kwacha = 100 tambala

MALAYSIA (Asia)
Area: 127,316 sq miles
Population: 22,662,365
Capital city: Kuala Lumpur

Main languages: Bahasa Melayu, English, Chinese dialects, Tamil
Main religions: Muslim, Buddhist, Daoist
Government: constitutional monarchy
Currency: 1 ringgit = 100 sen

MALDIVES (Asia)
Area: 116 sq miles
Population: 320,165
Capital city: Male
Main languages: Maldivian, English
Main religion: Sunni Muslim
Government: republic
Currency: 1 rufiyaa = 100 laari

MALI (Africa)
Area: 478,764 sq miles
Population: 11,340,480
Capital city: Bamako
Main languages: Bambara, Fulani, Songhai, French
Main religion: Muslim
Government: republic
Currency: 1 CFA* franc = 100 centimes

MALTA (Europe)
Area: 122 sq miles
Population: 397,499
Capital city: Valletta
Main languages: Maltese, English
Main religion: Roman Catholic
Government: republic
Currency: 1 Maltese lira = 100 cents

MARSHALL ISLANDS (Australasia/Oceania)
Area: 70 sq miles
Population: 73,630
Capital city: Majuro
Main languages: Marshallese, English
Main religion: Protestant
Government: republic
Currency: 1 U.S. dollar = 100 cents

MAURITANIA (Africa)
Area: 397,953 sq miles
Population: 2,828,858
Capital city: Nouakchott
Main languages: Arabic, Wolof, French
Main religion: Muslim
Government: republic
Currency: 1 ouguiya = 5 khoums

MAURITIUS (Africa)
Area: 788 sq miles
Population: 1,200,206
Capital city: Port Louis
Main languages: Mauritius Creole French, French, Hindi, Bhojpuri, Urdu, Tamil, English
Main religions: Hindu, Christian, Muslim
Government: parliamentary democracy
Currency: 1 Mauritian rupee = 100 cents

MEXICO (North America)
Area: 761,602 sq miles
Population: 103,400,165
Capital city: Mexico City
Main languages: Spanish, Mayan, Nahuatl

Malaysia

Maldives

Mali

Malta

Marshall Islands

Mauritania

Mauritius

GAZETTEER OF STATES CONTINUED

Mexico

Main religion: Roman Catholic
Government: federal republic
Currency: 1 Mexican peso = 100 centavos

MOLDOVA (Europe)
Area: 13,067 sq miles
Population: 4,434,547
Capital city: Chisinau
Main languages: Moldovan, Russian, Gagauz
Main religion: Eastern Orthodox
Government: republic
Currency: 1 Moldovan leu = 100 bani

Moldova

MONACO (Europe)
Area: 0.75 sq miles
Population: 31,987
Capital city: Monaco
Main languages: French, Monegasque, Italian
Main religion: Roman Catholic
Government: constitutional monarchy
Currency: 1 euro = 100 cents

MONGOLIA (Asia)
Area: 604,247 sq miles
Population: 2,694,432
Capital city: Ulan Bator
Main language: Khalkha Mongol
Main religion: Tibetan Buddist Lamaist
Government: republic
Currency: 1 tugrik = 100 mongos

Monaco

MOROCCO (Africa)
Area: 172,413 sq miles
Population: 31,167,783
Capital city: Rabat
Main languages: Arabic, Berber, French
Main religion: Muslim
Government: constitutional monarchy
Currency: 1 Moroccan dirham = 100 centimes

Mongolia

MOZAMBIQUE (Africa)
Area: 309,494 sq miles
Population: 19,607,519
Capital city: Maputo
Main languages: Makua, Tsonga, Portuguese
Main religions: indigenous, Christian, Muslim
Government: republic
Currency: 1 metical = 100 centavos

Morocco

NAMIBIA (Africa)
Area: 318,694 sq miles
Population: 1,820,916
Capital city: Windhoek
Main languages: Afrikaans, German, English
Main religions: Christian, indigenous
Government: republic
Currency: 1 Namibian dollar = 100 cents

Mozambique

NAURU (Australasia/Oceania)
Area: 8 sq miles
Population: 12,329
Capital city: Yaren
Main languages: Nauruan, English
Main religion: Christian
Government: republic
Currency: 1 Australian dollar = 100 cents

Namibia

NEPAL (Asia)
Area: 54,363 sq miles
Population: 25,873,917
Capital city: Kathmandu
Main languages: Nepali, Maithili
Main religions: Hindu, Buddhist
Government: constitutional monarchy
Currency: 1 Nepalese rupee = 100 paisa

NETHERLANDS (Europe)
Area: 16,036 sq miles
Population: 16,067,754
Capital cities: Amsterdam, The Hague
Main language: Dutch
Main religion: Christian
Government: constitutional monarchy
Currency: 1 euro = 100 cents

NEW ZEALAND (Australasia/Oceania)
Area: 103,737 sq miles
Population: 3,908,037
Capital city: Wellington
Main languages: English, Maori
Main religion: Christian
Government: parliamentary democracy
Currency: 1 New Zealand dollar = 100 cents

NICARAGUA (North America)
Area: 49,998 sq miles
Population: 5,023,818
Capital city: Managua
Main language: Spanish
Main religion: Roman Catholic
Government: republic
Currency: 1 gold cordoba = 100 centavos

NIGER (Africa)
Area: 489,189 sq miles
Population: 10,639,744
Capital city: Niamey
Main languages: Hausa, Djerma, French
Main religion: Muslim
Government: republic
Currency: 1 CFA* franc = 100 centimes

NIGERIA (Africa)
Area: 356,667 sq miles
Population: 129,934,911
Capital city: Abuja
Main languages: Hausa, Yoruba, Igbo, English
Main religions: Muslim, Christian, indigenous
Government: republic
Currency: 1 naira = 100 kobo

NORTH KOREA (Asia)
Area: 46,540 sq miles
Population: 22,224,195
Capital city: Pyongyang
Main language: Korean
Main religions: Buddhist, Confucianist
Government: authoritarian socialist
Currency: 1 North Korean won = 100 chon

NORWAY (Europe)
Area: 125,181 sq miles
Population: 4,525,116
Capital city: Oslo
Main language: Norwegian

Nauru

Nepal

Netherlands

New Zealand

Nicaragua

Niger

Nigeria

North Korea

Norway

Oman

Pakistan

Palau

Panama

Papua New Guinea

Main religion: Evangelical Lutheran
Government: constitutional monarchy
Currency: 1 Norwegian krone = 100 oere

OMAN (Asia)
Area: 82,031 sq miles
Population: 2,713,462
Capital city: Muscat
Main languages: Arabic, English, Baluchi
Main religion: Muslim
Government: monarchy
Currency: 1 Omani rial = 1,000 baiza

PAKISTAN (Asia)
Area: 310,401 sq miles
Population: 147,663,429
Capital city: Islamabad
Main languages: Punjabi, Sindhi, Urdu, English
Main religion: Muslim
Government: federal republic
Currency: 1 Pakistani rupee = 100 paisa

PALAU (Australasia/Oceania)
Area: 177 sq miles
Population: 19,409
Capital city: Koror
Main languages: Palauan, English
Main religions: Christian, Modekngei
Government: democratic republic
Currency: 1 U.S. dollar = 100 cents

PANAMA (North America)
Area: 30,193 sq miles
Population: 2,882,329
Capital city: Panama City
Main languages: Spanish, English
Main religions: Roman Catholic, Protestant
Government: democracy
Currency: 1 balboa = 100 centesimos

PAPUA NEW GUINEA
(Australasia/Oceania)
Area: 178,703 sq miles
Population: 5,172,033
Capital city: Port Moresby
Main languages: Tok Pisin, Hiri Motu, English
Main religions: Christian, indigenous
Government: parliamentary democracy
Currency: 1 kina = 100 toea

PARAGUAY (South America)
Area: 157,046 sq miles
Population: 5,884,491
Capital city: Asuncion
Main languages: Guarani, Spanish
Main religion: Roman Catholic
Government: republic
Currency: 1 guarani = 100 centimos

PERU (South America)
Area: 496,223 sq miles
Population: 27,949,639
Capital city: Lima
Main languages: Spanish, Quechua, Aymara
Main religion: Roman Catholic
Government: republic
Currency: 1 nuevo sol = 100 centimos

PHILIPPINES (Asia)
Area: 115,830 sq miles
Population: 84,525,639
Capital city: Manila
Main languages: Tagalog, English, Ilocano
Main religion: Roman Catholic
Government: republic
Currency: 1 Philippine peso = 100 centavos

POLAND (Europe)
Area: 120,727 sq miles
Population: 38,625,478
Capital city: Warsaw
Main language: Polish
Main religion: Roman Catholic
Government: democratic republic
Currency: 1 zloty = 100 groszy

PORTUGAL (Europe)
Area: 35,672 sq miles
Population: 10,084,245
Capital city: Lisbon
Main language: Portuguese
Main religion: Roman Catholic
Government: parliamentary democracy
Currency: 1 euro = 100 cents

QATAR (Asia)
Area: 4,416 sq miles
Population: 793,341
Capital city: Doha
Main languages: Arabic, English
Main religion: Muslim
Government: monarchy
Currency: 1 Qatari riyal = 100 dirhams

ROMANIA (Europe)
Area: 91,699 sq miles
Population: 22,317,730
Capital city: Bucharest
Main languages: Romanian, Hungarian, German
Main religion: Romanian Orthodox
Government: republic
Currency: 1 leu = 100 bani

RUSSIA (Europe and Asia)
Area: 6,592,735 sq miles
Population: 144,978,573
Capital city: Moscow
Main language: Russian
Main religions: Russian Orthodox, Muslim
Government: federal government
Currency: 1 ruble = 100 kopeks

RWANDA (Africa)
Area: 10,169 sq miles
Population: 7,398,074
Capital city: Kigali
Main languages: Kinyarwanda, French, English, Swahili
Main religions: Roman Catholic, Protestant, Adventist
Government: republic
Currency: 1 Rwandan franc = 100 centimes

SAINT KITTS AND NEVIS
(North America)
Area: 101 sq miles
Population: 38,736

Paraguay

• Peru

Philippines

Poland

Portugal

Qatar

Romania

GAZETTEER OF STATES CONTINUED

Russia

Capital city: Basseterre
Main language: English
Main religions: Protestant, Roman Catholic
Government: constitutional monarchy
Currency: 1 East Caribbean dollar = 100 cents

SAINT LUCIA (North America)
Area: 239 sq miles
Population: 160,145
Capital city: Castries
Main languages: French patois, English
Main religion: Roman Catholic
Government: parliamentary democracy
Currency: 1 East Caribbean dollar = 100 cents

Rwanda

SAINT VINCENT AND THE GRENADINES (North America)
Area: 150 sq miles
Population: 116,394
Capital city: Kingstown
Main languages: English, French patois
Main religions: Protestant, Roman Catholic
Government: parliamentary democracy
Currency: 1 East Caribbean dollar = 100 cents

SAMOA (Australasia/Oceania)
Area: 1,104 sq miles
Population: 178,631
Capital city: Apia
Main languages: Samoan, English
Main religion: Christian
Government: constitutional monarchy
Currency: 1 tala = 100 sene

Saint Kitts and Nevis

SAN MARINO (Europe)
Area: 24 sq miles
Population: 27,730
Capital city: San Marino
Main language: Italian
Main religion: Roman Catholic
Government: republic
Currency: 1 euro = 100 cents

SAO TOME AND PRINCIPE (Africa)
Area: 386 sq miles
Population: 170,372
Capital city: Sao Tome
Main languages: Crioulo* dialects, Portuguese
Main religion: Christian
Government: republic
Currency: 1 dobra = 100 centimos

Saint Lucia

SAUDI ARABIA (Asia)
Area: 756,987 sq miles
Population: 23,513,330
Capital city: Riyadh
Main language: Arabic
Main religion: Muslim
Government: monarchy
Currency: 1 Saudi riyal = 100 halalah

Saint Vincent and the Grenadines

SENEGAL (Africa)
Area: 75,749 sq miles
Population: 10,589,571
Capital city: Dakar
Main languages: Wolof, French, Pulaar
Main religion: Muslim
Government: democratic republic
Currency: 1 CFA* franc = 100 centimes

Samoa

• San Marino

SERBIA AND MONTENEGRO (Europe)
Area: 39,517 sq miles
Population: 10,656,929
Capital city: Belgrade
Main language: Serbian
Main religions: Orthodox, Muslim
Government: republic
Currency: 1 Yugoslavian new dinar = 100 paras

SEYCHELLES (Africa)
Area: 176 sq miles
Population: 80,098
Capital city: Victoria
Main languages: Seselwa, English, French
Main religion: Roman Catholic
Government: republic
Currency: 1 Seychelles rupee = 100 cents

SIERRA LEONE (Africa)
Area: 27,699 sq miles
Population: 5,614,743
Capital city: Freetown
Main languages: Mende, Temne, Krio, English
Main religions: Muslim, indigenous, Christian
Government: constitutional democracy
Currency: 1 leone = 100 cents

SINGAPORE (Asia)
Area: 267 sq miles
Population: 4,452,732
Capital city: Singapore
Main languages: Chinese, Malay, English, Tamil
Main religions: Buddhist, Muslim
Government: parliamentary republic
Currency: 1 Singapore dollar = 100 cents

SLOVAKIA (Europe)
Area: 18,859 sq miles
Population: 5,422,366
Capital city: Bratislava
Main languages: Slovak, Hungarian
Main religion: Roman Catholic
Government: parliamentary democracy
Currency: 1 koruna = 100 halierov

SLOVENIA (Europe)
Area: 7,827 sq miles
Population: 1,932,917
Capital city: Ljubljana
Main language: Slovenian
Main religion: Roman Catholic
Government: democratic republic
Currency: 1 tolar = 100 stotins

SOLOMON ISLANDS (Australasia/Oceania)
Area: 10,985 sq miles
Population: 494,786
Capital city: Honiara
Main languages: Solomon pidgin, Kwara'ae, To'abaita, English
Main religion: Christian
Government: parliamentary democracy
Currency: 1 Solomon Islands dollar = 100 cents

SOMALIA (Africa)
Area: 246,199 sq miles
Population: 7,753,310
Capital city: Mogadishu
Main languages: Somali, Arabic, Oromo

Sao Tome and Principe

Saudi Arabia

Senegal

Serbia and Montenegro

Seychelles

Sierra Leone

Singapore

*CFA = Communaute Financiere Africaine; Crioulo = a blend of Portuguese and West African

Slovakia

• **Slovenia**

Solomon Islands

Somalia

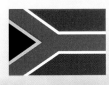

South Africa

South Korea

• **Spain**

Main religion: Sunni Muslim
Government: currently has no government
Currency: 1 Somali shilling = 100 cents

SOUTH AFRICA (Africa)
Area: 471,008 sq miles
Population: 43,647,658
Capital cities: Pretoria, Cape Town, Bloemfontein
Main languages: Zulu, Xhosa, Afrikaans, Pedi, English, Tswana, Sotho, Tsonga, Swati, Venda, Ndebele
Main religions: Christian, indigenous
Government: republic
Currency: 1 rand = 100 cents

SOUTH KOREA (Asia)
Area: 38,023 sq miles
Population: 48,324,000
Capital city: Seoul
Main language: Korean
Main religions: Christian, Buddhist
Government: republic
Currency: 1 South Korean won = 100 chun

SPAIN (Europe)
Area: 194,898 sq miles
Population: 40,077,100
Capital city: Madrid
Main languages: Castilian Spanish, Catalan
Main religion: Roman Catholic
Government: constitutional monarchy
Currency: 1 euro = 100 cents

SRI LANKA (Asia)
Area: 25,332 sq miles
Population: 19,576,783
Capital cities: Colombo, Sri Jayewardenepura Kotte
Main languages: Sinhala, Tamil, English
Main religions: Buddhist, Hindu
Government: republic
Currency: 1 Sri Lankan rupee = 100 cents

SUDAN (Africa)
Area: 967,493 sq miles
Population: 37,090,298
Capital city: Khartoum
Main languages: Arabic, English
Main religions: Sunni Muslim, indigenous
Government: Islamic republic
Currency: 1 Sudanese dinar = 100 piastres

SURINAM (South America)
Area: 63,039 sq miles
Population: 436,494
Capital city: Paramaribo
Main languages: Sranang Tongo, Dutch, English
Main religions: Christian, Hindu, Muslim
Government: constitutional democracy
Currency: 1 Surinamese guilder = 100 cents

SWAZILAND (Africa)
Area: 6,704 sq miles
Population: 1,123,605
Capital cities: Mbabane, Lobamba

Main languages: Swati, English
Main religions: Christian, indigenous, Muslim
Government: monarchy
Currency: 1 lilangeni = 100 cents

SWEDEN (Europe)
Area: 173,731 sq miles
Population: 8,876,744
Capital city: Stockholm
Main language: Swedish
Main religion: Lutheran
Government: constitutional monarchy
Currency: 1 Swedish krona = 100 oere

SWITZERLAND (Europe)
Area: 15,942 sq miles
Population: 7,301,994
Capital city: Bern
Main languages: German, French, Italian
Main religions: Roman Catholic, Protestant
Government: federal republic
Currency: 1 Swiss franc = 100 centimes

SYRIA (Asia)
Area: 71,498 sq miles
Population: 17,155,814
Capital city: Damascus
Main languages: Arabic, Kurdish
Main religions: Muslim, Christian
Government: republic under military regime
Currency: 1 Syrian pound = 100 piastres

TAIWAN (Asia)
Area: 13,892 sq miles
Population: 22,548,009
Capital city: Taipei
Main languages: Taiwanese, Mandarin Chinese, Hakka Chinese
Main religions: Buddhist, Confucian, Daoist
Government: democracy
Currency: 1 New Taiwan dollar = 100 cents

TAJIKISTAN (Asia)
Area: 55,251 sq miles
Population: 6,719,567
Capital city: Dushanbe
Main languages: Tajik, Russian
Main religion: Sunni Muslim
Government: republic
Currency: 1 somoni = 100 dirams

TANZANIA (Africa)
Area: 364,898 sq miles
Population: 37,187,939
Capital cities: Dar es Salaam, Dodoma
Main languages: Swahili, English, Sukuma
Main religions: Christian, Muslim, indigenous
Government: republic
Currency: 1 Tanzanian shilling = 100 cents

THAILAND (Asia)
Area: 198,455 sq miles
Population: 62,354,402
Capital city: Bangkok
Main languages: Thai, English, Chaochow
Main religion: Buddhist
Government: constitutional monarchy
Currency: 1 baht = 100 satang

Sri Lanka

Sudan

Surinam

Swaziland

Sweden

Switzerland

Syria

GAZETTEER OF STATES

Taiwan

Tajikistan

Tanzania

Thailand

Togo

Tonga

TOGO (Africa)
Area: 21,925 sq miles
Population: 5,285,501
Capital city: Lome
Main languages: Mina, Ewe, Kabye, French
Main religions: indigenous, Christian, Muslim
Government: republic
Currency: 1 CFA* franc = 100 centimes

TONGA (Australasia/Oceania)
Area: 289 sq miles
Population: 106,137
Capital city: Nukualofa
Main languages: Tongan, English
Main religion: Christian
Government: constitutional monarchy
Currency: 1 pa'anga = 100 seniti

TRINIDAD AND TOBAGO (North America)
Area: 1,980 sq miles
Population: 1,163,724
Capital city: Port-of-Spain
Main languages: English, French, Spanish, Hindi
Main religions: Christian, Hindu
Government: parliamentary democracy
Currency: 1 Trinidad and Tobago dollar = 100 cents

TUNISIA (Africa)
Area: 63,170 sq miles
Population: 9,815,644
Capital city: Tunis
Main languages: Arabic, French
Main religion: Muslim
Government: republic
Currency: 1 Tunisian dinar = 1,000 millimes

TURKEY (Europe and Asia)
Area: 301,382 sq miles
Population: 67,308,928
Capital city: Ankara
Main language: Turkish
Main religion: Muslim
Government: democratic republic
Currency: 1 Turkish lira = 100 kurus

TURKMENISTAN (Asia)
Area: 188,455 sq miles
Population: 4,688,963
Capital city: Ashgabat (Ashkhabad)
Main languages: Turkmen, Russian
Main religion: Muslim
Government: republic
Currency: 1 Turkmen manat = 100 tenesi

TUVALU (Australasia/Oceania)
Area: 10 sq miles
Population: 11,146
Capital city: Funafuti
Main languages: Tuvaluan, English
Main religion: Congregationalist
Government: constitutional monarchy
Currency: 1 Tuvaluan dollar or 1 Australian dollar = 100 cents

UGANDA (Africa)
Area: 91,135 sq miles
Population: 24,699,073

Capital city: Kampala
Main languages: Luganda, English, Swahili
Main religions: Christian, Muslim, indigenous
Government: republic
Currency: 1 Ugandan shilling = 100 cents

UKRAINE (Europe)
Area: 233,089 sq miles
Population: 48,396,470
Capital city: Kiev
Main languages: Ukrainian, Russian
Main religions: Ukrainian Orthodox
Government: republic
Currency: 1 hryvnia = 100 kopiykas

UNITED ARAB EMIRATES (Asia)
Area: 32,000 sq miles
Population: 2,445,989
Capital city: Abu Dhabi
Main languages: Arabic, English
Main religion: Muslim
Government: federation
Currency: 1 Emirati dirham = 100 fils

UNITED KINGDOM (Europe)
Area: 94,525 sq miles
Population: 59,778,002
Capital city: London
Main language: English
Main religions: Anglican, Roman Catholic
Government: constitutional monarchy
Currency: 1 British pound = 100 pence

UNITED STATES OF AMERICA (North America)
Area: 3,717,792 sq miles
Population: 280,562,489
Capital city: Washington D.C.
Main language: English
Main religions: Protestant, Roman Catholic
Government: federal republic
Currency: 1 U.S. dollar = 100 cents

URUGUAY (South America)
Area: 68,039 sq miles
Population: 3,386,575
Capital city: Montevideo
Main language: Spanish
Main religion: Roman Catholic
Government: republic
Currency: 1 Uruguayan peso = 100 centesimos

UZBEKISTAN (Asia)
Area: 172,741 sq miles
Population: 25,563,441
Capital city: Tashkent
Main languages: Uzbek, Russian
Main religions: Muslim, Eastern Orthodox
Government: republic
Currency: 1 Uzbekistani sum = 100 tyyn

VANUATU (Australasia/Oceania)
Area: 4,706 sq miles
Population: 196,178
Capital city: Port-Vila
Main languages: Bislama, French, English
Main religion: Christian
Government: republic
Currency: 1 vatu = 100 centimes

Trinidad and Tobago

Tunisia

Turkey

Turkmenistan

Tuvalu

Uganda

*CFA = Communaute Financiere Africaine

Ukraine

VATICAN CITY (Europe)
Area: 0.17 sq miles
Population: 900
Capital city: Vatican City
Main languages: Italian, Latin
Main religion: Roman Catholic
Government: led by the Pope
Currency: 1 euro = 100 cents

VENEZUELA (South America)
Area: 352,143 sq miles
Population: 24,287,670
Capital city: Caracas
Main language: Spanish
Main religion: Roman Catholic
Government: federal republic
Currency: 1 bolivar = 100 centimos

VIETNAM (Asia)
Area: 127,243 sq miles
Population: 81,098,416
Capital city: Hanoi
Main languages: Vietnamese, French,
English, Khmer, Chinese
Main religion: Buddhist
Government: Communist state
Currency: 1 new dong = 100 xu

YEMEN (Asia)
Area: 203,849 sq miles
Population: 18,701,257
Capital city: Sana
Main language: Arabic
Main religion: Muslim
Government: republic
Currency: 1 Yemeni rial = 100 fils

ZAMBIA (Africa)
Area: 290,584 sq miles
Population: 9,959,037
Capital city: Lusaka
Main languages: Bemba, Tonga, Nyanja,
English
Main religions: Christian, Muslim, Hindu
Government: republic
Currency: 1 Zambian kwacha = 100 ngwee

ZIMBABWE (Africa)
Area: 150,803 sq miles
Population: 11,376,676
Capital city: Harare
Main languages: Shona, Ndebele, English
Main religions: Christian, indigenous
Government: republic
Currency: 1 Zimbabwean dollar = 100 cents

Vanuatu

Vatican City

Venezuela

Vietnam

Yemen

Zambia

Zimbabwe

**United
Arab Emirates**

United Kingdom

**United States
of America**

Uruguay

Uzbekistan

THE UNITED NATIONS

The United Nations (U.N.) is an organization that aims to bring countries together to work for peace and development. Of the world's 193 states, 191 belong to the U.N. Those that don't belong are Taiwan and the Vatican City.

Internet links

For a link to a website where you can match countries and their flags in a game, go to
www.usborne-quicklinks.com

Kofi Annan, the Secretary-General of the U.N., with U.N. ambassador Pele

163

These statues of Buddha stand in a temple in Bangkok, Thailand.

WORLD
HISTORY DATES

PREHISTORIC WORLD

Scientists believe that the Earth was formed about 4,550 million years ago. Experts divide prehistoric time into several periods, each lasting many millions of years. The diagram on these two pages shows the main prehistoric periods. You can also see when different plants and animals appeared on the Earth.

440 MILLION YEARS AGO

SILURIAN PERIOD

The first land plants

ORDOVICIAN PERIOD

The first fish

408 MILLION YEARS AGO

360 MILLION YEARS AGO

The first amphibians

DEVONIAN PERIOD

The first creatures on land

510 MILLION YEARS AGO

CAMBRIAN PERIOD

The first creatures with skeletons

550 MILLION YEARS AGO

The first soft-bodied creatures

PRECAMBRIAN PERIOD

The first living cells

The Earth's surface is covered with volcanoes.

4,550 MILLION YEARS AGO
The Earth is formed.

Internet links

For a link to a website where you can be a virtual time traveler and explore the Universe from its creation to the present day and into the future, go to
www.usborne-quicklinks.com

The first flying insects

CARBONIFEROUS PERIOD

290 MILLION YEARS AGO

The first forests

The first swimming reptiles

PERMIAN PERIOD

245 MILLION YEARS AGO

TRIASSIC PERIOD

The first dinosaurs

200 MILLION YEARS AGO

JURASSIC PERIOD

The first reptiles

The first mammals

The first birds

144 MILLION YEARS AGO

CRETACEOUS PERIOD

The first flowering plants

66 MILLION YEARS AGO

The first humans

The first horses

TERTIARY PERIOD

The first elephants

The first grasses

The first cats

1.8 MILLION YEARS AGO

QUATERNARY PERIOD

The dinosaurs died out around 65 million years ago.

ANCIENT WORLD

DATE	THE AMERICAS	EUROPE	AFRICA
BEFORE 10,000BC	By c.13,000BC People arrive in North America.		
10,000BC	c.6000BC Farming begins in Central America.	c.6000BC Farming begins in Greece and spreads across Europe.	c.6000BC People in the Sahara tame cattle.
			Saharan rock painting
5000BC		c.3000–1500BC Stonehenge is built in Britain.	c.5000BC Farming begins in the Nile Valley.
			c.3100BC King Menes unites Upper and Lower Egypt.
			c.2686BC The Old Kingdom begins in Egypt.
		c.1900–1450BC The Minoans build palaces on Crete.	c.2530BC The Egyptians start building the Great Pyramid at Giza.
			c.2040BC The Middle Kingdom begins.
		c.1600BC The Mycenaeans become powerful in Greece.	c.1720BC The Hyksos invade Egypt. The Middle Kingdom ends.
	Olmec ball-players	*Mycenaean woman*	c.1570BC The New Kingdom begins.
	c.1200BC The Olmecs build temples. The Chavín way of life begins.	c.1450BC The Mycenaeans invade Crete. c.1100BC The Greek Dark Ages begin.	c.1450BC The Egyptian Empire is at its largest under King Tuthmosis III.
1000BC	c.1000BC The Adena build earth mounds.	c.800BC The Celtic way of life spreads across western Europe.	c.814BC The city of Carthage is built by the Phoenicians.
	The Great Serpent Mound	c.776BC The first Olympic Games	
		753BC The city of Rome is set up, according to legend.	
		c.509BC Rome becomes a republic.	
500BC		c.500–350BC The Greeks are at their most successful.	*Nok sculpture*
	c.300BC The Hopewell take over from the Adena.	431–404BC The Peloponnesian War	c.500BC The Nok way of life begins.
		356BC Alexander the Great is born.	332BC Alexander the Great conquers Egypt.
	c.200BC The Nazca start to draw lines in the desert.	44BC Julius Caesar is murdered.	146BC The Romans destroy Carthage.
		27BC Augustus becomes the first Emperor of Rome.	30BC The Romans conquer Egypt.
AD1	c.AD1–700 The Moche are ruled by warrior-priests.	AD117 The Roman Empire is at its largest under the Emperor Trajan.	c.AD100 The kingdom of Axum becomes powerful.
	c.AD250–900 The Maya are at their most successful.	AD395 The Roman Empire splits permanently in two.	
	c.AD500 Teotihuacán is the sixth-largest city in the world.	AD476 The Western Roman Empire collapses.	c.AD500 The Bantu people reach southern Africa.

ASIA			AUSTRALASIA
THE MIDDLE EAST	SOUTH ASIA	THE FAR EAST	

c.40,000BC People known as Aboriginals arrive in Australia.

Australian Aboriginal

c.10,000BC Farming begins in the Fertile Crescent.

c.9000BC The Jomon people of Japan hunt and fish for food.

c.3500BC The wheel is invented in Sumer. *Sumerian wheel*

c.3500BC Farmers settle in the Indus Valley.

c.5000BC Farming begins in China.

c.3300BC Writing is invented in Sumer.

c.2700BC Silk is first made.

c.2350BC Sargon of Akkad creates the world's first empire.

c.2500–1800BC The Indus Valley people are at their most successful.

c.2000BC The Hittites settle in Anatolia.

c.1792–1750BC King Hammurabi rules Babylon.

1766–1027BC The Shang kings rule China.

c.1400BC The first alphabet is invented in Canaan.

c.1500BC The Aryans arrive in the Indus Valley.

c.1400BC People in China write on oracle bones.

c.1250BC The Hebrews arrive in Canaan.

c.1500BC People begin settling on islands in the Pacific Ocean.

c.1200BC The Phoenicians become successful sailors and traders.

c.1000–663BC The Assyrians build up a strong empire.

1027BC The Zhou kings take control of China.

c.965–928BC King Solomon rules Israel.

605–562BC King Nebuchadnezzar II rules the Babylonian Empire.

c.560BC Siddhartha Gautama (the Buddha) is born.

559–530BC King Cyrus II rules Persia and builds up an empire.

Confucius

551BC Confucius is born.

490–479BC Wars between the Persians and the Greeks

c.500BC Farming begins in Japan.

481–221BC The Warring States Period in China

331BC Alexander the Great defeats the Persians.

221BC Qin Shi Huangdi becomes China's first emperor.

Alexander the Great

272–231BC Asoka rules the Mauryan Empire.

202BC The Han Dynasty begins.

64BC The Romans conquer parts of the Middle East.

c.AD29 Jesus Christ is crucified.

c.AD100 Paper is invented in China.

Yamato warrior

Jesus on the cross

AD320-535 The Gupta Empire in India

c.AD300 The Yamato tribe rules in Japan.

MEDIEVAL WORLD

DATE	THE AMERICAS	EUROPE	AFRICA
Before 500		c.450 The Angles, Saxons and Jutes begin to rule Britain.	429 The Vandals invade North Africa.
500	c.600 The Maya are at their most successful. *Mayan mask*	481–511 Clovis creates the kingdom of the Franks. 507 The Visigoths invade Spain. 527–565 Justinian rules the Byzantine Empire. *Coin showing Justinian*	533 The Byzantines conquer North Africa. 697 The Arabs conquer North Africa.
700	c.700 The Mississippi people start to build towns. c.850 Many Mayan towns are abandoned.	711 The Moors invade Spain. c.790 The Vikings begin raiding Europe. 800–814 Charlemagne rules his Empire. c.862 Rurik creates a kingdom in Russia.	c.700 The kingdom of Ghana is at its most successful.
900	c.900 The Pueblo people start to build towns. c.900–1200 The Toltecs are powerful. c.1000 Leif Ericson reaches North America.	962–973 Otto I is the first Holy Roman Emperor. *Emperor Otto's crown* 1037–1492 The Christians win back Spain from the Moors. 1054 The Church in eastern Europe splits from the Church in western Europe. 1066 The Normans conquer England.	969–1171 The Fatimids rule Egypt. c.1000 The kingdoms of Benin and Ife are created.
1100	c.1100 The Chimú start to build their Empire.	c.1100 The Viking raids end. 1215 King John of England signs Magna Carta. c.1250–1480 The Mongols rule southern Russia. *King John*	c.1200 The kingdom of Mali is created. 1250–1517 The Mamelukes rule Egypt.
1300	c.1300 The Pueblo people abandon their towns. c.1345 The Aztecs start to build their Empire. *Aztec warrior* 1438 The Incas start to build their Empire.	c.1300 The city of Moscow starts to become powerful. 1337–1453 The French and the English fight the Hundred Years' War. 1347–1353 The Black Death spreads through Europe. c.1350 The Renaissance begins in Italy. 1378–1417 Rival popes rule in Avignon and Rome. *Florence Cathedral*	c.1350 The city of Great Zimbabwe is at its largest.
1450	1492 Columbus discovers the West Indies.	1453 The Ottoman Turks capture Constantinople and the Byzantine Empire collapses.	c.1450 The Portuguese start trading in West Africa.

	ASIA		AUSTRALASIA
THE MIDDLE EAST	**SOUTH ASIA**	**THE FAR EAST**	
			c.400 Settlers reach Easter Island.
c.570–632 The life of Mohammed		*Sui Emperor's boat*	
632 Arab caliphs (rulers) start to build the Islamic Empire.		581 The Sui dynasty begins in China. 618 The Tang dynasty begins in China.	
750 The Abbasid Caliphs start to rule the Islamic Empire from Baghdad.	711 The Arabs invade northern India. 886 The Chola kingdom is created in southern India.	802 The Khmer kingdom is created in Cambodia. 858 The Fujiwara family takes control in Japan. 868 The earliest printed book is produced in China.	c.750 The Maoris reach New Zealand. *Maori good luck charm*
1055 The Seljuk Turks capture Baghdad and control the Islamic Empire. 1071 The Seljuk Turks defeat the Byzantines at the Battle of Manzikert. 1096 The Crusades begin. 1099 The Crusaders capture parts of Palestine.		960 The Sung dynasty begins in China. *Painting in the style of the Sung dynasty era*	c.1000 The Easter Islanders start to build stone heads.
Osman I 1258 The Mongols capture Baghdad. 1290 Osman I starts to build the Ottoman Empire. 1291 The Crusades end.	1206 The Sultans of Delhi start to rule northern India.	1192 Shoguns start to take control in Japan. c.1230 The Sukhothai kingdom is created in Thailand. 1206–1226 Genghis Khan builds the Mongol Empire. 1279–1368 The Mongols rule China.	
1360–1405 Tamerlane builds a new Mongol Empire. *Tamerlane*	1336 The kingdom of Vijayanagar is created in southern India. 1398 Tamerlane invades northern India.	*Statue from the Sukhothai kingdom* 1368 The Ming dynasty begins in China.	

THE LAST 500 YEARS

DATE	THE AMERICAS	EUROPE	AFRICA
1500	1500s Portuguese settlers arrive in Brazil. 1519–1521 Spanish conquistadors conquer the Aztecs. 1532–1534 Spanish conquistadors conquer the Incas. *Inca priest* 1580s The Slave Trade begins.	1520s The Reformation begins. 1545 The Counter-Reformation begins. 1547–1584 Ivan the Terrible is Tsar of Russia. 1556 Charles V divides the Habsburg Empire in two. *Flag of the Habsburg Empire* 1558–1603 Elizabeth I is Queen of England. 1581 The Republic of the United Netherlands is created.	1505 The Portuguese establish ports on the coast of East Africa. 1516–1560 The Ottoman Turks conquer large areas of North Africa.
1600	1603 French settlers start to set up colonies in Canada. 1620 The *Mayflower* arrives in North America carrying English pilgrims. 1699 The French create the colony of Louisiana.	1618–1648 The Thirty Years' War 1630s Galileo proves that the Earth travels around the Sun. 1642–1646 The English Civil War 1643–1715 Louis XIV is King of France. 1660s Isaac Newton discovers the laws of gravity. 1689–1725 Peter the Great is Tsar of Russia.	1616 Dutch and French traders set up trading posts in West Africa. 1652 Dutch settlers conquer Cape Colony.
1700	1759 British troops capture Quebec from the French. 1776 American colonists sign the Declaration of Independence. 1789 George Washington becomes the first President of the U.S.A.	1740–1780 Maria Theresa rules the Habsburg Empire. 1740–1786 Frederick the Great is King of Prussia. 1750s The Industrial Revolution begins in Britain. 1762–1796 Catherine the Great is Tsarina of Russia. 1789 The French Revolution begins. 1799–1815 Napoleon Bonaparte rules France. *Ribbons worn by French Revolutionaries*	1700–1800 The African kingdoms of Benin, Oyo and Ashanti flourish. *Ashanti gold ornament*
1800	1816–1824 Simon Bolivar and José de San Martín win independence for colonies in South America. 1860 Abraham Lincoln becomes President of the U.S.A. 1861–1865 The American Civil War 1888 Slavery ends throughout the Americas. *U.S. President Abraham Lincoln*	1848 Revolutions in many parts of Europe 1861 Italy is unified. 1871 Germany is unified. 1895 Karl Benz, a German engineer, builds the first motor car. 1895 The Lumière brothers give the first ever movie show, in Paris. *Benz's first motor car*	1806 Britain takes control of Cape Colony. 1836 The Boers set out on the Great Trek. 1841 David Livingstone starts to explore Africa. 1879 The Zulus are defeated by the British and the Boers. 1899 The Boer War begins.

ASIA

AUSTRALASIA

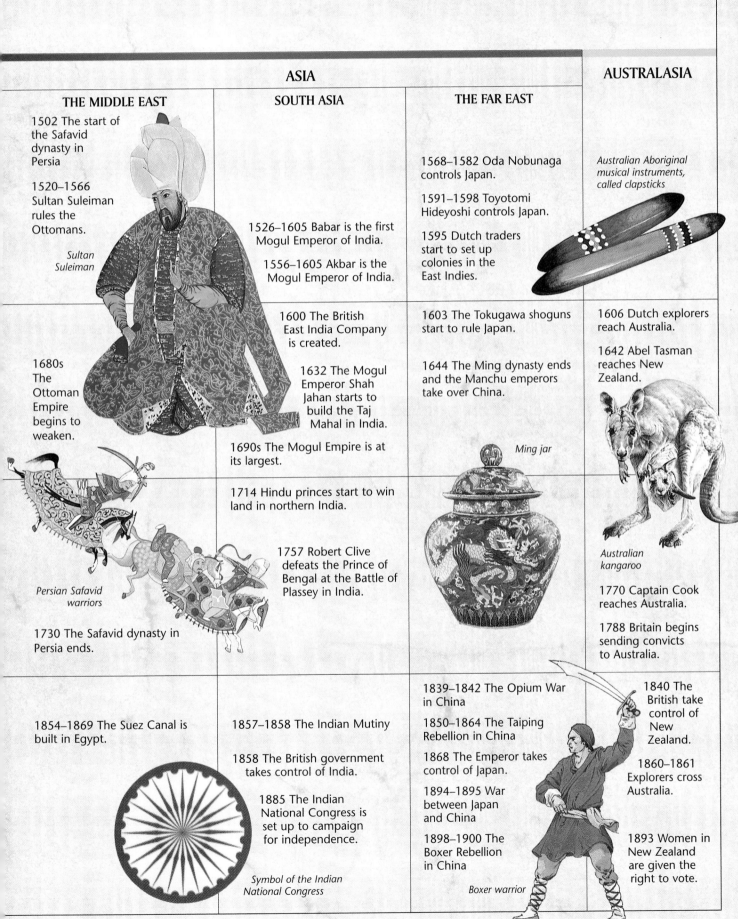

THE MIDDLE EAST

1502 The start of the Safavid dynasty in Persia

1520–1566 Sultan Suleiman rules the Ottomans.

Sultan Suleiman

1680s The Ottoman Empire begins to weaken.

Persian Safavid warriors

1730 The Safavid dynasty in Persia ends.

1854–1869 The Suez Canal is built in Egypt.

Symbol of the Indian National Congress

SOUTH ASIA

1526–1605 Babar is the first Mogul Emperor of India.

1556–1605 Akbar is the Mogul Emperor of India.

1600 The British East India Company is created.

1632 The Mogul Emperor Shah Jahan starts to build the Taj Mahal in India.

1690s The Mogul Empire is at its largest.

1714 Hindu princes start to win land in northern India.

1757 Robert Clive defeats the Prince of Bengal at the Battle of Plassey in India.

1857–1858 The Indian Mutiny

1858 The British government takes control of India.

1885 The Indian National Congress is set up to campaign for independence.

THE FAR EAST

1568–1582 Oda Nobunaga controls Japan.

1591–1598 Toyotomi Hideyoshi controls Japan.

1595 Dutch traders start to set up colonies in the East Indies.

1603 The Tokugawa shoguns start to rule Japan.

1644 The Ming dynasty ends and the Manchu emperors take over China.

Ming jar

1839–1842 The Opium War in China

1850–1864 The Taiping Rebellion in China

1868 The Emperor takes control of Japan.

1894–1895 War between Japan and China

1898–1900 The Boxer Rebellion in China

Boxer warrior

Australian Aboriginal musical instruments, called clapsticks

1606 Dutch explorers reach Australia.

1642 Abel Tasman reaches New Zealand.

Australian kangaroo

1770 Captain Cook reaches Australia.

1788 Britain begins sending convicts to Australia.

1840 The British take control of New Zealand.

1860–1861 Explorers cross Australia.

1893 Women in New Zealand are given the right to vote.

DATE	THE AMERICAS	EUROPE	AFRICA
1900	1914 Opening of the Panama Canal	1914–1918 World War I	1902 The Boer War ends.
	1917 U.S.A. joins World War I.	*Poppies from the battlefields of World War I*	1942 The Allies defeat the Germans at El Alamein in North Africa.
		1917 The Russian Revolution	
		1922 Benito Mussolini takes control of Italy.	1949 Apartheid is introduced in South Africa.
	1920 Prohibition begins in the U.S.A.	1928–1953 Josef Stalin controls the Soviet Union.	
	1927 *The Jazz Singer* is the first major movie with sound.	*Symbol of the Soviet Union*	
	1929 The Wall Street Crash	1933 Adolf Hitler becomes Chancellor of Germany.	
	1933 U.S. President Roosevelt launches the New Deal.	1939–1945 World War II	
		1948 Communists come to power in Czechoslovakia, Hungary, Romania, Bulgaria and Poland.	
	1941 The U.S.A. joins World War II after Pearl Harbor is bombed.	1949 Germany is divided into East and West.	
1950	1958 Jack Kilby invents the microchip.	1953 The structure of DNA is discovered in Britain by Francis Crick and James Watson.	1951 Libya becomes independent.
	1962 The Cuban Missile Crisis	1957 The Soviet Union launches *Sputnik I* into space.	1952–1955 Rebellion in Kenya against British rule
	1963 U.S. President Kennedy is assassinated.	1961 Yuri Gagarin of the Soviet Union is the first person in space.	1957 Ghana becomes independent.
	1968 Martin Luther King is assassinated.		1960–1980 Most African states become independent.
	1969 U.S. astronaut Neil Armstrong is the first man on the Moon.	1980 Solidarity is set up in Poland.	1967–1970 Civil war in Nigeria
	This photograph, of the U.S. astronaut Buzz Aldrin on the Moon, was taken by Neil Armstrong.	1985 Mikhail Gorbachev becomes leader of the Soviet Union.	
		1989 The Berlin Wall falls.	1984–1985 Ethiopia, Sudan and Chad suffer from serious famine (following 10 years of drought and civil war). Thousands die.
	1981 The U.S. space shuttle makes its first flight.	1989 Tim Berners-Lee invents the World Wide Web.	
	2001 Terrorists destroy the World Trade Center in New York, killing thousands of people.	1991 The Soviet Union splits up.	1990 Apartheid ends in South Africa.
		1991–1995 War in Yugoslavia	1991–1999 Civil war in Sierra Leone
		1998–1999 War in Kosovo	1994–1999 Nelson Mandela is President of South Africa.
Present day			

ASIA

AUSTRALASIA

THE MIDDLE EAST

SOUTH ASIA

THE FAR EAST

1918 The Turkish Ottoman Empire ends.

1922 The Republic of Turkey is formed.

1948 Israel is created.

1948–1949 Arab–Israeli War

Mahatma Gandhi

1920 Mahatma Gandhi starts a non-violent campaign for Indian independence.

1947 India and Pakistan become independent.

1904–1905 War between Japan and Russia

1910 Japan gains control of Korea.

1911 The Kuomintang start a revolution in China.

1912 The last Manchu Emperor of China gives up his throne.

1934 Communists in China set out on the Long March.

1941–1945 Japan fights the Allies in World War II.

1945 The first ever atomic bomb is dropped, on Hiroshima in Japan.

1949 Mao Zedong sets up the People's Republic of China.

1914–1918 Troops from Australia and New Zealand fight in World War I.

1939–1945 Troops from Australia and New Zealand fight in World War II.

1950–1953 The Korean War

1956 Second Arab–Israeli War

1967 Six-Day War between Israel and the Arab states

Israeli fighter plane

1973 Yom Kippur War between Israel and the Arab states

1979 Ayatollah Khomeini takes control of Iran.

1980–1988 Iran–Iraq War

1990 Iraq invades Kuwait.

1991 The Gulf War

1993 Peace agreement between Israel and the Palestinians.

1960 Mrs Bandaranaike of Ceylon is the first woman prime minister in the world.

1971 Bangladesh is formed.

1954 The Vietnam War starts.

1966 The Cultural Revolution in China

A Chinese Red Guard from the time of the Cultural Revolution

1973 The Vietnam War ends.

1976 Death of Mao Zedong

1989 Hundreds of Chinese protesters are killed in Tiananmen Square.

2002 East Timor becomes independent.

East Timorese women celebrate independence.

1993 The Native Titles Bill gives some land rights to Aboriginals in Australia.

1999 Australians vote to keep the British Queen as head of state.

This is Tokyo, Japan. It is currently the largest city in the world, with a population of over 26 million.

FACTS AND LISTS

TIME ZONES

We divide the Earth into many different time zones. Within each zone, people usually set their clocks to the same time. If you fly between two zones, you change your watch to the time in the new zone.

DIVIDING UP TIME

There are 25 main time zones. They are separated by one-hour intervals and there is a new time zone roughly every 15 degrees of longitude. There are 12 one-hour zones both ahead of and behind Greenwich Mean Time, or GMT, which is the time at the Prime Meridian Line. Governments can change their countries' time zones. So, for convenience, whole countries usually keep the same local time instead of sticking to the zones exactly. For example, China could be divided into several time zones, but instead the whole country keeps the same time. A few areas, such as India, Iran and parts of Australia, use non-standard half hour deviations.

SUMMER TIME

Some countries adjust their clocks in summer. For example, in the U.S. everybody's clocks go forward one hour. This is known as Daylight Saving Time or Summer Time. It is a way of getting more out of the days by having an extra hour of daylight in the evening. It reduces energy use because people don't use as much electricity for lights.

CHANGING DATES

On the opposite side of the world from the Prime Meridian Line is the International Date Line, which runs mostly through the Pacific Ocean and bends to avoid the land. Places to the west of it are 24 hours ahead of places to the east. This means that if you travel east across it you lose a day and if you travel west across it you gain a day.

This map shows the time zones. The times at the top of the map tell you the time in the different zones when it is noon at the Prime Meridian Line. There are two midnight zones, one for each day on either side of the International Date Line.

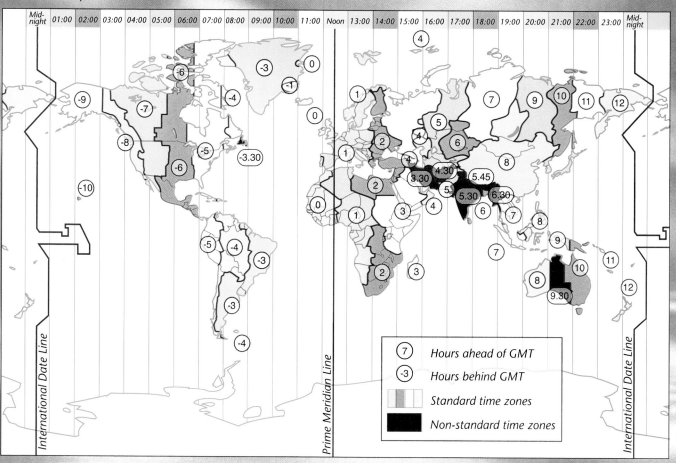

MEASUREMENTS

Measuring things, such as distance and area, is one of the most important parts of science. There are two main systems of measurement:

U.S. customary units and metric, used in Europe. This page shows how each system works, and also how to convert from one into the other.

U.S. CUSTOMARY UNITS

Length and distance
12 inches (")	= 1 foot (')
3 feet	= 1 yard (yd)
1,760 yards	= 1 mile
3 miles	= 1 league

Area
144 square inches	= 1 square foot
9 square feet	= 1 square yard
4,840 square yards	= 1 acre
640 acres	= 1 square mile

Mass
16 drams (dr)	= 1 ounce (oz)
16 ounces	= 1 pound (lb)

Volume and capacity
1,728 cubic inches	= 1 cubic foot (ft³)
27 cubic feet	= 1 cubic yard (yd³)
20 fluid ounces (fl oz)	= 1 pint (pt)
2 pints	= 1 quart (qt)
8 pints	= 1 gallon (gal)

METRIC MEASUREMENTS

Many metric measurements are spelled ending "er" in American English and "re" in British English.

Length and distance
10 millimeters (mm)	= 1 centimeter (cm)
100 centimeters	= 1 meter (m)
1,000 meters	= 1 kilometer (km)

Area
100 square mm (mm²)	= 1 square cm (cm²)
10,000cm²	= 1 square m (m²)
10,000m²	= 1 hectare (ha)
100 hectares	= 1 square km (km²)

Mass
1,000 grams (g)	= 1 kilogram (kg)
1,000 kilograms	= 1 tonne (t)

Volume and capacity
1 cubic cm (cm³/cc)	= 1 milliliter (ml)
1,000 milliliters	= 1 liter (l)
1,000 liters	= 1 cubic meter (m³)

CONVERSIONS

To convert between U.S. and metric figures, use this table with a calculator.

To convert	into	multiply by	To convert	into	multiply by
inches	cm	2.54	cm	inches	0.394
yards	m	0.914	m	yards	1.094
miles	km	1.609	km	miles	0.621
ounces	grams	28.35	grams	ounces	0.035
pounds	kilograms	0.454	kilograms	pounds	2.205
tons	tonnes	1.016	tonnes	tons	0.984
square inches	cm²	6.452	cm²	square inches	0.155
square yards	m²	0.836	m²	square yards	1.196
square miles	km²	2.59	km²	square miles	0.386
acres	hectares	0.405	hectares	acres	2.471
pints	liters	0.5683	liters	pints	1.76

MEASURING NATURE

It is not always easy to measure natural forces and substances precisely. The scales shown here work by measuring their effects or properties.

THE BEAUFORT SCALE OF WIND FORCE

The Beaufort scale was developed in 1805 by Sir Francis Beaufort, a British Navy Commander, to estimate wind speed at sea. In the 1920s it was extended to include precise wind speeds and adapted for use on land. While it is now rarely used by meteorologists (weather scientists), it is still a popular means of calculating wind speed without using instruments.

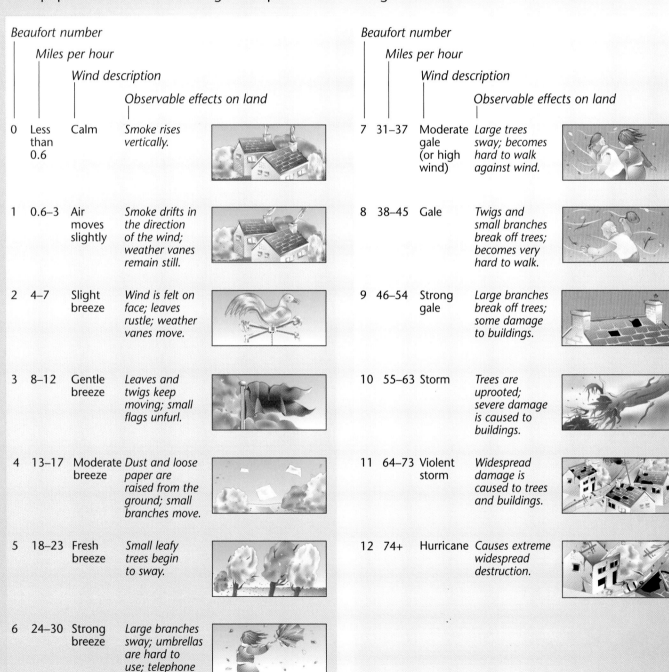

Beaufort number
  Miles per hour
    Wind description
      Observable effects on land

Beaufort number	Miles per hour	Wind description	Observable effects on land
0	Less than 0.6	Calm	Smoke rises vertically.
1	0.6–3	Air moves slightly	Smoke drifts in the direction of the wind; weather vanes remain still.
2	4–7	Slight breeze	Wind is felt on face; leaves rustle; weather vanes move.
3	8–12	Gentle breeze	Leaves and twigs keep moving; small flags unfurl.
4	13–17	Moderate breeze	Dust and loose paper are raised from the ground; small branches move.
5	18–23	Fresh breeze	Small leafy trees begin to sway.
6	24–30	Strong breeze	Large branches sway; umbrellas are hard to use; telephone wires whistle.

Beaufort number
  Miles per hour
    Wind description
      Observable effects on land

Beaufort number	Miles per hour	Wind description	Observable effects on land
7	31–37	Moderate gale (or high wind)	Large trees sway; becomes hard to walk against wind.
8	38–45	Gale	Twigs and small branches break off trees; becomes very hard to walk.
9	46–54	Strong gale	Large branches break off trees; some damage to buildings.
10	55–63	Storm	Trees are uprooted; severe damage is caused to buildings.
11	64–73	Violent storm	Widespread damage is caused to trees and buildings.
12	74+	Hurricane	Causes extreme widespread destruction.

MOHS HARDNESS SCALE

The hardness of minerals is measured on the Mohs scale, named after the German mineralogist, Friedrich Mohs (1773–1839). The scale has a sample mineral for each value, ranging from 1 (soft, crumbly talc) to 10 (diamond, the hardest mineral).

1. Talc
Very easily scratched with a fingernail.

2. Gypsum
Can be scratched by a fingernail.

3. Calcite
Very easily scratched with a knife, and just with a copper coin.

4. Fluorite
Easily scratched with a knife.

5. Apatite
Just scratched with a knife.

6. Orthoclase
Cannot be scratched with a knife. Just scratches glass.

7. Quartz
Scratches glass easily.

8. Beryl or topaz
Scratches glass very easily.

9. Corundum
Cuts glass.

10. Diamond
Cuts glass very easily. Will scratch corundum.

MEASURING EARTHQUAKES

Scientists use a device called a seismometer to measure the ground's vibrations during an earthquake. The vibrations are compared using a scale known as the Richter scale. Every whole value on the scale is equal to about 10 times the value below it, so for example an earthquake measuring 3 on the Richter scale is 10 times more powerful than one measuring 2. The Mercalli scale is also sometimes used. This compares the effects above ground, such as how badly buildings are damaged. This scale isn't considered as scientific though, as it relies on eyewitness accounts.

Mercalli	Effects	Richter	
1	Detectable only by seismometers.	0–2.9	
2	Only a few people on the upper floors of buildings will notice.	3–3.4	
3	Comparable to a heavy truck passing by. Hanging lights may swing.	3.5–4	
4	Comparable to a heavy truck crashing into a building. Windows and dishes rattle.	4.1–4.4	
5	Sleepers wake up. Almost everyone notices. Small objects move and drinks spill.	4.5–4.8	
6	Many people are frightened and run outdoors. Heavy furniture moves and pictures fall off walls.	4.9–5.4	
7	Cracks appear in walls. Tiles and bricks fall from buildings and it becomes difficult to stand up.	5.5–6	
8	Chimneys and some weaker buildings collapse. Mass panic may break out.	6.1–6.5	
9	Well-built houses collapse and underground pipes are damaged. Cracks appear in the ground.	6.6–7	
10	Landslides occur, railroad tracks buckle, rivers overflow and many stone buildings collapse.	7.1–7.3	
11	Most buildings and bridges are destroyed, and large cracks appear in the ground.	7.4–8.1	
12	The ground moves in waves, causing total destruction to land and buildings.	8.2+	

TEMPERATURE SCALES

There are three main scales for measuring temperature: the Fahrenheit scale (U.S.), the Celsius scale (metric) and the absolute temperature scale (SI), which is measured in kelvins.

The absolute temperature scale is seen as the most scientific because 0 kelvin (-273°C) is absolute zero: the temperature at which no more heat can be extracted from an object. Scientific theory holds that this point of absolute cold would be impossible to reach in practice.

Celsius (°C)	Fahrenheit (°F)	Kelvin (K)
110	230	383
100	212	373
90	194	363
80	176	353
70	158	343
60	140	333
50	122	323
40	104	313
30	86	303
20	68	293
10	50	283
0	32	273
-10	14	263
-20	-4	253
-30	-22	243
-40	-40	233
-50	-58	223
-60	-76	213
-70	-94	203
-80	-112	193
-90	-130	183
-100	-148	173
-110	-166	163

CONVERSIONS

Convert	into	calculation
°F	°C	-32,x5,÷9
°F	K	-32,x5,÷9,+273
°C	°F	x9,÷5,+32
°C	K	+273
K	°C	-273
K	°F	-273,x9,÷5,+32

SCIENTIFIC LAWS

Some scientific facts are accepted by all scientists as being true. They are often expressed as simple sentences (and/or mathematical equations). These are known as scientific laws.

COMMON SCIENTIFIC LAWS

Archimedes' principle The upthrust acting on an object is equal to the weight of the fluid that the object displaces.

Avogadro's law All gases of the same volume at the same temperature and pressure must contain the same number of molecules.

Bernoulli's principle When the flow of a fluid gets faster, its pressure is reduced.

Boyle's law The pressure and volume of a gas at a constant temperature are inversely proportional.

Charles' law (or **law of volumes**) The volume of an ideal gas at a constant pressure is proportional to its kelvin temperature.

Hooke's law The extension of a material is proportional to the force stretching it.

Law of conservation of energy Energy cannot be created or destroyed. It can only be changed into a different form.

Law of conservation of mass Matter cannot be created or destroyed in a chemical reaction.

Law of conservation of momentum After two objects have collided, their combined momentum remains the same.

Newton's first law of motion (or **principle of inertia**) If an object is not being acted on by a force, it will either stay still or continue moving at a constant speed in a straight line.

Newton's law of universal gravitation There is a gravitational force of attraction between any two objects with mass, which depends on the masses of the objects and the distance between them.

Newton's second law of motion Any resultant force acting on an object will change its motion. How much the motion changes depends on the object's mass and the size of the resultant force.

Newton's third law of motion When an object A exerts a force on an object B, then B exerts an equal and opposite force on A.

Pythagorean theorem The area of the square on the hypotenuse (side c in the diagram) of a right-angled triangle is equal to the sum of the areas of the squares on the other sides ($a^2 + b^2 = c^2$).

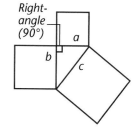

Right-angle (90°)

182

GEOMETRICAL SHAPES

There are two kinds of geometrical shapes. Planes are flat shapes with only two dimensions – length and width. Solids have three dimensions – length, width and height.

PLANES

Polygons
A polygon is a plane with three or more straight sides.

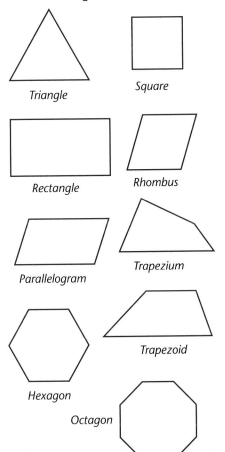

Triangle

Square

Rectangle

Rhombus

Parallelogram

Trapezium

Trapezoid

Hexagon

Octagon

Triangles
A triangle is a three-sided polygon.

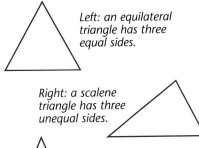

Left: an equilateral triangle has three equal sides.

Right: a scalene triangle has three unequal sides.

Left: an isosceles triangle has two equal sides.

Circles
A circle is a curved line on which all points are equally distant from the center. The parts of a circle are shown below.

The circumference is the length of the outer edge of the circle.

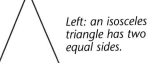

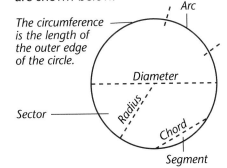

Arc

Diameter

Radius

Sector

Chord

Segment

SOLIDS

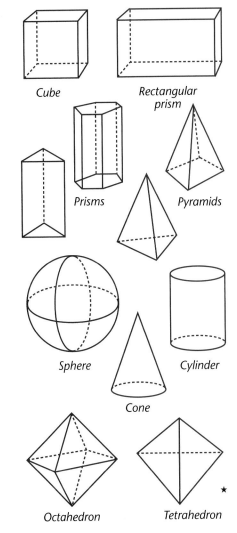

Cube

Rectangular prism

Prisms

Pyramids

Sphere

Cylinder

Cone

Octahedron

Tetrahedron

GEOMETRICAL FORMULAS

In these formulas, b = base, h = height, r = radius, π = pi (3.142), θ = an angle.

Area of circle = πr^2

Circumference of circle = $2\pi r$

Area of sector = $\dfrac{\theta \pi r^2}{360}$

Length of arc = $\dfrac{\theta \pi r}{180}$

Volume of cylinder = $\pi r^2 h$

Volume of cone = $\frac{1}{3} \pi r^2 h$

Volume of sphere = $\frac{4}{3} \pi r^3$

Surface area of sphere = $4\pi r^2$

Volume of pyramid = $\frac{4}{3} h \times$ base area

Area of triangle = $\frac{1}{2} bh$

Area of parallelogram = bh

WORLD RECORDS

Some of the Earth's longest rivers, highest mountains and other amazing world records are listed on these two pages. You may find slightly different figures in different books.

This is because the world is always changing; mountains wear down, rivers change shape and new buildings are constantly being constructed. Ways of measuring things can also change.

HIGHEST MOUNTAINS

Everest, Nepal/China	29,035ft
K2, Pakistan/China	28,251ft
Kanchenjunga, India/Nepal	28,208ft
Lhotse I, Nepal/China	27,923ft
Makalu I, Nepal/China	27,824ft
Lhotse II, Nepal/China	27,560ft
Dhaulagiri, Nepal	26,810ft
Manaslu I, Nepal	26,760ft
Cho Oyu, Nepal/China	26,750ft
Nanga Parbat, Pakistan	26,660ft

LONGEST RIVERS

Nile, Africa	4,145 miles
Amazon, South America	4,000 miles
Chang Jiang (Yangtze), China	3,964 miles
Mississippi/Missouri, U.S.A.	3,741 miles
Yenisey/Angara, Russia	3,442 miles
Huang He (Yellow), China	3,395 miles
Ob/Irtysh/Black Irtysh, Asia	3,362 miles
Amur/Shilka/Onon, Asia	2,744 miles
Lena, Russia	2,734 miles
Congo, Africa	2,718 miles

BIGGEST NATURAL LAKES

Caspian Sea	143,243 sq miles
Lake Superior	31,820 sq miles
Lake Victoria	26,724 sq miles
Lake Huron	23,010 sq miles
Lake Michigan	22,400 sq miles
Lake Tanganyika	12,650 sq miles
Lake Baikal	12,162 sq miles
Great Bear Lake	12,096 sq miles
Lake Nyasa	11,555 sq miles
Aral Sea	11,042 sq miles

DEEPEST OCEAN

The Mariana Trench, part of the Pacific Ocean, is the deepest part of the sea at 35,797ft deep.

DEEPEST LAKE

Lake Baikal, in Russia, is the deepest lake in the world. At its deepest point, it is 5,370ft deep.

BIGGEST ISLANDS

Greenland	840,000 sq miles
New Guinea	309,000 sq miles
Borneo	290,000 sq miles
Madagascar	226,656 sq miles
Baffin Island	195,928 sq miles
Sumatra	184,706 sq miles
Great Britain	90,506 sq miles
Honshu	88,000 sq miles
Victoria Island	83,896 sq miles
Ellesmere Island	75,767 sq miles

TALLEST INHABITED BUILDINGS

Petronas Towers, Malaysia	1,483ft
Sears Tower, U.S.A.	1,454ft
Jin Mao Building, China	1,378ft
CITIC Plaza, China	1,283ft
Shun Hing Square, China	1,260ft
Plaza Rakyat, Malaysia	1,254ft
Empire State Building, U.S.A.	1,250ft
Central Plaza, China	1,227ft
Bank of China, China	1,209ft
Emirates Tower, U.A.E.	1,148ft

BIGGEST CITIES/URBAN AREAS

Tokyo, Japan	26.4 million
Mexico City, Mexico	18.1 million
Bombay, India	18.1 million
Sao Paulo, Brazil	17.8 million
New York, U.S.A.	16.6 million
Lagos, Nigeria	13.4 million
Los Angeles, U.S.A.	13.2 million
Calcutta, India	12.9 million
Shanghai, China	12.9 million
Buenos Aires, Argentina	12.6 million

FAMOUS WATERFALLS

	HEIGHT
Angel Falls, Venezuela	3,212ft
Sutherland Falls, New Zealand	1,904ft
Mardalfossen, Norway	1,696ft
Jog Falls, India	830ft
Victoria Falls, Zimbabwe/Zambia	355ft
Iguacu Falls, Brazil/Argentina	269ft
Niagara Falls, Canada/U.S.A.	187ft

NATURAL DISASTERS

Natural disasters can be measured in different ways. For example, some earthquakes score highly on the Richter scale, while others cause more destruction. The earthquakes, volcanic eruptions, floods, hurricanes and tornadoes listed here are among the most destructive disasters in history.

Internet links

Website 1 Watch animations that explain why some natural disasters occur.

Website 2 Read more amazing animal facts.

For links to these websites, go to **www.usborne-quicklinks.com**

RECENT EARTHQUAKES	RICHTER SCALE	DISASTROUS EFFECTS
Gujarat, India, 2001	8.0	20,000 died
Kobe, Japan, 1995	6.8	6,400 died; buildings destroyed
Manjil-Rudbar, Iran, 1990	7.7	50,000 died; caused landslides
Mexico City, Mexico, 1985	8.1	20,000 died; buildings destroyed
Tangshan, China, 1976	7.9	655,200 died
Coast of Peru, 1970	7.8	18,000 died; Yungay town buried
Concepcion, Chile, 1960	8.7	2,000 died; strongest ever recorded
Quetta, Pakistan, 1935	7.5	30–60,000 died
Tokyo-Kanto, Japan, 1923	8.3	142,800 died; Great Tokyo fire
Ningzia-Kansu, China, 1920	8.6	200,000 died; caused landslides

VOLCANIC ERUPTIONS	DISASTROUS EFFECTS
Mount Vesuvius, Italy, AD79	Pompeii flattened; up to 20,000 died
Tambora, Indonesia, 1815	92,000 people starved to death
Krakatau, Indonesia, 1883	36,500 drowned in resulting tsunami
Mount Pelee, Martinique, 1902	Nearly 30,000 people buried in ash flows
Kelut, Indonesia, 1919	Over 5,000 people drowned in mud
Agung, Indonesia, 1963	1,200 people suffocated in hot ash
Mount St. Helens, U.S.A., 1980	Only 61 died but a large area destroyed
Ruiz, Colombia, 1985	25,000 people died in giant mud flows
Mt. Pinatubo, Philippines, 1991	800 killed by collapsing roofs and disease
Island of Montserrat, 1995	Most of the island left uninhabitable

FLOODS	DISASTROUS EFFECTS
Holland, 1228	100,000 drowned by a sea flood
Kaifeng, China, 1642	300,000 died after rebels destroyed a dyke
Johnstown, U.S.A., 1889	2,200 killed in a flood caused by rain
Italy, 1963	Vaoint Dam overflowed; 2–3,000 killed
East Pakistan, 1970	Giant wave caused by cyclone killed 250,000
Bangladesh, 1988	1,300 died, 30m homeless in monsoon flood
Southern U.S.A., 1993	$12bn of damage after Mississippi flooded
China, 1998	Chang Jiang overflow left 14m homeless
Papua New Guinea, 1998	Tsunamis killed 2,000 people
Venezuela, 1999	Floods and mudslides killed 5,000–20,000

STORMS	DISASTROUS EFFECTS
Caribbean "Great Hurricane", 1780	20,000 died; Biggest ever hurricane
Hong Kong typhoon, China, 1906	10,000 people died
Killer tornado, U.S.A., 1925	Up to 700 people died in Missouri
Tropical Storm Agnes, U.S.A.,1972	$3.5bn damage, 129 died
Hurricane Fifi, Honduras, 1974	8,000 people died; 100,000 homeless
Hurricane Georges, U.S.A., 1998	Caused $5bn of damage
Hurricane Mitch, C. America, 1998	9,000 died across Central America

ANIMAL FACTS

- **Fastest animal on land**
  Cheetahs can run at speeds of up to 70mph.

- **Fastest animal in the air**
  Peregrine falcons can fly at 112mph.

- **Fastest animal in water**
  Sailfish can swim at speeds of 68mph.

- **Slowest animal on land**
  The three-toed sloth moves along the ground at a speed of about 0.07mph.

- **Most deadly animal**
  The venom from a single sea wasp jellyfish can kill up to 60 people. Once stung, a person can die within minutes.

- **Largest animal**
  Blue whales can grow to over 98ft long, which is about the length of a Boeing 737 plane.

- **Smallest animal**
  Fairyflies are tiny wasps. They are only around 0.006in long.

- **Strongest animal**
  Rhinoceros beetles can carry up to 850 times their own body weight.

- **Longest-living animal**
  Giant tortoises have been known to live for more than 180 years.

SCIENTISTS AND INVENTORS

Here you can find out about people who have made important contributions to scientific discoveries and inventions.

Internet links

For a link to a website where you can explore interactive pictures to find out who invented many of the everyday objects around the home and office, go to **www.usborne-quicklinks.com**

al-Haytham, Ibn (Alhazen) (965–1038) An Arab physicist who made great advances in optics, explaining refraction, and the role of reflection in vision.

Ampère, André Marie (1775–1836) A French mathematician and physicist who did pioneering work on electricity and magnetism. The unit of electric current, called the ampere, is named after him.

Anaxagoras (c.500–428BC) This Greek philosopher was the first to explain the phases and eclipses of the Sun and Moon as the result of their movements.

Archimedes (c.287–212BC) A Greek mathematician and inventor who formulated the scientific principle that explains how a floating object displaces its own weight in water.

Aristotle (c.384–322BC) A Greek philosopher who made many contributions to physics, zoology and scientific theory.

Avogadro, Amedeo (1776–1856) This Italian chemist first theorized that all gases of the same volume at the same temperature and pressure must contain the same number of molecules. This is called Avogadro's law.

Babbage, Charles (1792–1871) An English mathematician and inventor who worked on a calculating machine called the Analytical Engine. The machine anticipated the modern computer.

Bain, Alexander (1811–1877) This Scottish clockmaker registered his design for the first fax machine (1843).

Baird, John Logie (1888–1946) A Scottish engineer who invented the television (1926).

Becquerel, Antoine (1852–1908) A French physicist who discovered radioactivity (1896).

Bell, Alexander Graham (1847–1922) A Scottish–American inventor who invented the telephone (1872–76).

Benz, Karl (1844–1929) A German inventor who designed the first car to be driven by an internal combustion engine.

Berliner, Émile (1851–1929) This German–American engineer invented the gramophone.

Biro, Lazlo (1900–1985) This Hungarian artist and journalist invented the ballpoint pen (1938).

Bohr, Niels (1885–1962) A Danish physicist who applied the quantum theory of physics to Rutherford's structure of the atom (1913).

Booth, Hubert (1871–1955) This Scottish engineer invented the first successful vacuum cleaner.

Boyle, Robert (1627–1691) This Irish scientist proposed that matter is made up of tiny particles. He also formulated Boyle's law, which states that the pressure and volume of a gas are inversely proportional.

Braun, Wernher von (1912–1977) A German engineer who was a pioneer of rocket-building and space flight.

Brown, Robert (1773–1858) A Scottish biologist who noted the apparently random motion of particles suspended in liquids.

Brunel, Isambard Kingdom (1806–1859) This English engineer designed many great bridges and ocean-going steamships.

Carlson, Chester (1906–1968) The American inventor of the photocopier.

Cavendish, Henry (1731–1810) This English chemist and physicist discovered hydrogen, the chemical make-up of air and water and estimated the weight of the Earth.

Celsius, Anders (1701–1744) This Swedish astronomer invented the first temperature scale to be divided into 100 degree units. It was named the Celsius scale.

Chadwick, James (1891–1974) An English physicist who worked on radioactivity and discovered the neutron.

Charles, Jacques (1746–1823) A French physicist who formulated Charles' law, which states the relationship between temperature and volume in gases.

Cockerell, Christopher (1910–1999) An English engineer who invented the hovercraft.

Copernicus (1473–1543) This Polish astronomer developed the theory that the planets move around the Sun, not around the Earth (1530).

Crick, Francis (1916–2004) This English biologist, along with his colleague, James Watson, discovered the structure of DNA. (See also *Franklin, Rosalind and Wilkins, Maurice.*)

Cugnot, Nicolas-Joseph (1725–1804) A French army engineer who, in 1769, invented the steam tractor. This was the first vehicle to move on land by its own power.

Curie, Marie (1867–1934) A pioneering Polish scientist who carried out work in radiation and discovered the radioactive material radium (1898).

Dalton, John (1766–1844) This English chemist suggested that elements are made of atoms, which combine to form compounds.

Darwin, Charles (1809–1882) The English naturalist who first suggested that species evolve and change by natural selection.

Drew, Richard (1886–1956) The American inventor of clear tape (1928).

Edison, Thomas (1847–1931) This American inventor made over a thousand devices, including the phonograph, an early version of the gramophone.

Einstein, Albert (1879–1955) A German-born physicist who published the Special Theory of Relativity (1905) and General Theory of Relativity (1915), revising previous ideas of time and space.

Fahrenheit, Gabriel (1686–1736) A German physicist who invented the mercury thermometer (1714) and devised the Fahrenheit temperature scale.

Faraday, Michael (1791–1867) An English scientist who invented the dynamo, generating an electric current by spinning a coil of wire in a magnetic field.

Fermi, Enrico (1901–1954) This Italian physicist was the first to control nuclear energy in a nuclear reactor.

Fleming, Alexander (1881–1955) This Scottish doctor discovered penicillin, a substance important in making antibiotics.

Ford, Henry (1863–1947) An American automobile engineer who built the Ford Model T and pioneered mass-production techniques in industry.

Franklin, Benjamin (1706–1790) This American inventor and politician proved that lightning is a form of electricity.

Franklin, Rosalind (1920–1958) This English scientist, along with her colleague, Maurice Wilkins, carried out research crucial to the discovery of the structure of DNA. (See also *Crick, Francis and Watson, James.*)

Galilei, Galileo (1564–1642) An Italian astronomer and scientist who made many discoveries. He proved that all falling bodies descend with equal acceleration. His studies of planetary motion supported the Copernican theory that the planets move around the Sun.

Gerbert (c.945–1003) This French monk invented the first mechanical clock. He became Pope Sylvester II in 999.

Gilbert, William (1544–1603) This English physicist, also doctor to Queen Elizabeth I of England, founded the scientific study of magnetism. He was the first to suggest that the Earth itself is magnetic.

Hahn, Otto (1879–1968) A German chemist who, together with Fritz Strassman, discovered nuclear fission. (See also *Meitner, Lise.*)

Halley, Edmund (1656–1742) An English astronomer and mathematician who charted and predicted the orbit of a comet. Halley's Comet is named after him.

Harvey, William (1578–1657) This English doctor discovered how blood circulates through the body.

Hawking, Stephen (1942–) An English physicist who has advanced the understanding of the origin of the Universe.

Herschel, William (1738–1822) This German-born astronomer and telescope-maker mapped the stars of the northern hemisphere and, in 1781, discovered the planet Uranus. He also discovered infrared radiation in 1800. His sister, **Caroline (1750–1848)**, did important work in assisting him.

Hertz, Heinrich (1857–1894) This German physicist began the research that demonstrated the existence of radio waves.

Hooke, Robert (1635–1703) An English physicist and chemist who discovered the relationship between elasticity and force, as formulated by Hooke's law.

Hubble, Edwin (1889–1953) An American astronomer who proved the existence of galaxies beyond our own. The Hubble Space Telescope is named after him.

Huygens, Christiaan (1629–1695) This Dutch physicist and astronomer invented the first accurate pendulum clock, recognized Saturn's rings and was the first person to suggest that light travels in waves.

Jenner, Edward (1749–1823) This English doctor invented the first vaccine.

Joule, James (1818–1889) An English physicist who did important work on heat, and helped to establish the principle of the conservation of energy. The joule, a unit of measurement of work and energy, is named after him.

Kelvin, Lord See *Thomson, William.*

Kepler, Johannes (1571–1630) A German astronomer who discovered the laws of planetary motion.

Lavoisier, Antoine (1743–1794) This French lawyer and scientist named oxygen and hydrogen, and explained the role of oxygen in combustion.

Leeuwenhoek, Antony van (1632–1723) A Dutch scientist who was the first to examine bacteria, sperm and blood cells with a microscope.

Lemaître, Georges (1894–1966) A Belgian astrophysicist, mathematician and priest who first suggested the big-bang theory of the origin of the Universe.

Linnaeus, Carolus (Carl von Linné) (1707–1778) This Swedish botanist introduced the method of classifying living things into genus, species and other sub-divisions.

Lister, Joseph (1827–1912) This English-born surgeon was the first to carry out antiseptic operations.

Lovelace, Ada (1815–1852) An English mathematician, Lovelace worked on the Analytical Engine designed by Charles Babbage, devising "programs" which anticipated computer programming.

Maiman, Theodore (1927–) An American scientist who built the first laser.

Malpighi, Marcello (1628–1694) Using a microscope, this Italian physiologist discovered that arteries and veins are connected by tiny blood vessels, called capillaries.

Marconi, Guglielmo (1874–1937) This Italian physicist developed radiotelegraphy and succeeded in sending signals across the Atlantic (1901).

Maxwell, James Clerk (1831–1879) A Scottish physicist who established the presence of electromagnetic radiation.

Meitner, Lise (1878–1968) This Austrian physicist explained nuclear fission for the first time (1939). (See also *Hahn, Otto and Strassman, Fritz.*)

Mendel, Gregor (1822–1884) An Austrian monk and naturalist who developed the laws of heredity.

Mendeleyev, Dmitri (1834–1907) This Russian chemist devised the first periodic table of the elements.

Mercator, Gerardus (1512–1594) This Flemish geographer and map-maker invented the Mercator projection: a way of accurately showing the Earth's round shape on a flat map.

Morse, Samuel (1791–1872) An American artist who invented a system of sending messages along electric telegraph wires by a coded system of dots and dashes (long and short electrical pulses), now called Morse code.

Newcomen, Thomas (1663–1729) An English inventor who built the first atmospheric steam engine.

Newton, Isaac (1642–1727) This English physicist and mathematician formulated fundamental laws of gravity and motion. He also discovered that light is made up of a spectrum of colors, and built the first reflecting telescope.

Nipkow, Paul (1860–1940) A German engineer and pioneer of television who invented the Nipkow disc, a mechanical scanning device.

Nobel, Alfred (1833–1896) A Swedish chemist who invented dynamite (1866), and founded the Nobel Prize program.

Ohm, Georg (1787–1854)
A German physicist who researched electrical resistance. The SI unit of electrical resistance, called the ohm, is named after him.

Pascal, Blaise (1623–1662)
A French mathematician and physicist who made contributions to hydraulics and the study of atmospheric pressure. The SI unit of pressure, called the pascal, is named after him.

Pasteur, Louis (1822–1895)
This French chemist showed that decay is caused by bacteria. He invented a process of preserving food by killing bacteria with heat, now called pasteurization.

Planck, Max (1858–1947)
This German physicist developed the quantum theory.

Priestley, Joseph (1733–1804)
An English chemist who discovered oxygen (1774). He also invented carbonated drinks.

Pythagoras (6th century BC)
A Greek scientist who made many discoveries, and devised the Pythagorean theorem, a formula for calculating the unknown length of one side of a right-angled triangle.

Röntgen, Wilhelm (1845–1923) This German physicist discovered X-rays (1895).

Ruska, Ernst (1906–1988) A German engineer who invented the electron microscope (1933).

Rutherford, Ernest (1871–1937) A New Zealand-born physicist who demonstrated the structure of the atom.

Savery, Thomas (c.1650 –1715) An English engineer who built the first steam engine.

Sikorsky, Igor (1889–1972)
A Russian-born American aeronautical engineer who built the prototype for the modern helicopter (1939).

Slipher, Vesto (1875–1969) An American astronomer who took the first clear photographs of Mars, and discovered the Universe was vastly bigger than previously thought.

Stephenson, George (1781–1848) An English inventor who invented the first successful steam locomotive (1814) and, with his son Robert, built Stephenson's Rocket (1829).

Strassman, Fritz (1902–1980)
A German chemist who, with Otto Hahn, discovered nuclear fission (1938). (See also *Meitner, Lise.*)

Talbot, William Fox (1800–1877) This English scientist invented the method of reproducing photographs from a negative image.

Tesla, Nikola (1856–1943)
A Croatian electrical engineer who invented the AC motor and high-voltage electrical generation.

Thomson, William (Lord Kelvin) (1824–1907) A British mathematician and physicist who did important work in thermodynamics, and established the absolute temperature scale.

Tombaugh, Clyde (1906–1997)
An American astronomer who discovered Pluto in 1930.

Torricelli, Evangelista (1608–1647) An Italian physicist who devised the principle of the barometer (1644).

Turing, Alan (1912–1954)
This English mathematician was an important pioneer of computer science.

Vesalius, Andreas (1514–1564)
This Flemish medical researcher founded the modern science of anatomy (the study of the body).

Villard, Paul (1860–1934)
A French physicist who discovered gamma radiation (1900).

Volta, Alessandro (1745–1827)
An Italian physicist who built the first electric battery. The volt, which measures electric potential, is named after him.

Watson, James (1928–) This American scientist, together with Francis Crick, discovered the structure of DNA (1953). (See also *Franklin, Rosalind and Wilkins, Maurice.*)

Watt, James (1736–1819)
A Scottish inventor who made substantial improvements to the steam engine. After he died, the watt, a unit of electrical power, was named after him.

Wegener, Alfred (1880–1930)
A German meteorologist who first suggested the theory of continental drift.

Whittle, Frank (1907–1996)
An English inventor who devised the jet engine (1930).

Wilkins, Maurice (1916–)
This New Zealand-born British biologist and physicist, along with Rosalind Franklin, carried out research crucial to the discovery of the structure of DNA. (See also *Crick, Francis and Watson, James.*)

Wright, Orville (1871–1948) and **Wilbur (1867–1912)** In 1903, these American brothers flew the first powered aircraft.

Yale, Linus (1821–1868)
This American inventor introduced the type of pin lock still used today.

KEY DATES IN SCIENCE

On these two pages, you can read about some of the most important dates in the history of scientific invention and discovery, from the introduction of the calendar to the mapping of the human genome.

Internet links

For a link to a website where you can follow the history of flight in an interactive timeline, as well as fly a simulation of the plane the Wright brothers invented, go to,
www.usborne-quicklinks.com

4241BC The Egyptian calendar was introduced, making this the first year in which events could be dated precisely.

c.4000BC The alloy bronze was first made in Mesopotamia.

c.3500BC The first wheels were made out of sections of tree trunks.

c.3000BC The Babylonians divided the day into 24 hours. They also invented the abacus, the first adding machine.

c.1600BC The first records were made of the study of astronomy.

c.1500BC Iron smelting was first developed in Asia Minor (Turkey).

c.700BC The *Ayurveda*, an early medical text, was written in India.

c.600BC The Greek philosopher Thales of Miletus described the magnetic properties of lodestone, a form of iron ore, which later became known as magnetite.

c.530BC Pythagorean, a Greek mathematician, made various important discoveries, including Pythagoras' theorem.

c.400BC The pulley was invented in Greece.

c.335BC The Greek philosopher Aristotle made many important scientific observations, including how levers work.

c.300BC Gears were first used in Egypt.

c.235BC Archimedes, a Greek scientist, invented the Archimedes' screw, which could move water upward. It was used for bailing out water from flooded ships and in irrigation systems for farming.

c.10BC The Roman architect Vitruvius described a crane.

c.200 The earliest known use was made of cast iron – to make a Chinese cooking stove.

c.635 Quill pens were used for writing.

c.700 The Catalan forge was used in Spain for smelting iron. It was an early version of the modern blast furnace.

c.950 Gunpowder was used by the Chinese to make fireworks and signals.

1000 The optical properties of lenses were first observed by the Arab physicist Ibn al-Haytham.

1088 The first known clock, which was powered by water, was invented in China by Han Kung-Lien.

1090 Compasses were first used by the Chinese and the Arabs to navigate at sea.

1202 The Italian scholar Leonardo Fibonacci published his *Liber Abaci*, the first European book to suggest the use of the Hindu-Arabic decimal number system.

1230 In China, gunpowder was first used as an explosive, to make bombs for attacking city walls.

1286 The first pair of glasses was made in Italy, probably by an Italian physicist named Salvino degli Armati.

1326 Early guns were in use in Italy.

1451 Johann Gutenberg invented the printing press in Germany.

1500 The Italian artist and scientist Leonardo da Vinci designed many devices, including a type of helicopter.

1540 The first artificial limbs were made for wounded soldiers, by the French doctor Ambroise Paré.

1543 The Polish astronomer Copernicus published his theory that the planets revolve around the Sun, not the Earth.

1590 The microscope was invented in the Netherlands.

1592 The Italian astronomer Galileo invented the first thermometer based on the expansion and contraction of air.

1608 The telescope was first demonstrated in the Netherlands.

1610 Galileo used a telescope to make astronomical observations.

1616 The English doctor William Harvey lectured on the circulation of blood.

1618 A German astronomer, Johannes Kepler, published laws describing the planets' elliptical orbits around the Sun.

1623 The first mechanical calculator was invented in Germany by Wilhelm Schickard.

1644 Evangelista Torricelli, an Italian physicist, discovered the principle of the barometer.

1682 The English astronomer Edmund Halley described and charted the orbit of a comet, later named after him.

1687 The English physicist Isaac Newton published his book *Principia*, in which he proposed the laws of motion and gravity.

1704 Isaac Newton wrote *Opticks*, a book about prisms and light.

1712 The English inventor Thomas Newcomen built the first atmospheric steam engine.

1752 The American scientist Benjamin Franklin showed that lightning is a form of electricity.

1769 The Scottish inventor James Watt produced the first version of his improved steam engine.

1774 An English chemist, Joseph Priestley, discovered and isolated oxygen gas.

1783 The first flight in a hot-air balloon took place in Paris, France.

1789 Antoine Lavoisier, a French lawyer and scientist, published his *Elementary Treatise on Chemistry*, which became the basis for modern chemistry.

1796 In England, Edward Jenner performed the first vaccination.

1799 Alessandro Volta, an Italian physicist, built the first battery.

1808 The English chemist John Dalton published *A New System of Chemical Philosophy*, containing his theories of atomic structure.

1810 The first electric lamp was displayed in London, England.

1820 A Danish scientist, Hans Ørsted, observed that a wire with an electric current running through it behaved like a magnet, an effect later called electromagnetism.

1821 Michael Faraday, an English scientist, invented the electric motor.

1831 Michael Faraday invented the dynamo.

1833–4 English mathematicians Charles Babbage and Ada Lovelace worked on the Analytical Engine, a forerunner of the computer.

1837 The electric telegraph, used to send messages along wires, was invented in England.

1839 In England and France, the invention of photography was announced.

1852 The first airship, powered by steam and filled with hydrogen, made its maiden flight in France.

1859 The internal combustion engine was invented in France.

1859 Charles Darwin, an English naturalist, published *On the Origin of Species by Natural Selection*. It contained his theories of evolution.

1862 The first celluloid plastic was exhibited in London, England.

1869 The Russian scientist Dmitri Mendeleyev developed the first periodic table of the elements.

1876 The first telephone message was transmitted by Alexander Graham Bell in Boston, U.S.A.

1877 The first sound recording was made in the U.S.A. by Thomas Edison on his prototype phonograph machine.

1877 A German–American scientist, Émile Berliner, invented the microphone.

1879 Thomas Edison invented the first successful light bulb.

1881 The first power station was built in Surrey, England.

1884 The first artificial fibers, made from cellulose, were exhibited in London, England.

1885 The petrol-driven car was invented by the German Karl Benz.

1888 Heinrich Hertz, a German physicist, demonstrated the existence of radio waves.

1895 Moving pictures were first shown in public in France.

1895 X-rays were discovered by the German physicist Wilhelm Röntgen, and the first X-ray photograph was taken.

1895 The Italian physicist Guglielmo Marconi developed and demonstrated radio transmission.

1896 Antoine Becquerel, a French physicist, discovered radioactivity.

1903 The American Wright brothers made the first powered aircraft flight.

1905 German-born physicist Albert Einstein published scientific works including the Special Theory of Relativity.

1911 Marie Curie, a Polish scientist, won the Nobel prize for her work on radioactivity.

1911 Ernest Rutherford, a New Zealand-born scientist, showed that atoms have a central nucleus.

1926 John Logie Baird, a Scottish engineer, transmitted the first black and white television picture across the Atlantic.

1929 Edwin Hubble, an American astronomer, showed that galaxies are moving away from each other. This became the foundation of the big-bang theory.

1936 The first helicopter flight was made in Germany by the Focke Fa-61.

1938 Nuclear fission was discovered by Otto Hahn and Fritz Strassman. Lise Meitner explained the discovery in 1939.

1941 Frank Whittle invented the turbojet aircraft engine in England.

1945 The U.S.A. tested the atomic bomb in New Mexico, U.S.A., and used it on Hiroshima, Japan.

1948 Three American scientists, John Bardeen, Walter Brattain and William Shockley, invented the transistor, making miniature electronics possible.

1953 Francis Crick and James Watson discovered the structure of the DNA molecule, which forms living cells, later proved by Rosalind Franklin.

1957 The first satellite, the Russian Sputnik I, was launched.

1959 The integrated circuit was invented in the U.S.A.

1961 Vostok I, the first manned spacecraft, was launched. Yuri Gagarin became the first person to travel into space.

1969 An American astronaut, Neil Armstrong, became the first person to walk on the Moon.

1969 The Internet, in the form of ARPANET, an American military computer network, was born.

1975 The first home computer, the Altair, became available.

1981 The first reusable spacecraft, the Space Shuttle, was launched.

1990 The first transmission of high-definition television (HDTV) was made.

1992 The World Wide Web, invented by the English computer scientist Tim Berners-Lee, went online for the first time.

2000 Scientists announced the completion of the first draft of the human genome sequence.

GLOSSARY

This glossary explains some key words used in this book. Words in *italic* type have their own entry elsewhere in the glossary.

airfoil A shape that is curved on top and flatter underneath. It helps to create *lift*.

alloy A mixture of two or more metals, or a metal and a nonmetal.

amphibian Any of a class of cold-blooded, soft-skinned animals that live both on land and in water. Frogs and toads are amphibians.

amplitude The size of vibrations a sound makes.

anther A pod at the end of a *stamen*, containing *pollen*.

anus The opening at the end of the digestive tract through which waste is released.

artery A strong *blood vessel* through which blood flows away from the heart.

asterism Smaller patterns of *stars* within a *constellation*.

asteroid A rock that travels around the *Sun*. There are thousands of asteroids in the part of the *Solar System* known as the Asteroid Belt.

asthenosphere A weak, partly molten layer in the Earth's upper *mantle*.

atmosphere A layer of gases that surrounds the Earth.

atom The smallest unit of an *element*.

aurora Flickering lights, caused by magnetic particles from the *Sun*, that often appear in the sky near the poles.

axon A *nerve fiber* that carries information away from a *neuron*.

bacterium (plural: **bacteria**) A tiny *organism* found in soil, in the air and in plants and animals.

bandwidth The number of *bytes* a microprocessor can process at once.

big-bang theory The theory that all the matter in the *Universe* came into being with a massive explosion known as the big bang.

bile A green liquid, produced by the liver, that breaks up fat into tiny drops, which *enzymes* can digest.

binary code The representation of information using the digits 1 and 0.

biome An area with a *climate* that supports a particular range of plants and animals.

bit A single piece of information in *binary code* – a 0 or a 1.

blood vessel A tube in the body that blood travels along.

bond A *force* that holds together two or more *atoms*.

bronchus Either of the two thick tubes that lead from the windpipe into the lungs.

bus An electronic pathway that carries information between the *CPU* and other parts of a computer.

byte A group of eight *bits* of information in *binary code*.

camouflage Patterns or features that help plants and animals to look like their backgrounds and avoid being seen. For example, a tiger's stripes blend in with long grass.

capillary A tiny *blood vessel* that carries oxygen to *cells*, and carries carbon dioxide and waste away in the blood.

carbohydrate The part of food that gives you energy. Bread and pasta contain carbohydrates.

carnivore An animal or plant that feeds on other animals.

carpel The female reproductive organ of a flower, made up of a *stigma*, *style* and *ovary*.

cell The smallest unit of an *organism* that can carry out chemical processes vital to life.

chemical reaction An interaction between substances in which their *atoms* combine to form new substances.

chlorophyll The green chemical in plants that enables them to convert sunlight into food.

cholesterol A fat-like substance found in some foods. Too much cholesterol in the body can cause heart disease.

chromosome A bundle of *DNA* in the middle of a *cell* containing information needed for an *organism* to develop.

cirrus A wispy cloud that forms high in the sky.

classification A method of dividing things up into groups with similar features.

climate The typical weather conditions in a particular region.

clock speed The number of instructions a microprocessor can process in one second.

clone Make an identical copy of an *organism*.

cochlea A spiral-shaped tube inside the ear through which sound waves travel.

comet A chunk of dirty ice mixed with dust and grit that travels around the *Sun*.

compass A device used to find your direction. It usually has a magnetic needle.

compound A substance made up of two or more *elements* joined together by a chemical *bond*.

condensation The process of a gas cooling to form a liquid.

conductor A substance that *electricity* or heat can flow through easily.

constellation A group of *stars* that form an easily recognizable pattern. There are 88 constellations altogether.

coral reef A structure made up of the skeletons of small sea animals called coral polyps. A reef builds up gradually as old polyps die and new ones grow on top.

core The central part of the inside of the Earth, which scientists think is made up of the metals iron and nickel.

cornea A thin, clear layer covering the eyeball.

corona A layer of gas around the *Sun*, visible as a faint halo during a total solar *eclipse*.

CPU (Central Processing Unit) The main circuits in a computer, which control the operation of the computer.

crater A hole in the surface of a *planet*, *moon* or *asteroid*, caused by the impact of a *meteorite* or an *asteroid*.

crust The Earth's solid outer layer. It consists of continental crust, which forms the land, and oceanic crust, which forms the seabed.

cumulus A fluffy, white cloud that forms high in the sky during warm, sunny weather.

delta A fan-shaped system of streams, created when a river splits up into many smaller branches and deposits debris as it nears the sea.

dendrite A *nerve fiber* that carries information toward a *neuron*.

density A measure of the amount of matter in a substance compared to its volume.

desert An area that has little vegetation, because of low rainfall.

diaphragm A flat sheet of muscle under the lungs.

dietary fiber A type of *carbohydrate* that helps the digestive system to work properly.

DNA (deoxyribonucleic acid) A set of coded instructions in the *cells* of living things that contains the information the cells need to function and develop.

drag A type of *friction*, caused by air resistance, that slows planes down while they are in the air.

ear canal A passage in the ear that channels sound waves toward the *eardrum*.

eardrum A thin layer of tissue in the ear that vibrates in reponse to sound waves.

earthquake A sudden movement of the Earth's *crust*, releasing energy.

echo A sound wave that has reflected off a surface and is heard after the original sound.

echolocation A method of locating an object by detecting the return of an *echo*.

eclipse The total or partial blocking of one object in space by another. For example, when the Moon passes in front of the *Sun*.

ecosystem A living system that includes a group of plants and animals and the area where they live.

EEG (electroencephalogram) A chart used by doctors to record brain wave patterns.

electric charge A property of matter that causes *electric forces* between particles.

electric current A flow of electrically charged particles.

electric field The area around an *electric charge* in which its electrical effects can be detected.

electric force The force that causes electrically charged particles to attract or repel each other.

electricity The effect caused by the presence or movement of charged particles.

electromagnetism The effect caused by an *electric current* flowing through a wire, forming a *magnetic field*.

electron A negatively charged particle that whizzes around the *nucleus* of an *atom*.

element A substance, such as iron or oxygen, made of only one type of *atom*.

email A message sent over the *Internet* using a computer.

enzyme A kind of protein that speeds up *chemical reactions* in living things.

epidermis The outer layer of skin.

Equator An imaginary line around the middle of the Earth, halfway between the North Pole and the South Pole.

estuary A wide channel that joins a river to the sea.

evaporation The process where a liquid changes into a vapor.

evolution The gradual development of plants and animals over many generations, to fit in better with their *habitats*.

exosphere The outermost layer of the *atmosphere*.

extinction The death of a *species* of plant or animal.

fault A large crack in the Earth's *crust*.

ferromagnetism A form of magnetism. Ferromagnetic metals become magnetic when they are near to a magnet.

fiber optic cable A cable made up of many glass or plastic fibers.

food chain A series of *organisms* in an *ecosystem,* each member of which feeds on another in the chain and is in turn eaten by another.

food web A vast network of interlinked *food chains*.

force Something that can push or pull an object. A force can make an object move faster or slower, or make it stop, change direction, or change size or shape.

fossil The shape or remains of a plant or animal that died long ago, hardened and preserved in rock.

fossil fuel A fuel made from the compressed bodies of plants and animals that died many years ago.

frequency The number of vibrations something makes per second, measured in hertz (Hz).

friction The *force* of resistance that slows down moving objects that are touching.

fungus (plural: **fungi**) A type of *organism*, including mushrooms, that feeds on dead or living animals and plants.

galaxy A huge group of *stars* and *planets*. There are millions of galaxies in the *Universe*.

gall bladder A sac in the body that stores *bile*.

gastric juice An acidic liquid in the stomach that breaks down food and kill germs.

gene A segment of *DNA* containing a specific instruction for building part of an *organism*.

genetic engineering Changing the *DNA* of plants and animals to benefit medicine, farming and industry.

genome All the *DNA* that makes up a particular *organism*.

geyser A spring that ejects hot water and steam.

global warming An increase in average global temperature, possibly due to the *greenhouse effect*.

gorge A deep, narrow valley, shaped by a river gradually cutting down into the land it flows across.

gravity The pulling *force* that attracts small objects to much bigger objects.

greenhouse effect The trapping of heat by carbon dioxide, ozone and other gases in the Earth's *atmosphere.*

habitat The place where an animal or plant *species* lives.

hard disk A set of disks in a computer where information is stored.

hardware The equipment that makes up a computer, such as the keyboard, monitor and mouse.

hemisphere Half of the Earth.

herbivore An animal that eats plants.

hibernation A sleep-like state that enables animals to survive the winter cold.

HTML (HyperText Markup Language) A language used to create web pages.

igneous rock Rock formed from *magma* that has cooled and hardened.

inner planets Mercury, Venus, Earth and Mars.

insulator A substance that heat or *electricity* cannot flow through easily.

International Date Line An imaginary line on the Earth's surface, to the east of which the date is one day earlier than to the west. It runs on the opposite side of the world to the *Prime Meridian Line.* It lies at 180° of longitude, except where it bends to avoid time change in populated areas.

Internet A vast network that links together computers all over the world.

invertebrate An animal without a spine.

iris The colored part of the eye. It contains muscles that control the size of the pupil.

ISP (Internet Service Provider) A company that provides people with access to the *Internet.*

joint The place where bones meet.

kidney An organ that removes waste from the blood and regulates the body's fluid levels.

kinetic energy The energy an object has when it is moving.

kingdom One of the five groups into which all living things can be divided.

landslide A sudden slippage of rocks and soil down a hillside, usually caused by heavy rain or an *earthquake.*

larva A young insect, before it has undergone *metamorphosis.*

lava Hot, molten rock ejected by a *volcano.*

life cycle The different stages of development an *organism* goes though during its lifetime.

lift A *force* that pushes up on things that move through the air.

ligament A tough band of tissue that holds together two bones at a *joint.*

lightning A flash of light in the sky, caused by *static electricity.*

light year The distance that light travels in one year.

lithosphere The solid outer layer of the Earth, made up of the *crust* and upper *mantle.*

magma Hot, molten rock inside the Earth.

magnetic field The area around a magnet in which its magnetic effects can be detected.

magnetic poles The ends of a magnet, where the magnetic field is strongest.

magnetism An invisible *force* that attracts certain kinds of metals.

mammal Any of a class of hairy, warm-blooded animals that suckle their young with milk.

mantle The thick layer of rock under the Earth's *crust.* Some of it is solid and some is molten.

mass The amount of matter contained in an object.

mass extinction An event in which huge numbers of living things die out in a short time.

meander A bend or loop in a river.

Mediterranean A *climate* characterized by warm winters and hot summers. It is named after a region around the Mediterranean Sea, but is also found in other parts of the world.

mesosphere A layer in the Earth's *atmosphere* that lies between the *stratosphere* and the *thermosphere*.

metalloid An *element* that shares some of the properties of both metals and nonmetals.

metamorphic rock Rock that has been changed by heat or pressure.

metamorphosis A complete change of an animal's body, such as when a tadpole turns into a frog.

meteor A *meteoroid* that has entered the Earth's *atmosphere*. Meteors are also called shooting stars.

meteorite A *meteor* that has fallen to Earth.

meteoroid A chunk of rock that travels around the *Sun*.

migration Moving from one place to another. Many animals migrate each season to find food or to breed.

Milky Way The galaxy that contains our *Solar System*.

mineral A non-living substance found in the Earth, such as salt or iron.

modem A device that enables a computer to send and receive information along telephone lines.

molecule A tiny particle consisting of two or more *atoms* bonded together.

moon Any natural *satellite* of a *planet*.

natural selection The survival of individual plants and animals that are best suited to their environment.

nectar A sweet, sticky substance produced by flowers, which some animals drink.

nerve A bundle of *nerve fibers*.

nerve fiber A strand that links one *neuron* to the next. There are two kinds of nerve fibers: *axons* and *dendrites*.

neuron A nerve *cell*, consisting of a cell body surrounded by *nerve fibers*. Neurons carry information from the brain to different parts of the body and vice versa.

neutron A particle in the *nucleus* of an *atom* that has no electrical charge.

niche A particular plant or animal *species*' place in an *ecosystem*.

nitrate A type of salt found in soil that helps plants to grow.

nucleus 1. The core of an *atom*, made up of *protons* and *neutrons*. 2. The part of a *cell* that controls its processes.

omnivore An animal that eats both meat and plants.

opaque Not allowing light to pass through.

operating system A piece of *software* that controls how a computer works.

orbit The path of an object as it travels around another.

organism A living thing, such as a plant, animal, or *bacterium*.

outer planets Jupiter, Saturn, Uranus, Neptune and Pluto.

ovary The reproductive part of an animal or plant that contains eggs.

oxbow lake A curved lake created when a river *meander* is cut off from the rest of the river. Also called a billabong.

Pangaea A huge continent that once existed on Earth. It began to break up around 200 million years ago, and gradually formed the continents we have today.

peninsula A narrow strip of land that juts out into the sea.

photosynthesis A chemical process in plants that converts sunlight into food.

pigment A substance that absorbs some colors of light and reflects others.

pistil The female reproductive part of a flower, made up of one or more *carpels*.

planet A celestial body that orbits a *star*. For example, Earth and Mars are *planets* that orbit the *Sun*.

plate One of the large pieces of *lithosphere* that make up the Earth's surface.

plate tectonics The study of the structure of the *lithosphere*, exploring how *plates* move around in relation to each other.

pollen A plant's male reproductive cells.

pollination The transfer of pollen from an *anther* to a *stigma*. This enables a plant to begin to make a seed.

potential energy Energy that is stored, ready to used.

precipitation Rain, snow, hail or any other water falling from the sky.

Prime Meridian Line An imaginary line that runs from north to south through Greenwich, England, at zero degrees of longitude.

program A set of instructions that enables a computer to carry out certain tasks.

proton A positively charged particle in the *nucleus* of an *atom*.

refraction The change in direction of light rays as they enter a different medium.

reptile Any of a class of scaly, cold-blooded animals that lay eggs.

rift valley A valley formed when land collapses between two *faults* in the Earth's *crust*.

satellite An object that orbits a *planet* or *star*. Some, such as the Moon, are natural, but many are built to do particular jobs, such as monitoring the weather.

scale The size of a map in relation to the area it represents. If a map's scale is 1:100, 1in on the map represents 100in of the area shown.

sedimentary rock Rock made up of particles of sand, mud and other debris that have settled on the seabed and been squashed down.

software The *programs* used by a computer.

Solar System The *Sun* and the *planets* and other objects that orbit it.

solar wind A constant stream of invisible particles blown out into space from the *Sun*.

sonar A method of bouncing sounds off objects and measuring the results. Sonar is used to map the seabed.

species A type of animal or plant.

stamen The male reproductive organ of a plant, consisting of a stalk with an *anther* at the end.

star A huge ball of gas in space that gives out heat and light. The *Sun* is a star.

static electricity Electrical charge held by a material.

stigma The sticky part of a *carpel* that catches *pollen*.

stratosphere A layer in the middle of the *atmosphere*. It contains the ozone layer.

stratus A type of cloud that forms low in the sky in flat, gray layers.

streamlined Designed to allow a gas or a liquid to flow smoothly around something.

style The part of a *carpel* that connects the *stigma* to the *ovary*.

Sun The *star* that lies in the middle of our *Solar System*.

temperate A *climate* that is characterized by mild temperatures.

tendon A tough band of tissue that attaches a muscle to a bone.

thermosphere A layer in the *atmosphere* between the

mesosphere and the *exosphere*, where the temperature can reach up to 2,732°F.

thrust The *force* that moves some vehicles forward.

time zone A region where the same standard time is used.

translucent Allowing some light to pass through.

transparent Allowing light to pass through.

trench A long, deep channel in the ocean floor.

tributary A river that flows into a bigger river.

trophic level A level of a *food chain*.

troposphere The lowest layer of the Earth's *atmosphere*.

tsunami A giant wave caused by an *earthquake*, *landslide* or volcanic activity on the seabed.

tundra A *climate* characterized by harsh winds and low winter temperatures.

Universe The collection of everything that exists in space.

vein A *blood vessel* that carries blood to the heart.

vertebrate An animal with a spine.

volcano An opening in the Earth's surface from which lava, rock fragments, ash and gases are ejected.

weight A measure of the strength of the pull of *gravity* on an object.

INDEX

In this index, words that have several page numbers may have a number in **bold** to show where to find the main explanation.

A

Africa, 38, 39, 168, 170, 172, 174
    map, 146–147
aileron, 121
air, 46, 47, 49, 50, 51, 52, 61, 66, 67, 68, 84, 85, 91, 94, 96, 110, 111, 113, 114, 115, 117, 120, 121, 186
airfoil, **120**, 121, 192
alloy, **118**, 190, 192
Alpha Orionis, *see Betelgeuse*
ampere, 186
amphibian, 60, 68, **72**, 166, 192
amplitude, 110, 192
Analytical Engine, **126**, 186, 188, 191
Andromeda Galaxy, 20
Angel Falls, 138
animal, 14, 40, 41, 45, 49, 50, 56, 57, 58, 59, **60–61**, 62, 63, 64–65, 66, 67, 68, 69, 70, 71, 72, 73, 109, 110, 111, 112, 113, 166
    classification, 70–73
    communication, 61, 113
    kingdom, 71
Antarctica, 47
antenna, 122, 123
anther, **58**, 192, 196, 197
anus, 81, 192
area, **179**, 182, 183
artery, 78, **79**, 188, 192
Asia, 38, 52, 169, 171, 173, 175
    map, 142–143
asterism, 22, 192
asteroid, **11**, 16, 69, 192, 193
Asteroid Belt, 11, 192
asthenosphere, **36**, 38, 192
atmosphere, 14, 16, 17, **46–47**, 48, 49, 53, 67, 114, 122, 192, 194, 195, 196, 197

atom, 104, 105, 106, 107, 108, **116**, 186, 187, 189, 191, 192, 194, 196, 197
atria, 78
aurora, **13**, 46, 192
    australis, *see southern lights*
    borealis, *see northern lights*
Australasia, 169, 171, 173, 175
    map, 140
axon, 86, 192, 196

B

baby, 77, 82, 111
bacterium, **66**, 68, 71, 188, 189, 192, 196
balance, 95
bandwidth, **125**, 127, 192
battery, **108**, 109, 189, 191
Bell, A. G., 110
Betelgeuse, 12
big bang, 188, 191, 192
bile, **81**, 192, 194
binary code, 123, **127**, 192
binoculars, 13, 16, 19, 28
bioluminescence, 113
biome, **62**, 192
bird, 60, 61, 65, 68, 71, **72**, 109, 110, 120, 167
blood, 73, **78–79**, 80, 81, 82, 84, 85, 187, 188, 190, 192, 195, 197
    clotting, 79
    vessel, 77, 78, **79**, 81, 83, 84, 90, 91, 188, 192
boiling, 104, 107
bone, 41, **76–77**, 93, 94, 111, 195, 197
brain, 86, 87, **88–89**, 90, 92, 94, 95, 96, 97, 194, 196
    stem, 88
    waves, 89
breathing, 61, 65, 67, **84–85**, 87, 88, 96
bronchiole, 84
bronchus, 84
bud, 58

C

cable, 116, **123**, 124, 125
    broadcasting, 123
    fiber optic, 123, 124, **125**, 194
    network, 123
camouflage, **60**, 69, 192
capillary, **79**, 188, 192
carbohydrate, 67, **82**, 192, 193
carnivore, **60**, 62, 72, 192
Cartwheel Galaxy, 21
cathode ray tube, 123
CD, 125, 127
cell, 70, 77, 83, 86, 90, 91, 94, 95, **98**, 115, 166, 188, 191, 192, 193, 196
    red blood, 79
    white blood, 79
central processing unit, *see CPU*
cerebellum, 88
cerebrum, 88, 89
chemical reaction, 79, **108**, 113, 182, 192, 194
cholesterol, 82, 193
chromosome, 193
circle, 183
circulatory system, 78–79
circumference, 183
climate, 46, **52–53**, 62, 69, 192, 193, 197
cloning, 101, 193
cloud, 14, 15, 46, 47, 48, 49, **50–51**, 117, 193, 197
coal, **67**, 109, 116
coast, **44**, 53, 142
cochlea, 94, 193
colon, 80, 81
color, 9, 92, **114–115**, 188, 196
    complementary, 114
    primary, 114, 115, 123
    secondary, 114, 115
comet, **11**, 16, 187, 190, 193
compass, **37**, 119, 190, 193
compound, **107**, 187, 193
computer, 49, 107, 111, 116, 123, 124, 125, **126–127**, 128, 186, 188, 189, 191, 192, 193, 194, 195, 196, 197

bit, 127, 192
bus, 127, 192
byte, 127, 192
clock speed, 127, 193
condensation, 104, 193
conductor, 106, 107, **116**, 117, 193
cone (eye), 92
constellation, **22–23**, 24, 25, 26, 27, 29, 30, **32**, 192, 193
consumer (in a food web), 63
continent, 38, 196
continental shelf, 44
convective zone, 12
Copernicus, 16
coral reef, **45**, 193
cornea, 92, 193
corona, 19
coughing, 85
CPU, **127**, 193
crater, 11, **16**, 193
cuticle, 91
cycle,
    carbon, 67
    life, **64–65**, 195
    nitrogen, **66**, 67
    water, 50

D

Darwin, Charles, **69**, 187, 191
Daylight Saving Time, 178
delta, 42, 193
dendrite, **86**, 193, 196
density, 49, **105**, 106, 193
dermis, 90
desert, 49, **52**, 57, 138, 144, 146, 193
diaphragm, 85, 193
diet, **82–83**
digestion, **80–81**, 82, 83, 84, 87, 96
digestive tract, **80**, 81, 193
digital,
    broadcasting, 123
    signal, **123**, 124, 125
dinosaur, 57, **68**, 69, 167
distance (measuring), 179
DNA, **98–101**, 187, 189, 191, 193, 194
domain name, 129
downloading, 128
drag, **120**, 121, 193
drought, 48, 65

E

ear, 86, **94–95**, 125, 193
eardrum, 94, 193
Earth, 8, 9, 10, 11, 12, 13, **14–15**, 16, 17, 18, 19, 22, 33, **36–37**, **38**, **39**, 40, 42, 43, 47, 48, 50, 51, 52, 53, 56, 57, 66, 68, 69, 79, 105, 106, 107, 114, 120, 122, 166, 184, 186, 187, 188, 190, 192, 195
    core, **36**, 37, 193
    crust, 36, 37, **38–39**, 40, 106, 193, 194, 195, 197
    mantle, **36**, 38, 39, 192, 195
earthquake, **37**, 181, 185, 193, 195, 197
echo, 111, 193
echolocation, 111, 193
eclipse, **18–19**, 186, 193
    annular, 19
    diamond ring effect, 19
    lunar, 18
    solar, 18, 19
ecosystem, **62–63**, 193, 194, 196
EEG chart, 89, 194
egg, 45, 58, 64, 65, 72, 82, 194, 196, 197
elasticity, 188
electric,
    charge, **116**, 117, 194
    current, **116**, 119, 126, 186, 187, 191, 194
    field, 116, 194
    force, 116, 194
electricity, 106, 107, **116–117**, 122, 178, 186, 187, 191, 193, 194, 195
    static, **117**, 195, 197
electromagnet, 119
electromagnetism, **119**, 188, 191, 194
electron, **116**, 117, 189
electronic circuit, 126
element, 41, **106–107**, 187, 188, 191, 192, 193, 194
elevator, 121
email, **129**, 194
energy, 12, 13, 46, 47, 56, 63, 80, 82, 84, **108–109**, 110, 116, 178, 182, 188, 192, 193

chemical, **108**, 109
    elastic, 108
    gravitational, 108
    heat, 108, 109
    kinetic, **108**, 195
    light, 108, 109
    nuclear, 187
    potential, 108, 197
enzyme, **81**, 192, 194
epidermis, **90**, 91, 194
epiglottis, 80
Equator, 46, 49, 52, 194
estuary, 42, 194
Europe, 14, 44, 168, 170, 172, 174
    map, **144–145**
evaporation, 50, **104**, 107, 194
evolution, **68–69**, 191, 194
exhalation, 85
exosphere, 46, 194, 197
extinction, 69, 194
eye, 86, **92–93**, 95, 115, 195

F

fat, 81, **82**, 90, 111, 192
fault, **39**, 194, 197
fax, 125, 186
fiber, 83, 193
fish, 44, 45, 60, 61, 68, 71, **72**, 111, 113, 166
flight, 46, 47, **120–121**, 186, 189, 191
floating, **105**, 107, 186
flood, 48, 185
flower, 56, 57, **58–59**, 71, 115, 167, 196
focus (sight), 93
follicle, 91
food, 44, 45, 56, 57, 60, 61, 62, 63, 65, 66, 67, 71, 77, 78, 79, 80, 81, **82–83**, 90, 97, 108, 109, 192, 193
    chain, **62**, 63, 194
    web, 62, 194
force, 10, 105, 118, 120, 180, 182, 188, 192, 194, 195, 197
fossil, **40–41**, **68**, 194
    fuel, 67, 194
freckle, 91
freezing, 50, 51, **104**
frequency, **110**, 125, 194
friction, 119, 120, 193, 194
fruit, 52, **59**, 60, 83

fuel, 67, 82, 108, 116, 194
fungus, **71**, 194

G

galaxy, **8**, 9, 10, **20–21**, 27,
  28, 188, 191, 194, 196
    barred spiral, 20
    elliptical, 20
    irregular, 20
    spiral, 20, 21
gall bladder, 81, 194
gas, 8, 9, 11, 12, 14, 21, 45,
  46, 47, 50, 53, 61, 66,
  104–105, 107, 111, 116,
  120, 182, 186, 187, 191,
  193, 195, 197
gastric juice, 81
gene, **98–101**, 194
generator, 109, 116
genetic engineering, 100
genome, 100, 190, 191, 194
geologist, 37, 38
germ, 79, 81, 84, 85, 93, 194
geyser, 104, 194
gigabyte, 127
glacier, 40
glass, 113, 114
glasses, 93, 190
glider, 120
global warming, **53**, 67, 194
glucose, 82
GMT, *see Greenwich Mean Time*
gorge, 42, 43, 194
Grand Canyon, 40–41
grassland, 52
gravity, **10**, 20, 46, 105, 108,
  120, 172, 182, 188, 190,
  195, 197
greenhouse effect, **67**, 194,
  195
Greenwich Mean Time, 178
groundwater, 42
gullet, 80, 81, 84

H

habitat, **62**, 69, 73, 194, 195
hemoglobin, 79
hail, 50, **51**, 197
hair, 70, **90–91**, 94, 95, 96
hard disk, 127, **195**
hardware, **126**, 195
hearing, 86, **94–95**, 110, 117
heart, 76, **78**, 83, 84, 192, 193,
  197

heat, 9, 12, 15, 41, 46, 49, 50,
  53, 67, 90, 91, **104**, 106,
  107, 108, 109, 116, 188,
  189, 193, 195, 196, 197
helicopter, 120, 189, 190, **191**
herbivore, **60**, **62**, 195
hibernation, 65, 195
Himalayas, 142
hovercraft, 187
HTML, *see HyperText Markup
  Language*
Hubble Space Telescope, 21,
  188
hurricane, 15, **49**, 180, 185
hyperlink, *see link (Internet)*
HyperText Markup Language,
  128, 195
hypothalamus, 88

I

ice, 11, 14, 40, 42, 50, 53, **104**,
  117
insect, 58, 60, 61, **64**, 68, 167,
  195
insulator, 107, 116, 117, 195
International Date Line, 178, 195
Internet, **128–129**, 191, 194,
  195
    Service Provider, **128**, 129,
    195
intestine, **80–81**, 83
inventor, 186–189
ionosphere, 122
iris, **92–93**, 195
ISP, *see Internet Service Provider*

J

joint, **77**, 195
Joule, J. P., **109**, 188
Jupiter, 11, 196

K

keratin, 90, 91
keyboard (computer), 126
kidney, 79, 195
kilobyte, 127

L

lake, 184

laptop, 126
Large Magellanic Cloud, 20, 27
larynx, 84, **85**
lava, 16, 33, 195, 197
leaf, 50, 52, **56**, 57, 58
length (units of measurement),
  179
lens, 90, 92, **93**, 190
    contact, 93
lift, **120**, 121, 192, 195
ligament, 77, 195
light, 8, 9, 12, 13, 15, 17, 18,
  21, 45, 46, 53, 56, 59, 63,
  71, 109, **112–113**, 114,
  115, 116, 117, 178, 188,
  190, 191, 195, 197
    brightness, **112**
    dispersion, 114
    intensity, **112**
    year, **8**, 9, 10, 20, 21, 22,
    195
lightning, 116, **117**, 187, 191,
  195
link (Internet), 129
liquid, 11, 14, 50, 78, 84, 94,
  95, **104–105**, 107, 111,
  113, 186, 193, 194, 197
lithosphere, **36**, **38–39**, 195,
  196
liver, 80, **81**, 82, 192
long-sighted, 93
loudness, **110**
luminosity, **112**
lung, 61, 64, 78, **84–85**, 96,
  192, 193

M

maglev (train), 119
magma, 36, 38, 40, 41, 195
magnet, **118–119**, 191, 194,
  195
magnetic, 187, 190
    field, 37, **118**, 119, 187,
    195
    flux line, 118
magnetism, 13, 37, 107,
  118–119, 186, 187, 194,
  195
magnetoscope, 13
mammal, 60, 68, 69, 70, 72,
  167, 194, 195
map, 33, 38, **132–147**, 188
Marconi, 122
marconiphone, 122

Mars, 10, 11, 189, 195, 196
mass, **105**, 179, 182, 195
matter, **105**, 182, 186, 193, 194
meander, **42**, 43, 195, 196
measurement, 105, 109, **179–181**, 182, 184, 185, 188, 189
    converting, 179, 182
    imperial, 179, 182
    metric, 179, 182
megabyte, 127
melanin, 91
memory, 88, **89**, 96, 127
Mercury, 10, 195
mesosphere, **46**, 196, 197
metal, 10, 11, **106**, 107, 116, 118, 119, 192, 193, 194
    ferromagnetic, 118, 119
metalloid, *see semimetal*
metamorphosis, **64**, 195, 196
meteor, **11**, 46, 196
meteorite, **11**, 193, 196
meteoroid, **11**, 16, 196
meteorologist, **48**, 180
microprocessor, **127**, 192, 193
microscope, 188, 189, 190
migration, 64, 196
Milky Way, **8**, 10, 20, 21, 29, 31, 196
mineral, **40–41**, 45, 82, 83, 181, 196
mirror, 50, 112, **113**
mobile phone, 125
modem, 125, 196
molecule, **104**, 105, 106, 182, 186, 191, 196
monitor (computer), 126
Moon (Earth's), 9, 11, **16–17**, 18, 19, 22, **33**, 105, 186, 191, 193, 197
    phases, **17**, 186
moon, 10, **11**, 16, 193, 196
Morse code, 188
mountain, 11, 16, 38, **39**, 44, 53, 138, 142, 144, 184
mouse (computer), 126, 129
mouth, **80**, 84, 86, 97
MP3, 125
mucus, **84**, 96, 97
muscle, **76**, 78, 79, 80, 81, 85, 86, 87, 88, 90, 91, 92, 93, 95, 111, 193, 195, 197
    intercostal, 84, 85

N

nail, 90–91

nasal cavity, **96**, 97
natural selection, **69**, 187, 196
nectar, **58**, 59, 60, 196
Neptune, 11, 196
nerve, 77, **86**, 87, 92, 196
    fiber, **86**, 87, 89, 192, 193, 196
nervous system, **86–87**
neuron, **86**, 88, 192, 193, 196
neutron, **116**, 187, 196
Newton, Isaac, 114, 172, **188**, 190
Niagara Falls, 43
Nile River, 146
nitrate, 66, 196
nonmetal, 106, **107**, 192
North America, 52, 168, 170, 172
    map, 136–137
northern hemisphere, 15, 22, 24, 25, 26, 28, 30, 187
northern lights, 13
nose, 84, 86, 93, **96–97**
nostril, 96
nucleus, 71, 116, 194, **196**, 197
nutrient, 82, 84

O

ocean, 38, 42, **44–45**, 184
Oceania,
    map, 140–141
oceanic ridge, 38
oil, 67, 108
omnivore, 60, 196
opaque, 113, 196
operating system, 126, 196
orbit, **9**, 10, 11, 14, 15, 16, 17, 20, 22, 47, 187, 190, 196
organ, 76, 78, 81, 86, 90, 92, 94, 96, 192, 195
ovary, 58, 192, 196, 197
oxbow lake, 43, 196
oxyhemoglobin, 79
ozone layer, **47**, 195, 197

P

Palm Pilot, 126
pancreas, 80, 81
Pangaea, 38, 196
papilla, 97
parasite, 73
pasteurization, 189

PDA, *see Palm Pilot*
penumbra, 18
peripheral, 126
pharynx, 80
pheromone, 61
photocopier, 186
photosphere, 12
photosynthesis, 56, 196
pigment, 115, 196
pins and needles, 87
pistil, 58
pitch (sound), 110
pixel, 123
plane, 46, 47, **120–122**
planet, 8, 9, **10–11**, 12, 14, 15, 16, 19, 20, 22, 187, 190, 193, 194, 195, 196, 197
plant, 14, 40, 41, 45, 50, 52, **56–57**, **58–59**, 60, 62, 63, 66, 67, 68, 69, 71, 97, 109, 166, 192, 193, 194, 195, 197
plasma, 79
plate (Earth's crust), **38–39**, 41, 196
platelet, 79
Pluto, **11**, 189, 196
pole,
    magnetic, 37, **118**, 195
    north, 13, 37, 46, 118, 192
    south, 13, 37, 46, 118, 192
pollen, **58–59**, 85, 192, 196, 197
pollution, 46, 69
polygon, 183
power, 109, 187
    station, **109**, 116, 191
precipitation, 51
predator, **60**, 61, 69, 113
prey, **60**, 61, 113
primate, 72
Prime Meridian Line, **178**, 195, 197
prism, 114, 190
producer (in a food web), 63
program, **126**, 127, 128, 129, 188, 197
prominence (solar), 12
propeller, 120
protein, 66, 81, **82**, 194
proton, 116, 197
Proxima Centauri, 9
pupa, 64
pupil (eye), **92–93**, 195

Pythagorean theorem, **182**, 189, 190

R

radiative zone, 12
radio, 107, **122–123**, 191
    broadcasting, **122**, 123
rain, 40, 42, 48, 49, 50, **51**, 52, 114, 197
rainbow, 114, 115
rainforest, 15, 52, **62**, 138
random access memory (RAM), 127
receptor, 86, 90
rectum, 80, 81
recycling, 50, 121
reflex action, 87
refraction, **113**, 114, 186, 197
reptile, 60, 68, 69, **72**, 167, 197
respiratory system, **84–85**, 96
retina, 92, 93
river, 40, **42–43**, 50, 67, 146, 184, 193, 194, 196, 197
rock, 10, 11, 16, 36, 37, 39, **40–41**, 42, 43, 44, 46, 194, 195, 196, 197
    igneous, **40**, 41
    metamorphic, **40**, 41
    sedimentary, 40, **41**
rod (eye), 92
rodent, 72
rudder, 121

S

Sahara, 146
saliva, 80, 97
satellite, 14, **15**, 49, 123, 124, 191, 196, 197
    broadcasting, 123
Saturn, 11, 188, 196
scale, 105, 180, 186
    absolute temperature, 182, 189
    Beaufort, 180
    Celsius, 182, 186
    Fahrenheit, 182, 187
    Mercalli, 181
    Mohs hardness, 181
    Richter, 181, 185
scientist, 186–189
sea, 16, 40, 42, **44–45**, 50, 52, 57, 59, 65, 146, 180, 190, 193, 194, 196
sea level, 44, 52, 53
season, **15**, 22, 52, 65
seed, 56, 58, **59**, 194, 196
seismic waves, 37
seismogram, 37
seismometer, 181
semicircular canal, 95
semiconductor, 107
semimetal, 106, **107**
senses, 89, **92–97**
server, 128, 129
shadow, 18, 19, **113**
short-sighted, 93
sight, **92–93**
skeleton, 45, 68, **76–77**, 166, 193
skin, 64, 68, 80, 82, 86, **90–91**, 93, 194
skull, 60, 76, 88, 89, 93
sleep, 89
sleet, 51
Small Magellanic Cloud, 20, 27
smell, 86, **96**, 97
sneezing, 85
snow, 42, 48, 50, **51**, 197
software, 125, **126**, 196, 197
solar flare, 12
Solar System, 9, **10–11**, 14, 192, 196, 197
solar wind, 13, 197
solid, 50, **104–105**, 107, 111
sonar, 44, **111**, 197
sonic boom, 111
sound, 85, 95, 108, 109, **110–111**, 117, 120, 122, 123, 191, 192, 193
South America, 15, 38, 172
    map, 138–139
southern hemisphere, **15**, 22, 25, 27, 29, 31
southern lights, 13
space, **8–35**, 46, 48, 56, 106, 123, 124, 186, 191, 197
Space Shuttle, 47, 106, 191
species, **57**, 58, 60, 63, 69, 70, 71, 72, 187, 188, 194, 195, 196, 197
spectrum, 92, **114**, 115, 188
speech, 88, 96
spinal cord, 86
stamen, 58, 192, 197
star, 8, 9, 10, 12, **20–33**, 65, 187, 192, 193, 194, 196, 197

cluster, 20, **21**, 27
dwarf, 12
giant, 12
map, 22, 24–31
shooting, 30
supergiant, 12
starch, 80, 81, 82
steam, **104**, 109
    engine, 188, 189, 190, 191
stigma (flower), **58**, 59, 192, 196, 197
stomach, 80, **81**, 194
storm, 49, 117, 185
stratosphere, 46, **47**, 196, 197
stream, **42**, 50, 193
streamlined, 120
sugar, 80
Sun, 8, 9, 10, 11, **12–13**, 14, 15, 17, 18, 19, 20, 22, 46, 47, 49, 50, 53, 63, 65, 67, 91, 109, 112, 114, 186, 187, 190, 192, 193, 196, 197
    core, 12
    sunspot, 12
sweat, 83, 90, **91**
synovial fluid, 77

T

taste, 86, 96, **97**
teeth, 41, 60
telecommunications, 124, 125
telephone, 110, **124–125**, 128, 186, 191
telescope, 8, 13, 19, 21, 33, 187, 188, 190
television, 109, **122–123**, 186, 188, 191
    broadcasting, 123
    camera, 123
    decoder, 123
    interactive, 123
temperature (measurement), 182
tendon, **76**, 95, 197
thalamus, 88
thermosphere, 46, **47**, 196, 197
throat, **80**, 84, 97
thrust, 120, 197
thunder, 117
time, 187
    zone, **180**, 197
tissue, 82, 94, 193, 195
tongue, 96–97

tornado, 185
touch, 86
train, 119
translucency, 113, 197
transmitter (radio), 122
transparency, **113**, 197
tree, 52, 53, 57, 58, 63, 69, 71, 112, 138
trench, **38**, 197
triangle, **183**, 189
tributary, 42, 197
trophic level, **63**, 197
troposphere, 46, 197
twins, 99

U
ultrasound, 111
umbra, 18
Uniform Resource Locator, 129
Universe, **8–19**, 109, 112, 187, 188, 189, 192, 194, 197
Uranus, 11, 187, 196
urine, **79**, 83
URL, *see Uniform Resource Locator*
username, 129

V
vaccine, 188, 191
valley, 11, 42, 43, 44, 194
    rift, **39**, 197
vein, **79**, 188, 197
ventricle, 78
Venus, 10, 195
vestibular system, 95
vitamin, 82, **83**, 90
vocal cord, 85
voice box, *see larynx*
volcano, 16, 37, 40, 44, 166, 185, 197
volume (of matter), **105**, 179, 182, 183, 186, 187, 193

W
water, 14, 17, 42, 44, 45, 49, **50–51**, 56, 57, 59, 61, 66, 68, 72, 81, 83, 95, 97, 104, 105, 107, 109, 113, 114, 115, 117, 186, 190, 192, 194, 197
    cycle, 50
    vapor, 50, **104**

waterfall, 42, **43**, 138, 184
wave
    analog, **122**, 123, 124, 125
    radio, **122**, 123, 124, 188, 191
    sound, 94, **110**, 111, 122, 125
weather, 15, 46, **48–49**, 51, 52, 180, 193, 197
web browser, 128, 129
web page, 128, 129, 195
weight, **105**, 182, 185, 186, 197
wind, 40, 48, 49, 53, 59, 180
windpipe, **80**, 84, 85, 192
wing, 61, 64, 68, 69, 72, 110, **120–121**
world,
    physical map, 134–135
    political map, 132–133
    records, 184–185
World Wide Web, 128–129, 191

Y
yawning, 85

Z
zone of totality, 19

ACKNOWLEDGMENTS

Every effort has been made to trace the copyright holders of the material in this book. If any rights have been omitted, the publishers offer to rectify this in any subsequent edition, following notification. The publishers are grateful to the following organizations and individuals for their contributions and for permission to reproduce material (t=top, m=middle, b=bottom, l=left, r=right):

Title page: (Arts and Science City) © Jose Fuste Raga/CORBIS

2–3: (bottlenose dolphin) © Stuart Westmorland/CORBIS

6–7: (Horsehead Nebula) © NOAO/AURA/NSF/WIYN

8–9: p8 (distant galaxies) © NASA

12–13: p12tr (sunspot) © NASA; p12–13b (Sun's surface) © European Space Agency; p13tr (aurora) © Pekka Parviainen/Science Photo Library

14–15: p14tl (satellite view of forests) © NASA Landsat Pathfinder Humid Tropical Forest Project/Science Photo Library; p14tm (Earth's atmosphere) © Digital Vision; p14–15b (satellite view of Earth) © European Space Agency/PLI; p15t (hurricane clouds) © NOAA/Science Photo Library

16–17: p16bl (Apollo astronaut), p16m (Copernicus) and p16–17t (Moon) © NASA

18–19: p18–19 main (eclipse) © Rev. Ronald Royer/Science Photo Library; p18l (lunar eclipse) © G. Antonio Milani/Science Photo Library

20–21: p20bl (galaxy M100) © NASA; p20–21t (Cartwheel Galaxy) © Space Telescope Science Institute/NASA/Science Photo Library

34–35: (Wonder Lake) © Charles Mauzy/CORBIS

36–37: p36–37 main (Earth) © Digital Vision; p37b (compass) Howard Allman

38–39: p38–39b (Himalayas) © Galen Rowell/CORBIS; p39tr (rift valley) © Yann Arthus-Bertrand/CORBIS

40-41: p40–41t (rocks) Mike Freeman; p40–41b (Grand Canyon) © Dr. B Booth/G.S.F Picture Library

42–43: p42tr (river delta) © 1996 CORBIS – original image courtesy of NASA/CORBIS; p42bl (rounded rocks) © David Muench/CORBIS; p42–43 (Horseshoe Falls) © John and Dallas Heaton/CORBIS

44–45: p44tl (fish) © Lawson Wood/CORBIS; p44b (diver) © AMOS Nachoum/CORBIS; p45tl (turtle) and p45b (coral reef) © Digital Vision

46–47: p46tl (thermosphere) © Digital Vision; p46tl (mesosphere) © Jonathan Blair/CORBIS; p46ml (stratosphere); p46bl (troposphere) © NASA; p46–47 main (plane in clouds) © George Hall/CORBIS; p47t (ozone layer) © NASA/Science Photo Library

48–49: p48–49 (rainbow background) © Craig Aurness/CORBIS; p48l (rainbow dancer) © Michael Yamashita/CORBIS; p49t (clouds) © Digital Vision; p49b (parasols) © Wolfgang Kaehler/CORBIS

50–51: p50tr (snowflakes) © Scott Camazine/Science Photo Library; p50–51 (clouds background), p51tr (cumulonimbus clouds) Shuttle Views of the Earth: Clouds from Space, compiled by Pat Jones, courtesy of LPI; p51ml (stratus clouds) © Photodisc/Getty Images; p51tl (cumulus clouds) and p51bl (cirrus clouds) © Digital Vision

52–53: p52tm (giraffes) and p52–53b (cactus) © Digital Vision

54–55: (jaguar) © Michael & Patricia Fogden/CORBIS

56–57: p56tl (Earth), p56m (sunflower), p56tr (Sun) and p57t (aloe) © Digital Vision; p56br (stomata) © Ron Boardman, Frank Lane Picture Agency/CORBIS; p57r (tree) © Galen Rowell/CORBIS

58–59: p59t (hummingbird) © Tim Flach/Getty Images; p59bl (sunflower seeds) Howard Allman; p59br (coconut) © Kevin Schafer/CORBIS

60–61: p60–61m (eagle) © Stuart Westmorland/CORBIS; p60bl (seal skull) © Anthony Bannister; Gallo Images/CORBIS; p60br (horse skull) © Sally and David Waters/Horsepix Equestrian Photography, (vulture, bee-eater, butterfly, flowers, mushrooms) © Digital Vision

62–63: p62m (cheetahs and gazelle) © Tom Brakefield/CORBIS; p63b (elephant) © Digital Vision

64–65: p64–65b (migrating wildebeest) © Yann Arthus-Bertrand/CORBIS

66–67: p66tr (pea plant) © Dr. Jeremy Burgess/Science Photo Library; p66bl (dung beetle) © Karl Switak/ABPL/CORBIS; p67tl (charcoal) © Nick Cobbing/Still Pictures; p67br (algae) © Chinch Gryniewicz, Ecoscene/CORBIS

68–69: p68 (ammonite fossil) © James L. Amos/CORBIS

70–71: p71 (salmonella bacterium) © UDSA/Science Photo Library

72–73: p73t (tiger) and p73b (giraffes) © Digital Vision

74–75: (chromosomes) © BSIP, DUCLOUX/Science Photo Library

76–77: p76 (skeleton) © Manfred Kage/Science Photo Library

78–79: p78–79t (blood cells) © National Cancer Institute/Science Photo Library

82–83: p82b (pasta) and p82–83t (fruit and vegetables) Howard Allman

84–85: p84–85t (lungs) © Alfred Pasieka/Science Photo Library; p85r (opera singer) © Richard Moran (Roderick Williams as Figaro in Opera North's production of The Barber of Seville)

86–87: p86–87m (nerve fibers) © CNRI/Science Photo Library; p87r (footballer) Howard Allman

88–89: p88 (brain) © Mehau Kulyk/Science Photo Library

90–91: p90–91b (hair and skin) © Prof. P Motta/Dept of Anatomy/University "La Sapienza", Rome/Science Photo Library; p91r (faces) Howard Allman

92–93: p92–93 (eye) © David Parker/Science Photo Library

94–95: p94 (ballerina) © Hulton-Deutsch Collection/CORBIS

96–97: p97 (man collecting petals) © Michael Freeman/CORBIS

98–99: p98b (twins) © Barbara Penoyar/Getty Images; (baby) © Royalty-free/CORBIS

100–101: p100tr (fruit fly) © Darwin Dale/Science Photo Library; p100bl (featherless chickens) © Reuters NewMedia Inc./CORBIS; p101bm (genetically engineered salmon) © Natalie Forbes/CORBIS; p101br (baby face) © Steve Grand/Science Photo Library

102–103: (molecule structure model) © I Dream Stock/Alamy

104–105: p104–105 (geyser) © W. Perry Conway/CORBIS

106–107: p106bl (chocolate eggs) © Jim Zuckerman/CORBIS; p106bm (rolled aluminum) © Lawson Mardon Star Ltd. Bridgnorth; p106–107 main

(Space Shuttle) and p107m (integrated circuit) © Digital Vision

108–109: p108bl (hammer), p108tr (Sun) and p109bl (power station) © Digital Vision

110–111: p110–111b (aircraft landing) © George Hall/CORBIS; p111ml (aircraft at supersonic speed) © American government; p111m (ultrasound scan) © Charlotte Tomlins; p111tr (dolphins) © Digital Vision

112–113: p112bl (train) © Lester Lefkowitz/CORBIS; p112tr (trees) © Digital Vision; p113r (fish) © Natural Visions/Peter David; (shrimp) © Nature Picture Library/David Shale

114–115: p114–115t (rainbow) © Joseph Sohm, ChromoSohm Inc./CORBIS; p114m (sunset) © Digital Vision

116–117: p116–117 main (lightning) © Kennan Ward/CORBIS

118–119: p118t (horseshoe magnet) © TEK IMAGE/Science Photo Library; p119t (electromagnet) © Alex Bartel/Science Photo Library; p119b (Maglev train) © Transrapid International

120–121: p120–121b (plane) © Digital Vision

122–123: p123b (television) © Two Way TV & Philips; p123b (picture on television screen) © Allsport UK Ltd.

124–125: p124tr (telephone) © Michael Denora/Getty Images; p125tr (fiber optic cables) © Royalty free/Corbis

126–127: p126bl (computer) © Gateway; p127m (CPU microprocessor) © Intel; p127br (CDs) © Digital Vision

128–129: p128tl (BrainPOP screenshot) © BrainPOP; p128tr (NASA screenshot) © NASA

130–131: Image courtesy of Earth Sciences and Image Analysis Laboratory, NASA Johnson Space Center

136–137: p136bl (hoodoos) © Richard Cummins/CORBIS; p137br (eagle) © W. Perry Conway/CORBIS

138–139: p138bl (guanaco) © Galen Rowell/CORBIS; p139tr (frog) © Eye Ubiquitous/CORBIS

140–141: p140–141t (island) © Pascal Kobeh/Still Pictures; p141br (fish) © Bates Littlehales/CORBIS

142–143: p142–143b (boat in port) © Michael S. Yamashita/CORBIS; p143b (flowers) © Keren Su/CORBIS

144–145: p144–145 (clouds background) © Digital Vision; p145b (cow) © Peter Dean/Agripicture

Managing editor: Gillian Doherty

Authors:
Jane Bingham, Fiona Chandler, Philip Clarke, Anna Claybourne, Susanna Davidson, Gillian Doherty, Emma Helbrough, Corinne Henderson, Laura Howell, Lisa Miles, Kirsteen Rogers, Alastair Smith and Sam Taplin

Designers:
Melissa Alaverdy, Sarah Cronin, Laura Fearn, Keith Newell, Susie McCaffrey, Stephen Moncrieff, Steve Page, Linda Penny, Chloe Rafferty, Jane Rigby, Ruth Russell, Karen Tomlins and Candice Whatmore

Illustrators:
Alan Baker, John Barber, Joyce Bee, Verinder Bhachu, Gary Bines, Simone Bowl, Isabel Bowring, Peter Bull, Andy Burton, Lorenzo Cecchi, Kuo Kang Chen, Barry Croucher, David Cuzik, Peter Dennis, Matthew Doyle, Inklink Firenze, Mark Franklin, Giacinto Gaudenzi, Jeremy Gower, Andy Griffin, Rebecca Hardy, Nicholas Hewetson, Ian Jackson, Cathy Jakeman, Chris Lyon, Malcolm MacGregor, Janos Marffy, Sean Milne, Stephen Moncrieff, Martin Newton, Mike Olley, Radai Parekh, Justine Peek, Luis Rey, Michael Saunders, Chris Shields, Guy Smith, Justine Torode, Robert Walster, Ross Watton, Sean Wilkinson and David Wright

Cover design: Zöe Wray

Cartography: Craig Asquith/European Map Graphics Ltd.

Additional thanks to: Georgina Andrews and Fiona Patchett